11-04

D0561948

Public Affairs

DATE DUE

DEMCO 38-296

edited by
Paul Apostolidis and
Juliet A. Williams

Public Affairs

Politics
in the Age of
Sex Scandals

Duke University Press   Durham & London

•

2004

© 2004 Duke University Press

All rights reserved

Printed in the United States of

America on acid-free paper ∞

Designed by C. H. Westmoreland

Typeset in Times Roman with

ITC American Typewriter display

by Tseng Information Systems, Inc.

Library of Congress Cataloging-in-

Publication Data appear on the last

printed page of this book.

Contents

Acknowledgments

We would like to thank a number of people who helped us conceptualize this project and bring it to fruition. Rose Corrigan, Cynthia Daniels, Judith Grant, David Gutterman, and Jill Locke provided helpful comments on our work at a panel for the Western Political Science Association. Thanks also go to the following faculty members at Whitman College, whose thoughtful reflections on our drafts were indispensable: Julia Davis, Tom Davis, Susan Ferguson, Tim Kaufman-Osborn, Jeannie Morefield, David Schmitz, Lynn Sharp, and Bob Tobin. At UC-Santa Barbara, we are especially grateful to the faculty members in the Law and Society Program and the Women's Studies Program, and to Constance Penley of the Film Studies Department. We are additionally grateful to Judith Grant and to three anonymous readers for all the hard work they devoted to this project and for their insightful criticisms. Finally, we thank our editor, Valerie Millholland, and all those at Duke University Press who have provided us with their invaluable professional assistance.

Some of the essays in this volume have been previously published elsewhere, either in whole or in part. Parts of Paul Apostolidis's essay "On 'The Dalliances of the Commander in Chief': Christian Right Scandal Narratives in Post-Fordist America" appeared as chapter 4 in Paul Apostolidis, *Stations of the Cross: Adorno and Christian Right Radio* (Durham, NC: Duke University Press, 2000), copyright 2000 by Duke University Press, and is reprinted with permission. Jodi Dean's essay "Making (It) Public" appeared in *Constellations* 6.2 (1999) and is reprinted with permission. Joshua Gamson's essay "Normal Sins: Sex Scandal Narratives as Institutional Morality Tales" appeared in *Social Problems* 48.2 (May 2001), copyright 2001 by The Society for the Study of Social Problems, and is reprinted with permission. Parts of Joshua D. Rothman's essay "Hardly Sallygate: Thomas Jefferson, Sally Hemings, and the Sex Scandal That Wasn't" appears in

Introduction
Sex Scandals and Discourses of Power

On the day before President Bill Clinton left office, the news broke that he had struck a deal with the Office of the Independent Counsel. Clinton admitted to having provided false testimony regarding his relationship with former White House intern Monica Lewinsky in the Paula Jones sexual harassment case. In exchange, the soon-to-be ex-president received immunity from prosecution for perjury and related offenses. Pundits wrangled over whom the deal favored, Clinton or his accusers. They agreed, however, that most of the public was simply relieved to see the matter of the Clinton-Lewinsky scandal finally—apparently—brought to a conclusion. Yet the dogged persistence of the scandal through the very last hours of the Clinton administration hardly allowed for much optimism that sex scandals would remain off the main docket of the electronic court of public opinion for very long. To the contrary, the timing of the deal transparently signaled the determination of the contestants to use every available advantage in fighting the battle at hand, and thus portended no ebbing of blood lust as similar occasions arise in the future.

The Deepening Muck of Scandal There is a general sense among politicians, commentators, and the American public at large that at some point during the past fifteen years, a line was crossed. After the exposure of Gary Hart's infidelity (on the good ship *Monkey Business*) ended his 1987 presidential primary run, after Anita Hill's charges of sexual harassment nearly derailed Clarence Thomas's confirmation to the U.S. Supreme Court, after Bob Packwood's ignominious exit from the U.S. Senate for just such behavior, and especially after Bill and Monica, Americans from most reaches of the ideological spectrum wonder whether so much fanfare over the sexual lives of political leaders is genuinely necessary to a well-functioning polity. For some, the problem is that U.S. politics has veered beyond commonly recognized bounds of good taste and propriety, filling TV and computer screens with an overabundance of explicit sexual content, even as major party politicians try to outdo one another in inveighing against the sexual excesses of Hollywood, the popular music industry, and online pornography. Others are concerned that political competition has become focused on matters that are trivial when compared to presumptively grander affairs of state, such as concluding international treaties or formulating industrial or banking policy. Some even suspect a bad faith effort by elites to divert the public's attention from these weighty issues by channeling public discourse into these foul and shallow waters. Politically diverse interests and individuals certainly find some of these scandals more defensible than others, but few seem happy about the extent to which the political culture as a whole has been sexualized.

This book grew out of a shared insistence among its contributors that a more nuanced critical engagement with the politics of sex scandals is both possible and urgently needed. Those who hope American public life might become more participatory and inclusive, and that it might provide more effective avenues for ordinary citizens to define the substance of public policy, should above all not react to the surfeit of sex in political discourse by ignoring it for fear that to address scandals directly only enhances their already undue influence. Nor is it wise simply to dismiss the intensified sexual scrutiny of political leaders as evincing a general regression of the public psyche, or as a tip-off to the manipulations of officials who want to insulate public policy from the citizenry. Again, these interpretations of recent events would logically prompt us to shift critical attention from sex scandals to other events in the shadows looming beyond the media spotlight's glare. We argue instead that sex scandals themselves provide particularly fructuous vantage points from which to gain critical perspective on structural aspects of public life in the United States: the narratives according to which ethical norms of the culture industries become effectual; the consumerist logic of the public sphere; the dynamics of the political party system in relation to the constitutional separation of powers; the institutions intended to ensure political leaders' accountability to the public for their official actions; the construction of citizenship as participation in the media spectacle; and the discourses enabling and constraining challenges to racial, gender, and sexual privilege. By charting a critical path through rather than around the muck of scandal, we not only attain clearer sightings of the complex dynamics of these major sites of political contestation, but we also grasp the reasons why, in these structural contexts, sex scandals have become anything but peripheral to American public life.

The Guilty Pleasures of the Public Some important work in cultural studies has drawn just this sort of needed attention to recent sex scandals. Toni Morrison's collection *Race-ing Justice, En-gendering Power* (1992) examined the multiple discourses of race, gender, and class that circulated through the scandal surrounding Clarence Thomas's Supreme Court nomination hearings. *Our Monica, Ourselves* (2001), edited by Lauren Berlant and Lisa Duggan, offered similar analyses of the Clinton-Lewinsky affair, with focused attention on discourses of sexuality. This collection is intended to bring together reflections on a variety of different sex scandals in U.S. political culture, though with an emphasis on the Clinton scandal, which was certainly the most avidly followed and consequential political sex scandal in this country's history. Together, these essays tease out the broad implications of sex scandal politics for the meaning, constitution, and agency of the public, or more concretely, for the prospects of cultural critique and democratic action by discrete, socially situated publics. The intellectual scope of this volume, moreover, extends beyond cultural studies, bringing critical cultural theory into a conversation with political-scientific writing on the role of scandal politics in general in the institutional development of liberal democracies.

We suggest that a scandal be understood as the publicization of a transgression of a social norm. Because a scandal is a public disgrace, what is at stake is the transgressor's public value, that is, her or his reputation. A sound reputation depends, above all, on conformity to established and generally held social norms. For this reason, accusations of hypocrisy typically do not produce scandals, for they involve the violation of particularized rather than universally shared norms, even though alleged or demonstrated hypocrisy certainly can detract from leaders' political viability by creating personal embarrassment and damaging their constituency's estimation of their moral stature. If, for example, vice presidential candidate Joseph Lieberman had campaigned on a Saturday, he surely would have been criticized for lacking character and selling out, and this might have adversely impacted both his vote totals in Connecticut's senatorial race and the electoral fortunes of the Gore-Lieberman ticket. Nonetheless, only those Americans who believe that a leader must observe the Sabbath to exercise legitimate political leadership would have considered his actions to be scandalous—or so it would seem. Interpreting this hypothetical situation becomes trickier if we take into account the majoritarian sentiment in the United States that to exercise legitimate authority political leaders must identify themselves with a mainstream religious institution and show themselves to be pious (or at least avoid being exposed as impious) within whatever faith tradition they embrace. Given this political-cultural context, such a departure from principled practice by Lieberman might well have sparked a general scandal. In any case, different kinds of censure flow from the violations of different norms, because specific norms are situated differently with respect to existing discourses of race, class, gender, and sexuality. For example, some have argued that Clinton's relationship with Lewinsky displayed distinctly "queer" aspects, for instance, their play with sexual objects, which contravene conventions of heteronormativity. These particular bodily transgressions of such norms doubtless signaled a more urgent threat than would have been presented by any digression by Lieberman from the weekly routine of the faithful family.[1]

Importantly, a transgression is necessary, but not sufficient, for a scandal. Publicity is essential. Every scandal thus involves a double boundary crossing: the violation of the norm involved in the scandalous act itself, and that act's exceptional manifestation before the public.[2] Some scandals presuppose—and capitalize on for shock value—an underlying societal expectation of respect for a distinction between personal or intimate affairs and matters that strangers have a legitimate interest in knowing. The events involving actor Hugh Grant discussed in Joshua Gamson's essay, as well as the simple fact of Clinton's adulterous relationship with Lewinsky (apart from the charges of perjury or obstruction of justice), were scandals of this order. In other scandals, publicity involves breaching the boundary dividing an institution's internal business from those aspects of the institution's operations that are subjected to regular public scrutiny. Teapot Dome and the Iran-Contra affair, analyzed here by Theodore J. Lowi, exemplify this sort of scandal, along with, arguably (given the normative structures of American pentecostalism), the revelations of Jimmy Swaggart's sexual and financial "sins."

What distinguishes sex scandals from other kinds of political scandals? Recent experience suggests that sex scandals have a singular capacity to capture the public imagination—in ways, to be sure, that make the public distinctly uncomfortable. Just think about the difference between the popular reception of Whitewater and Monicagate: had the details of the Whitewater probe held the public's interest, it is doubtful that Independent Counsel Kenneth Starr would have meandered into the tenuously related domain of the Paula Jones case in the first place. Part of the explanation for the prominence and tenacity of sex scandals lies in the fact that accusations of sexual impropriety are scandalous in and of themselves, unlike charges of financial misdealings or abuse of power, which generally need to be meticulously documented before being given even a fleeting place in the public's conception of the national agenda. However, the threshold for publicizing alleged sexual misconduct evidently is much lower than in the case of other kinds of misbehavior. When it comes to discussions of sexual impropriety, gossip is the prevailing lingua franca, regardless of whether the conversational venue is the proverbial water cooler or the national media.

But although the public consumes sex scandals avidly, it also does so ambivalently. And to the extent that citizens register not just prurient interest but disgust over the increasingly common occurrence of sex scandals, they are not sure whom to blame—and rightly so. On the one hand, sex scandals provoke frustration with the difficulty of challenging the corporations whose structural orientation toward the creation of private profit underlies and motivates these media events. The capacity of ordinary citizens to "choose" to follow sex scandals as news is highly compromised by the multiple ways consumer "choices" in this area are effects rather than determinants of the actions of culture industries and political parties. For many, sex scandals are detestable because they exemplify this pseudo-democratic aspect of American public life. Perhaps no recent scandal was more deserving of such reactions than the Gary Condit scandal. The mysterious disappearance of Chandra Levy in 2001 was perfect midsummer fare: a story fueled by innuendo, covered around the clock even in the absence of new or newsworthy developments, and baldly appealing to viewers' desire for juicy entertainment rather than their concern for the public interest. On the other hand, the public's desires, even (or perhaps especially) in this extreme case, are not wholly the products of strategic corporate and political action, however embedded such action is in fundamental social structures. Sex scandals depend on citizens' willingness, even eagerness, to indulge the guilty pleasure of watching them flower, and on some level the public knows that it bears some responsibility for the cupidity with which it seeks such pleasures. Indeed, the feelings of degradation and shame that accompany absorption in a sex scandal, as Foucault suggests, are very likely related in a positive way to the degree of pleasure that these events make possible, enhancing their capacity to fascinate. In other kinds of scandals, such as those regarding financial misdealings, the shame tends to stay confined to the individual charged with the misdeed. Not so with sex scandals. This mirroring effect, a special form of guilt by association, suggests that the boundaries enabling the public to view sex scandals from a safe and detached distance are unusually thin, unsteady, and permeable. When a sex scandal occurs, the public cannot depend on being able to stand apart in smug judgment of the alleged malefactor. Inevitably, the potential guilt of the accused becomes the spectators' guilt as well.

Because the shame in admitting that one "likes to watch" is peculiar to sex scandals, we suspect that the cries against sex scandals have more to do with the fact that politics has been sexualized than that it has been scandalized. But it is important to be clear about what it means to sexualize politics, for in more or less explicit terms, sex and sexuality have long been a constitutive feature of politics and political discourse in the United States. We have always expected our leaders to be potent and virile, and we have often taken pride in an official appetite for conquest, whether military or, more recently, corporate. Indeed, sexual metaphors have long pervaded political discourse in the United States. The imbrication of political and sexual talk is, in fact, a common feature of political scandals in general. Consider, for example, the Lincoln Bedroom controversy that arose during Clinton's first term of office. The Clintons were not simply denounced for using public facilities to raise campaign funds; they were specifically and repeatedly reviled for "prostituting" themselves to wealthy donors. Violating the sexual integrity of the national boudoir became a highly effective metaphor for the transgression of unofficial standards of propriety regarding the maintenance of a safe distance between political fundraising and state business. At the same time, the fact that this outcry was raised at all, when quite similar events went unreported during the preceding Republican administrations, may have betrayed a certain discomfort on the right with the "scandal" of Clinton's election as the representative of the nation despite his lack of wealth and prestige. As was the case with the Lewinsky scandal, criticism of Clinton's sexuality provided a comfortable way to attack him in a country notoriously squeamish about discussions of class: as embarrassing as it may be to talk about sex, with Clinton, it seemed easier than broaching the touchy matter of his unseemly origins. Sex talk, then, often furnishes the discourse in which other public controversies are encrypted. As such, it both expresses and reinforces the failure to address these scandals in an explicit and democratic manner, and it has functioned in these ways historically as well as in recent times. In the end, then, it may be more accurate to say that sex scandals do not so much sexualize politics as force us to confront the degree to which sex and sexuality permeate the political universe.

Even so, the role of sex in public discourse has mutated rapidly and in important ways in recent years. The sources of this shift are multiple and interrelated, including the advent of new communication technologies, the economic restructuring of the corporate media, and the particular political logics of the right wing in the United States. In the past, public discourse has been sexualized without necessarily focusing substantively on scandals involving the sexual activities of national leaders. Consider that scandals, in general, have been a fixture in U.S. politics since the earliest days of the republic, perhaps all too readily accepted as part of the price we must pay for living in a polity officially committed to freedom of the press. Yet even in a country that has long prided itself on protecting investigative journalism, until roughly fifteen years ago U.S. politics proved an inhospitable environment for scandalmongering of a sexual kind. Prior to the 1980s, leaders in politics and journalism minimized public discourse about the sexual hijinks of presidents and other principal figures in national politics. From Thomas Jefferson's affair with his slave Sally Hemings to John F. Kennedy's notorious indulgences, public officials strayed beyond the bounds of sexual propriety—with the knowledge, at least, of those in their intimate social and political circles. But it is only recently that these matters have attained the status of front-page news. Indeed, comparative studies of political scandal and corruption have often used the U.S. case, where until recently these phenomena were focused almost exclusively on the misuse of money and influence, as a foil for countries where political sex scandals were much more common, notably Great Britain.[3] Evidently, what has changed is not the behavior of public officials, which consistently has failed to live up to public standards, but rather American society's willingness and desire to talk about it.

Sex Scandals and the (De)Composition of the Public/Private Divide

At least on the surface, the increasingly commonplace occurrence of sex scandals in U.S. politics seems to reflect disruption and ambiguity in the politicocultural norms defining and separating the public and private realms. Pointing to a dwindling respect for a traditional public/private distinction is one powerfully resonant way to narrate the historical transition that has made sex scandals involving political leaders more mundane today than they were forty years ago. The story is that because Americans have lost a sense for the value of segregating public from private concerns, as well as a sense of where the dividing line lies, they imprudently indulge either their utopian desires for a government "administered by angels" or their carnal appetites by generating and following sex scandals.

Whether this account is adequate to recent events depends significantly on how the terms public and private are defined. We take it as both logically and empirically the case that the public and private realms are mutually constitutive: the realm of the public appears rational, orderly, and oriented toward universality precisely by differentiating itself from private matters, defined as irrational, disorderly, and guided by particularity. The public realm can be differentiated from the private realm by excluding the latter, but public matters can also be distinguished from private affairs insofar as the former include the latter in planned, disciplined ways, such that the regulation of the private is productive of power. Here we borrow from Foucault the notions that power is generated when disciplinary practices are institutionalized and normalized, and that power constitutes the agencies that are involved in these relational processes, rather than being simply a "thing" that one entity can possess and use instrumentally to influence another entity. To take the example of religion and the liberal state, the constitutional imperative to maintain a balance between freedom of religious expression and religious disestablishment means that public power comes into being as the power ensuring that religious expression is channeled into certain venues and not into others: religion is constituted as a private activity (even as the private realm is constituted as the sphere of faith and individual conscience), and in turn the public realm is constituted as the agency disciplining religion (and embodying a universal rationality that transcends private, particularistic spirituality). The myriad and continuing historical adjustments, through judicial decisions and public policy changes, of what is commonly thought of as "the state's power to intervene in religious affairs" reflect the fact that neither the public nor the private realm is an entity that exists with an enduring, stable self-identity; rather, both are continually being re-produced and refashioned as the relations of power linking them together in a disciplinary matrix are altered. A crucial effect of these power relations, finally, is the appearance of the legitimacy of the state, which hinges on the maintenance of a strict distinction between the rational, orderly, universally oriented public realm and the irrational, disorderly, particularistic private realm.

When a political scandal occurs, part of what is shocking is the fact that the revelation of this deed forces private desire to appear in a public space where it is supposed to be absent or invisible. This particular shock effect of scandal consists in the troubling sensation that the public/private binary might not be so natural and secure after all, that public agency ultimately may not operate in a (rational) manner wholly or sharply distinct from (irrational) private life. Indeed, often the transgression at the heart of a scandal is something quite commonplace, such as adultery; in these cases, for some people, this boundary crossing may actually be more of a shock than the violation itself. At the same time, a breach of the public/private boundary is only likely to seem worthy of publicity to scandalmongers when the private conduct at issue has attained a certain intensity of disciplinary intertwinement with the public realm, and hence has become constitutive of public agency to an especially significant degree. Thus, for example, if Lieberman's hypothetical decision to campaign on the Sabbath were in fact to touch off a scandal, this would reflect the great extent to which religious life in the United States is enmeshed in regulatory discourses involving state agency and establishing the public and private realms as separate and distinct entities.

These considerations point to a key reason studying scandals is valuable: analyzing scandals can reveal much about historically distinctive constructions of the public/private divide, shedding light on those elements of privacy whose containment, channeling, or sublimation has become especially generative of the power that constitutes public agency. More specifically, this framework of analysis can help us explain why sex scandals are proliferating in the contemporary United States. It suggests that we see these scandals as evidence that discourses of sexuality are pivotal today to the circulations of power reproducing the public and private realms and legitimating the social order, and it invites us to consider the particular forms of regulation of private sexual life on which the constitution of public agency depends. Some especially prominent regulatory forms of this sort are the growing though embattled awareness and discipline of sexual harassment; the discursive economy in which Christian conservatives and lesbian, gay, bisexual, and transgendered activists struggle over the meaning and legal definition of marriage; and the proliferation of sexually explicit and sex-focused talk shows in television culture. Certainly, the causes of the recent plenitude of sex scandals can be found in multiple and precedent historical events, for example, as some of our authors discuss, the cultural revolution of the 1960s, the feminist movement's insistence that "the personal is the political," changes in the law defining spheres of privacy, and the politics of family preservation waged by the Christian right. But we would argue as well that sex scandals now abound in the United States because it is to a significant extent through the discipline of sexuality that political power comes to seem normal, efficacious, and just at this historical juncture.

What are the consequences of sex scandals for these disciplinary discourses and for the public/private divide? Do sex scandals destabilize or reinforce established power relations—or both? On the one hand, sex scandals (re)enact the regulation of sexuality by defining temporary breakdowns in the network that binds public agency to sexual desire as crises and then focusing public forces on the problem of sorting out and maintaining the proper relationship between these two domains. Sex scandals thus reflect and reproduce hegemonic constructions of the public/private distinction, at least in part. They occasion the expression of displeasure at an evident disrespect for boundaries and thereby reproduce respect for those same boundaries, renewing and strengthening efforts to contain, channel, and sublimate the private conduct at issue. In doing so, they reinforce the legitimacy and perceived naturalness of making this distinction at all. On the other hand, sex scandals demonstrate that the public/private boundary can be breached and is in need of policing. They expose this limit and the realms it demarcates as fragile, historically mutable, and contingent on deliberately constructive effort rather than natural or existing in themselves. They demonstrate, moreover, that the power composing this boundary can be—indeed, is being—challenged. Sex scandals are thus symptomatic of contestation over where to draw the line between public and private with regard to sex, and insofar as they bring such contestation to light, they inherently deconstruct the notion of the public/private distinction as a universal truth that is simply given to the rational mind. They have the potential, then, to unsettle the discourses regulating sexuality that depend on this distinction to seem normal and legitimate.

The Clinton scandal illustrates the complex and sometimes contradictory effects of sex scandals on both historically particular constructions of the public/private divide and the reigning liberal ideology that such a distinction is necessary and foundational for a political community that values liberty, prosperity, and social order. Congressional Democratic leaders were for the most part in synch with majority, polled public opinion in declaring the scandal itself to be scandalous. For them, publicizing Clinton's affair with Lewinsky violated an existing norm defining marital infidelity and sexual behavior as private matters unsuited and irrelevant to the realm of public officialdom. Recall, for example, the comments in congressional chambers and to the media of House Minority Leader Richard Gephardt and House Minority Whip David Bonior, both of whom lamented the egregious disrespect for privacy and personal freedom that, in their view, the attack on Clinton exhibited. In the Clinton affair, it was thus most explicitly Democrats and liberals who set out to defend a particular distinction between public and private realms, a distinction grounded in traditional norms. These actors sought to refortify the normative status of these principles, although by explicitly invoking and attempting to vindicate them, they involuntarily acknowledged that these norms could no longer be taken for granted and thus underscored their contested and precarious status. Most obviously, this response was rooted in a combination of partisan interests and genuine commitment to the principles they claimed were at stake. Somewhat less evident, but perhaps more important, their responses may also have been symptoms of their investments, as elites in a society where the public/private distinction undergirds structural privileges based on class, gender, race, and sexuality, in maintaining public confidence in the stability of the public/private boundary — and of their attendant anxiety over the scandal's potential manifestation of this boundary's constitutive instability.

Such anxiety could logically be expected to have motivated Republicans to protect the traditional public/private distinction even more strongly, given the GOP's historical opposition to policies compromising these structural privileges. And yet Republicans in Congress closed ranks behind leaders who seemed hell-bent on tearing down the existing divide between public and private, perhaps even subverting the centrality of the public/private divide in the pantheon of American values. This apparent contradiction can be traced to a peculiarly conservative qualification of the right to privacy: the notion that privacy matters only to those among us with something to hide. Judge Starr's persecution of Clinton, then, served as an occasion to rehearse and reinforce this claim and advance a more comprehensive antiprivacy political project, albeit against the resistance of some leading Democrats.

Before Starr's campaign, it was all too easy to dismiss attackers of the value of privacy as marginal, impotent extremists. In the end, however, the widely held assumption that privacy is an unshakeable value left many unprepared for the verve and reach of the independent counsel's effort, an assumption that may prove misleading in the post–September II era as government scrambles to roll back civil liberties in the name of the war on terrorism. The increasingly fraught status of the value of privacy is further obscured by the understandable though erroneous belief that as long as the U.S. power and corporate elite remain committed to private property, privacy rights more generally will be accorded respect. However, though privacy rights might be thought to be a natural extension of the values that underwrite a defense of private property, for most of this nation's history a defense of private property has not been understood to entail anything like a right to privacy when it comes to the governance of domains like bodies, ideas, and actions. Indeed, it is only in the past four decades that privacy rights have been accorded legal recognition and constitutional protection in U.S. courts. And today, in cases ranging from access to abortion to the control of medical records to the enforcement of drug policy, many judges are returning to the position that privacy has a dubious grounding in the Constitution and should yield when conflicts arise with other values, such as public health, welfare, and safety.

One can hardly be surprised that government itself is attacking privacy, for privacy doctrine was born in the crucible of a fear of state power. The legitimacy of the U.S. state may still depend on maintaining faith in its ultimate, liberal commitment to respect for the public/private distinction. Nevertheless, jurisprudential trends, as well as official efforts to portray opponents of government DNA data banks and national ID cards as the enemies of security and community, suggest that other, increasingly important ideologies may well be dislodging the liberal respect for the boundary between public and private from its traditional place as one among the core elements of legitimation for the U.S. state and structures of social privilege.

Other analysts contend that, aside from its effects on privacy, the investigation and impeachment of Clinton proceeded by weakening core assumptions about how public power comes to be exercised legitimately. Specifically, these events jeopardized the presumption that conformity to the rule of law is both fundamental to legitimate public action and the key characteristic distinguishing public from private action. William E. Scheuerman argues that the impeachment made manifest certain problems deriving from the independent counsel statute that reach to the heart of the rule of law in the United States. A precise definition of the rule of law, according to Scheuerman, "requires that state action rest on norms that are *general, public*, relatively *clear*, and *stable*." Kenneth Starr baldly violated the standards of generality, clarity, and stability, respectively, by virtue of "aggressively pursuing 'crimes' typically ignored in other settings," enjoying a "vast, open-ended delegation of authority," and constantly altering the course of his investigation in a cavalier manner.[4] For Andrew Arato, the impeachment belongs to a more comprehensive conservative effort to revise the Constitution by informal means, the goal being to endow Congress with selected quasi-parliamentary powers.[5]

The hounding of Clinton both reflected and reinvigorated these broader tendencies in U.S. law and legislation, while at the same time strengthening parallel mutations in popular culture. Outside the realm of citizens and government, the public/private divide faces a different kind of challenge, one led by corporate powers who we might expect would strenuously favor maintaining a cultural commitment to the inviolability of the private sphere, which has always been understood to encompass the market. In recent years, however, corporate America has launched an aggressive and strategic campaign to undermine popular regard for privacy. The notion of the home as a sanctuary or refuge is under attack by corporations who seduce us with promises of "access" and "service" if only we will relinquish our antiquated attachment to the value of privacy. These days, every electronic portal in our homes, from the telephone to the television to the computer, provides a conduit through which corporations can hawk their wares. We are now constantly fed the idea—part Orwellian, part oxymoron—that freedom consists in the liberating opportunity to do business from the "privacy of one's own home." At the same time, we are being bombarded with a spate of reality television shows that allow the big media and their corporate backers to dangle the tantalizing rewards of fame before anyone willing to renounce privacy. In an era when people actually compete for the privilege of living in a house where there is a TV camera trained on the toilet, the value of privacy seems decidedly old-fashioned. Arguably, Starr's mission to expose the details of Clinton's anatomy and sex life to the public helped massage Americans' transition to a new level of comfort with markedly downsized spaces of personal privacy.

Meanwhile, the distinctively public-oriented features and functions of popular culture were revealed to be in a decrepit condition by media coverage of the scandal. Despite their almost manically reiterated concern for upholding their role as mediators of democratic deliberation (as Jodi Dean critically observes in her essay here), news organizations showed every sign of subordinating this mission to privatistic, profit-seeking interests. In an era of hard-fought competition, news organizations now face excruciating pressures to get and keep audiences while cutting costs. As Bill Kovach and Tom Rosenstiel show in their analysis of reporting on the Clinton scandal, these forces have induced even the major networks and leading national newspapers to lower their standards for verifying sources' claims; to emphasize opinion, allegation, and speculation over the reporting of well-researched and substantively new information; and to adopt a "blockbuster mentality" that tries "temporarily [to] reassemble the now-fragmented mass audience" by relying on cheaply produced "formulaic stories that involve celebrity, scandal, sex, and downfall, be it O. J., Diana, or Monicagate."[6] In short, the Clinton scandal paradoxically showed popular culture to be a site not only for the death of privacy but also for the withering of publicity, in the sense of a vibrant public sphere.

The Republicans' prosecution of the Clinton scandal thus displayed the multiple and varied dimensions of conservatism's general assault on the public/private divide. Nevertheless, it should not go without note that other dimensions of GOP-led conservatism aim to etch a new and enduring line separating public from private even while leaders like Kenneth Starr, Henry Hyde, and Rupert Murdoch strive to dismantle the boundary that has traditionally existed—and that sex scandals abet this project, too. In general, the right tends to define the common bonds of citizens with reference to matters of the private sphere: marriage, parenthood, work, investment, faith, and, of course, sex (or the renunciation of it). Doing this might seem to be just another way of muddying the public/private distinction, or hybridizing the two realms. But in a basic sense the public "material" in liberal society has always been drawn from the private realm, above all, the public responsibility to furnish the political preconditions for the system of private property. This deep structure of liberalism is a core element of Locke's theory; it is also precisely the aspect of bourgeois liberalism that the early Marx contended was its most dire flaw, because, for him, the elevation of "egoistic" concerns to the main substance of communal life nullified any chance that the polity could provide a genuine experience of human solidarity. The right's contemporary project registers this historical and intellectual inconsistency in liberalism in an extreme, albeit convoluted, way. Latter-day conservatism gives a jarringly explicit expression to the general, constitutive dependence in liberal society of the public realm on the private realm by the intensity with which it declares selected private affairs in the areas of sexuality and the family to be central to the conduct of public business. At the same time, the right reestablishes the foundationalist ideology of the public/private distinction insofar as the zealotry of its pursuit of moral regulation is matched by (and cryptically reflects) its fervor for making public initiatives subservient to the dominant, private economic interests, a project that advances under the banner of respecting the rights and freedoms of individual private property owners (even as it entails massive state subsidization of corporate concerns, and hence extensive state action in bureaucratically organized markets). Conservative policies advocating choice in education, housing, and other areas of social welfare can be seen as further attempts to reinscribe this basic ideology, and to inscribe a particular understanding of what the public/private divide should look like today, inasmuch as they enhance the prerogatives of the owners of private capital to dispose of their resources without public interference.

Seen in this context, the wider assault on privacy in civil liberties, abortion, and other areas that the attack on Clinton emblematized looks much less like a wholesale dismantling of the public/private distinction. In the most charitable interpretation, it can be seen as an attempt to compensate in an exaggerated (but dangerous) way for the stark indifference of conservative economic and social policies toward the liberal principle of employing civil government to safeguard the public good. In another sense, like a not-much-fun-house mirror, conservatives' scandal politics hyperbolically reflects liberalism's bad conscience: its legitimation of the interests of the powerful by invoking the good of all.

Expressions of mass opinion about the Clinton scandal yielded similarly crosscutting implications for the public/private divide. During the scandal, and especially in the context of unprecedented Democratic gains in the 1998 congressional elections, a solid majority of the public appeared more congenially disposed toward the Democrats' invocation of liberal values than Republican civic moralism.[7] Indeed, the rhetorical strategies of the president's antagonists betrayed an acknowledgment of this reality, insofar as Starr stressed that his investigation into the Lewinsky matter was not really about sex at all, but rather perjury and other more recognizably public offenses. Yet surely there was more ambivalence in the public's stance than poll figures, election results, and the independent counsel's turns of speech indicated. Just ask Al Gore, who was hamstrung in his efforts to identify himself with the Clinton administration's successes because of the need to distance himself from the president's perceived character flaws. The latter obviously had political relevance in 2000 not only for the roughly 30 percent of the public, mainly staunch Republicans and evangelicals, who consistently favored Clinton's removal, but, more important, for moderate swing voters who were likely among the majorities voicing both disapproval of the president's personal conduct and approval of his performance in office.

So ordinary citizens gave very mixed signals about how they received the Republicans' new version of the public/private division, with its shrunken realm of privacy in matters of personal conduct. At the same time, it is important to remember that the public offered few signs at all (the most notable being the small but fervent groundswell of support for Ralph Nader in 2000) of its readiness to depart from the traditional liberal ideology, to which both major parties subscribe, that uses the public/private distinction to rationalize corporate power. However, few citizens had the opportunity to hear alternative interpretations of the scandal itself from the left media. The structural incapacity of the mainstream media to engage in critical discussion about sexual matters (especially in masculine-gendered "hard news" contexts) aggravated its ordinary tendency to exclude voices of the left, which were attempting to initiate such discussion.[8] Meanwhile, the focus on sex probably made commentators on the left less willing to respond with full force to the right's crusade, not only because of a desire not to have their attention diverted from other causes like fighting poverty and promoting peace but also perhaps because of a faltering commitment on the left to sustained, critical moral reasoning on the links between erotic expression and universalist rights and values.[9] However one assesses the left's role vis-à-vis this problem, the situation remains that for most citizens, the controversies sex scandals raise over when and how invasions of privacy are justified, while vital concerns in themselves, have the added effect of reaffirming the overall discursive organization of political contestation in terms of a public/private boundary. In a historical situation when no counterhegemonic force exists that is capable of effectively challenging the general presupposition that private capital interests accord with the public good, this means that sex scandals buttress the popular legitimacy of the political-economic status quo.

Sex Scandals and the Citizen   Given these diverse impacts of sex scandals on the public/private distinction, what can the critical analysis of sex scandals tell us specifically about experiences of political citizenship in the contemporary United States? How do sex scandals constrain or expand opportunities for citizens to take democratic action, especially action that challenges the discourses mobilized by the politically and socially dominant?

Lauren Berlant provides one model of contemporary U.S. citizenship that is especially useful for critically assessing the implications of sex scandals for the citizen. Consistent with our conceptions of the mutually constitutive relationship of the public and private realms, the productivity of sex regulation for state power, and conservatism's emphatic definition of public concerns with reference to the familial sphere, Berlant argues that in the wake of the new right's rise, "intimate things" — especially behaviors, attitudes, and identities pertaining to sex — are increasingly invoked to define the meaning of "America" and the nature of American citizenship. Berlant perhaps exaggerates the extent to which the presence of intimate concerns in the public sphere is a phenomenon of the recent past. Earlier epochs of U.S. history certainly prepared the ground for this aspect of contemporary conservatism by generating a variety of enduring valences among family, state, and nation. Historical precedents for what Berlant calls the "intimate public sphere" of the 1980s and 1990s notably include Theodore Roosevelt's efforts to justify imperialism through a nationalist rhetoric centered on (white) women's duty to bear children, the maternalist antipoverty discourses that both predated and were carried forward by the New Deal, and cold war ideology's obsession with communism's threat to the American family.[10] Berlant shows, however, that the conservative age of Reagan-Bush-W. Republicans and Clinton-Gore Democrats has given a distinctive twist to these earlier strategies for rooting U.S. citizenship in private, familial commitments. Today, mainstream discourses reimagine the nation as populated by citizens who are identified *as* citizens not just by virtue of their orientations toward family and sexuality but more specifically through their "infantile" relationship to the nation.

Infantilizing the citizen means figuring the citizen as a being in grave peril and endangered by threats circulating within the private realm, above all, threats concerning childbearing and sexuality. For Berlant, the endlessly reproduced images of fetuses and children that saturate our popular culture furnish the key symbols for this mode of citizenship. Perpetually vulnerable to being traumatized by sexual predators and errant or unwilling mothers, the infantile citizen finds protection in the arms of the nation that gears up to monitor, reform, incapacitate, or expel these internal deviants.[11] Thus, when the discourses of national policy formation are mobilized to cleanse the Internet of pornography, "defend marriage" against homosexual incursions on its traditional meaning, provide "opportunities" to women and children "imprisoned" by cycles of "welfare dependency," and restrict abortion, the therewith infantilized resident acquires both self-knowledge and public recognition as a citizen.

Sex scandals, we would argue, reinvigorate this figure of the "citizen-victim" by providing occasions to rehearse the discourse of dismay over the exposure of children to sexually explicit material, which the reporting on the scandal inevitably enacts. The Clinton scandal recited the emergent norm of infantile citizenship in an additional way when conservatives attempted to portray Lewinsky as a vulnerable intern. Lewinsky thus in one sense came to typify the traumatized subject-position of the citizen-victim in desperate need of the state's paternalistic protection (even while, as the "stalker," she also personified a variety of aggressively feminine threats to sexual normativity). Clinton, too, was cast as a citizen-victim by various forces with divergent objectives. Some on the left tried to seize the victim narrative for Clinton's defense, portraying him as a "sex addict" in dire need of professional help. More commonly, the notion that Clinton fell prey to the exorbitancy of his own desires was woven into less sympathetic discourses stereotyping him (and his roaming, unmanageable, and putatively tasteless appetites) as the product of his "white trash" background.[12] Here, Clinton's identity as white trash, certified by his apparent inability to control his own body, served as a particular permutation of his more general infantilism. On the one hand, we might have expected efforts to infantilize Clinton (whether from the left or the right) to fail, for as the personification of the masculinized state the president's role was to lend succor to the feminized and infantilized nation, not to model its imperiled condition. On the other hand, insofar as U.S. citizenship increasingly takes shape as an experience of personal identification with the nation's leader rather than a more critical-rational experience of representation and agency, the characterization of Clinton as a citizen-victim can be seen as both inevitable and functional, in the sense of reproducing this mode of citizenship.[13]

Is it possible, however, that the Clinton scandal may have also nourished more autonomous and mature forms of citizenship by reawakening the public to a more traditionally liberal sense of the distinction between political leaders' private conduct and public responsibilities? Liberalism presumes that citizens are rational beings capable of dis-

cerning the public interest and holding accountable those public officials whose private conduct egregiously interferes with their public
duties or who misuse public powers to serve private ends. The Clinton
scandal generated open controversy over whether the president's actions had violated the public trust, and more generally over the proper
distinction between public and private affairs. In doing so, it arguably stimulated some citizens who otherwise would not have done so
to reflect critically on both the content of the public interest and its
categorical differences from private affairs. It rather more clearly motivated some to hold public officials accountable, by favoring the Democrats in the 1998 elections, for trying to make partisan advantage mas-
querade as the public good. To be sure, as we have argued, it would be
unwise to take at face value these election results and the polled majorities approving of Clinton's job performance and opposing his removal
from office while disapproving of his personal conduct. But these in-
dicators of critical thinking and action by citizens, crude though they
are, are still of some worth and suggest that many U.S. citizens may not
have regressed to the degree one would surmise from reading Berlant.

Even if this more optimistic view of citizens' responses to the Clinton scandal is warranted, however, sex scandals still contribute powerfully to the culture of depoliticization analyzed by Berlant. That is because the autonomously and critically reasoning citizen of liberalism is
not necessarily a democratic citizen who is inclined toward participatory and inclusive deliberation or communication. For Berlant, regular
exposure to the media's coverage of the events it defines as national
crises ensures that "the infantile citizen has a memory of the nation
and a tactical relation to its operation. But no vision of sustained individual or collective criticism and agency accompanies the national system here."[14] Insofar as the Clinton scandal resensitized people to their
rights, responsibilities, and capacities as citizens in a liberal polity, this
scandal actually may have bolstered "individual criticism and agency."
But even so, the scandal worked against this same effect, while intensifying the decline in "collective criticism and agency." It did this
by recirculating the discourse of citizen-victimhood and celebrating
citizenship as consumerism incited by "the national culture industry
[that] provides information about the United States but has no interest in producing knowledge that would change anything."[15] Further,
and ironically, precisely inasmuch as it restored vitality to the liberal
model of citizenship and the principle of an inviolable private sphere,
the Clinton scandal may have depressed democratic energies. For in a
liberal polity where the private realm furnishes the substance of public

life, there is necessarily an underdevelopment of political citizenship as a distinctive human activity in its own right—as something that is not reducible to the individual or factional pursuit of interest satisfaction.

Nevertheless, it is still possible for sex scandals to create opportunities for political interventions that enhance democracy. One way they can do this is by inspiring a critical awareness among ordinary citizens of the constructed and ideological character of the public/private divide. Party and media elites are unlikely to pursue the deconstruction of discourse organized around a distinction between public and private because of their investments in the social privileges this dichotomy supports. As we have argued, however, sex scandals inevitably bring the tenuousness of this binary to the fore. They thereby provide openings for ordinary citizens to use these events to develop their own critiques of the hegemonic versions of the public interest and the commonsense conceptions of privacy against which these reigning conceptions are defined. In addition, sex scandals can function as an occasion for the entry of new voices and new perspectives into public discourse, subverting exclusions that historically have been justified on the grounds that the relationships among power, sex, and sexuality are not proper subjects for political discussion. To be sure, sex scandals may reinforce masculinist, racist, and homophobic understandings of the public/private divide, as well as those conducive to class domination, by virtue of the categories mobilized to order the discursive relationship between sexuality and public power.[16] But at the same time, sex scandals can illuminate pathways citizens can take to reconstruct the public/private divide and its various valences with class, gender, race, and sexuality.

Sex Scandals and the Production of Political Identities Beyond reproducing and destabilizing hegemonic discourses concerning the meaning of public and private, sex scandals invariably bring to the surface certain specific ways in which regulation of the body geared toward the production of sexual, gender, and sex identities is central to the circulation of power in this society. On first sight, these effects appear focused on the male/masculine body: in U.S. politics, it seems that only men are capable of spawning a sex scandal, just as only women can beget "nannygates." However, the gendering of both kinds of scandal requires critical explanation given the undeniable fact that people of both sexes have tawdry affairs and hire illegal immigrants as domestic help. The gendering of scandal tells us something important about the ways gendered and sexed bodies are constructed via these media events.

For women, the process of gender/sex identity construction reflects deeply entrenched societal expectations that women devote themselves primarily to the nurture of children. Thus the nannygates of Zoë Baird (one of President Clinton's early choices for attorney general) and Linda Chavez (whom President George W. Bush originally tapped to head the Department of Labor), while scuttling the Senate's confirmation of these women to executive office, ritually reconfirmed various tropes in the construction of American femininity, including the obligatory guilt of mothers with professional careers and the responsibility of motherhood to safeguard the nation, embodied in the nuclear family, from "invasion" by foreign elements. In this way, nannygates serve to "put in their place" those women who disregard the enduring cultural imperative to stay within the boundaries of the home.

Like nannygates, sex scandals, too, are a way of keeping men in their proper place. Traditionally, the private sphere—the feminine realm—is concerned with satisfying bodily needs and pleasure, while the public sphere has been regarded as a higher realm governed by the logic of disembodied rationality. Sex scandals penalize public men who fall prey to carnal urgings. To be sure, virility is a core political value in the United States, but the man who *needs* sex undermines his own claim to manliness, a victim of desire rather than its master. Significantly, however, until the Clinton-Lewinsky scandal, with its revelations that Clinton had transgressed the norms of straight sex, sex scandals did not make an issue of the man's sexual behavior as such. This intensification of the regulation of the male body lends support to Berlant's insight that one of the key characteristics of the emergent "intimate public sphere" is that "formerly iconic" white/male/heterosexual citizens have lost "the freedom to feel unmarked" and "sense that they now have *identities*, when it used to be just other people who had them"—in this case, more diligently monitored *sexual* identities.[17] Clarence Thomas's alleged come-ons to Anita Hill were not only less noteworthy as sex acts in themselves; they were also inherently less shocking and consequential to a public historically accustomed to the discursive thematization and regulation of black male sexuality. This historical context made it very difficult for Thomas to try to defend his sexual conduct per se as adhering to the norm. Instead, he (and his advocates on the Senate Judiciary Committee) responded by emphasizing his personification of other norms of masculinity by stressing his devotion to his wife and narrating his personal history as a story of heroic, self-motivated, individual achievement in his chosen career.[18] Sex scandals thus further show men their social "place" by reaffirming the importance of both employment and marriage as such (rather than a family role that would include fatherhood) for normative masculinity. When Gary Hart and Bill Clinton launched public relations counteroffensives to media revelations regarding their affairs, respectively, with Donna Rice and Gennifer Flowers, in both cases it was crucially with their faithful wife by their side. Both candidates knew that strategically it was vital to respond to the charges of illicit *sex* by stressing their strong dedication to the institution of *marriage*.

Thomas also used the historical backdrop of racist discourse to his advantage, however, turning the tables on Hill by appealing to well-worn stereotypes of African American women as hypersexual (images deployed, for instance, to justify white men's rape of black women under slavery) to make her very accusations seem like evidence of her own sexual depravity.[19] Thomas's success in this regard points to another important aspect of the gendered (and engendering) aspects of sex scandals: although the direct targets of these stagings of regulatory practices are men, these events usually also rehearse gender norms pertaining to femininity—which is logically to be expected, given that in a basic sense the construction of masculinity depends on the establishment of its difference from the feminine other. Thus sex scandals reliably police women's sexual behavior, too, most frequently whenever the far-too-familiar type of the vamp rears her seductive head, as in the media's presentations of Rice, Flowers, and Lewinsky. And as the example of Thomas's successful demonization of Hill illustrates, sex scandals furnish scenes not simply for the recitation of gender norms defining femininity as such but more precisely for the reiteration of norms differentiating femininities (as well as masculinities) in terms of race (and class, as the endless derision lobbed at Clinton's "bimbos" with "big hair" typified).

It should additionally be noted that the reiteration of norms governing gender, racial, and sexual identity in the context of sex scandals does not exclusively depend on the performative recitation of normative identities by those directly involved in the scandal. Sex scandals call on members of the public, too, to join in this process of actualizing political-cultural identities. Martin Plot argues that the Clinton-Lewinsky affair generated a "deliberative scene," defined as an "extraordinary moment when a body politic is transversally mobilized and called upon to monitor and reflect upon its own rules for public life." Plot stresses that the outcomes of these processes are by their nature indeterminate and open to the efficacious involvement of the public, not simply despite the fact that they are set in motion by the corporate media but also because the media tend to abandon routine "scripts" and "turn from reporting to monitoring" in these contexts.[20] Plot's overexuberant optimism about the indeterminacy and substantively deliberative character of such "scenes" is, in our view, in need of some qualification. A hard look must be taken at how existing matrices of discursive power always already set the conditions of the possible when publics, "the public" as a general entity, or members of the public attempt to engage in self-reflection on the "rules for public life." Nevertheless, we heartily endorse the broader implication of Plot's argument: that sex scandals invariably involve ordinary citizens as active participants in nation-making processes. Indeed, the fact that sex scandals eagerly invite the public—and not just the protagonists in the tale of scandal—to perform and reiterate social norms is probably another important reason why the shame evoked in sex scandals never stays solely confined to the person accused of wrongdoing but invariably envelops the public as well.

Our approach to sex scandals thus takes it as axiomatic that a scandal never simply "is." Rather, a scandal is a discursive construct, a story that is told and may be retold by a variety of different narrators, including those who are not officially charged with the task of rehearsing the scandalous material in the media and in the halls of government. Unfortunately, conventional ways of interpreting the events occurring during a scandal tend to assume a hierarchy of agency that places citizens-consumers on the lowest, most passive rung. When a scandal is narrated as a story about government actions to investigate allegations of corruption, the characters usually fall into these familiar types: politicians are the primary agents, the media transmit information about political leaders' actions to the public, and the citizenry is generally passive, its contribution limited to the indirect power of judgment that it exercises through polls and the franchise.[21] Alternatively, scandals may be more cynically conceived as entertainment, a diversion for the masses from the obligations of work and other responsibilities, including that of substantive political engagement. From this perspective, scandals are complex cultural productions where the roles again seem easily identifiable: politicians are the leading actors, the media are the producers, and TV watchers make up the audience, whose role is to consume the spectacle obediently, perhaps occasionally expressing diffuse sentiments of satisfaction or dissatisfaction with the conduct or outcome of the investigation (and this more for the sake of seasoning the scandal story with a mildly savory subplot about the public's feelings than for the purpose of tangibly influencing the course of events).[22]

Both these modes of framing scandals obscure the possibility for discursive agency that a scandal provides ordinary citizens. To assess the political purchase of these opportunities, it is necessary to inquire into what sex scandals tell us about how public discourses reflect and reproduce the power of dominant institutions and normative identities. At the same time, it is essential to investigate openings for reappropriations of hegemonic discourses. Without denying the significance of the obstacles facing those outside the media elite who seek to be heard in public discourse—obstacles rooted in gross inequalities of resources as well as the less tangible but equally important disparities in access and privilege—the exclusion is not, and cannot be, total. For those committed to reversing the processes by which citizenship is being rendered entirely passive, virtual, and symbolic, the question is how to exploit the cracks in the regime of exclusion as opportunities for new voices to be heard.

It is clearly beyond our scope here either to provide a full assessment of the nature of the challenge that lies ahead or to offer a comprehensive solution. But we would like to highlight the following points as worthy of consideration for the development of such a counterhegemonic project. First, as suggested above, sex scandals threaten to expose the contingency of the public/private divide and thus to denaturalize the social privileges depending on this ideology. These privileges include not only those supported by a system of private property, but also protection from the regulation of oppressions practiced within the domestic sphere. Here, then, are opportunities for citizens to turn these events, which are otherwise salad days for the corporate media, into launching points for critiques of the very social inequalities that stratify access to the media. Of course, the trick is to contest the ideological implications of the public/private divide, especially with regard to private property, while at the same time vigorously defending the value and right of privacy as an aspect of individual freedom.

Second, citizens interested in a more democratic polity can highlight the ways sex scandals not only rearticulate given norms regarding gender, race, and sexuality, but also carry forward the necessary and constitutive contradictions within those norms. As Judith Butler argues, there is a "*de*constituting possibility in the very process of repetition" of "regulatory ideals" such as femininity, masculinity, whiteness, and heterosexuality. The invocation of a norm itself exposes the "gaps and fissures" within it, the impossibility of ever fully occupying the subject-position it articulates.[23] It should be possible, for instance, to amplify the static noise interfering with regnant codes of masculinity and male sexuality by representations of Clinton's body and desires in the Clinton-Lewinsky affair, while still avoiding any naïve heroization of the sexual and gender politics of the president who signed into law the Defense of Marriage Act and welfare "reform."

Third, at a time of increasingly mediated citizenship, it is clear that there is a new citizenship skill to be learned: how to reappropriate the news, how to use the media to tell our own stories. This seizure of voice can be accomplished only by citizens savvy about not just message but medium, citizens who know as much about news cycles as they do election cycles, citizens who not only appreciate the essential presence of "spin" in the delivery of the news but who are themselves capable of producing counterspin. This should not mean simply adapting to the rapidly evolving and disturbing structures of news reporting in the current era. As noted above, furious economic competition among media enterprises has spawned "the continuous news cycle, the growing power of sources over reporters, varying standards of journalism, and a fascination with inexpensive, polarizing argument."[24] Media coverage of the Clinton-Lewinsky scandal epitomized and intensified these tendencies. Simply to play along would yield at best a Pyrrhic victory for citizens concerned about expropriating the media as an instrument of popular accountability. Nevertheless, in a society populated by masses of people and stretching over vast territories, finding a way to use the media to broadcast messages to potentially sympathetic strangers, without having these messages completely altered by media routines, is simply an unavoidable element of any political strategy that has a chance of effecting widespread change.

Synopsis of the Book   In studying the politics of sex scandals, it is important to address the workings of those institutions explicitly charged with the authority to govern or to articulate the public's voice, as some recent writings on the Clinton-Lewinsky affair have done. It is also vital, however, to examine other significant institutional and cultural contexts in which sex scandals unleash and perpetuate effects of power—from Hollywood to Christian right radio; from feminist debates over core principles to African American struggles over the civil rights legacy; and in the rituals of citizenship, whether mediated by the consumption opportunities Americans are graced with in their public sphere or by their routine participation in the "society of the spectacle." *Public Affairs* both broadens the institutional focus and cuts across the realms traditionally distinguished as "state" and "culture." What institutional conditions give rise to sex scandals not as aberrations but as unintended by-products arising in the course of ordinary operations? What do these insights into institutional dynamics reveal about the challenges and possibilities for unsettling patterns of domination based on class, race, gender, and sexuality?

The essays in this collection have been arranged into three roughly defined groups. The essays in part 1 seek to furnish a variety of broader contexts within which to situate contemporary sex scandals in U.S. politics, including earlier political sex scandals, the history of U.S. political scandals in general, and narrations of sex scandals in institutional spheres beyond the realm of politics. The authors in part 2 focus on how the Clinton scandal revealed and reinforced, but also potentially destabilized and refashioned, the discursive conditions for feminist and antiracist politics, as well as activism geared toward economic justice. Part 3 investigates the institutional parameters within which any attempts by citizens to contest the antidemocratic and illiberal effects of sex scandals must be mobilized. The final three essays thus reflect broadly on sex scandals, major media events, and the conditions of public interaction in the contemporary United States, debating the possibility of critical agency in the "society of the spectacle" and the functions of the concept of the public sphere as both normative ideal and ideological fetish.

Joshua Gamson demonstrates that sex scandals tend to follow strikingly similar narrative trajectories in a variety of institutional contexts, including the political, religious, and corporate-entertainment worlds. Gamson looks at news coverage of three recent scandals involving men whose dealings with prostitutes were exposed to the public: televangelist Jimmy Swaggart's encounter with prostitute Debra Murphree in 1988, actor Hugh Grant's liaison with prostitute Divine Brown in 1995, and presidential advisor Dick Morris's tryst with prostitute Sherry Rowlands in 1996. Gamson shows how, in some ways, scandal reportage yields disparate story-lines depending on the particular features of persons and events (in Swaggart's case, hypocrisy became the main issue, whereas Grant was criticized for excessive risk taking and Morris for his putative amorality). These cases also enable us to see, however, how, across institutional fields, news coverage tends to follow a similar pattern: sex as such rapidly disappears, while the scandalous behavior gradually becomes normalized as the institutional context for the sexual behavior comes into focus. Scandal stories thus become not so much tales of individual failings as demonstrations of the routine moral compromises required by specific, public institutional roles. These dramatizations of the perilous (but seemingly inevitable, hence in a keen sense tragic) consequences of institutional responsibility ironically end up buttressing rather than undercutting the legitimacy of these institutions, even while manifesting their deep corruption.

Theodore J. Lowi's essay furnishes a broad context for analyzing contemporary political sex scandals in another way, by examining the long history of political scandals in the United States. Lowi figures scandal as a commodity that is exchanged among political contestants under variable "market" conditions. U.S. history has thus witnessed an irregular succession of bull and bear markets in political scandal, when political actors have thought it relatively more or less profitable to invest political resources in scandal investigation. For Lowi, scandal-trading gains appeal in periods when the party system is "deranged": when the party system cannot effectively process political conflict because of great unevenness in the partisan balance of power (or, more recently, the creation of weakly contested party strongholds in different constitutionally defined institutional contexts under conditions of "divided government"). Political scandals sometimes call forth rivers of pious talk about constitutional principles and the rule of law, as the impeachment of President Clinton notoriously did. Reading Lowi, however, we learn that these events are symptomatic of a *failure* of confidence in the Madisonian thesis that private ambitions can be constitutionally channeled in ways that serve public purposes. They also reveal dysfunctions in that shadow institutional realm without which, Lowi contends, constitutional government could never operate democratically: the realm of political parties. Like Gamson, then, Lowi finds that scandals illuminate and further entrench the failings of U.S. public institutions, although he is more critical than Gamson of how these episodes affect the institutions' durability.

Joshua D. Rothman further fleshes out the historical context for contemporary sex scandals in U.S. politics by excavating relics from what could have been the nation's first major sex scandal: the revelation in 1802 of the relationship between President Thomas Jefferson and his slave Sally Hemings. Rothman asks why this turned out to be a "sex scandal that wasn't": why journalist James Callender's publicization of Jefferson's affair with Hemings elicited so little response of a serious nature from Jefferson's political opponents. Contemporary readers, Rothman stresses, must rid themselves of any illusions that earlier eras of U.S. political history were less tarnished by the politics of personal attack than the present; in this period, in particular, political conflict tended to be intensely personalized. Nonetheless, Jefferson's Federalist enemies declined to inflame the Hemings affair into a full-fledged scandal. They chose not to do this for a variety of reasons, Rothman argues, above all out of respect for the ethical obligation among white men of privilege to maintain a gentlemanly silence in the national public sphere about slave owners' routine sexual abuse of their female slaves both as a form of domination and for personal gratification. Although Rothman himself does not transpose this analysis into a critical-theoretical register, his revealing and finely wrought account nonetheless makes it quite clear that in this "classical" era (and locus) of the bourgeois-liberal public sphere, a robust construction of the public/private divide generated specific zones of privacy inflected by race and class—and, increasingly, regard for the bourgeois family. He shows, moreover, that sex scandals had a notably less significant role in the stabilization and destabilization of the public/private distinction. This was mainly because of the general unwillingness to challenge the pretense of sexual-moral rectitude that safeguarded the power of upper-class white men. Precisely the ability of such hypocrisy to function smoothly in this manner marks a key contrast between Jefferson's era and our own. Although the Clinton scandal, for example, arguably reaffirmed the privileges of bourgeois masculinity insofar as Clinton's presumed access to sexual favors from female subordinates reinstantiated and reinforced traditional practices, the fact that not only Clinton but also Representatives Hyde and Livingston were called upon to atone publicly for transgressing their marital vows reveals the extent to which times have indeed changed.

From here, the book turns to a focused analysis of the discursive environment generated and reproduced by the Clinton scandal and the consequences of these discursive power plays for a variety of counterhegemonic projects. Taking an in-depth look at evangelical conservative talk radio, Paul Apostolidis argues that stories of Watergate and the Iran-Contra affair furnished genealogical reference points for the Christian right's outraged reception of the Clinton scandals. Narratives of these earlier scandals channel egalitarian hopes toward personal identification with political leaders, seeking to justify authoritarian leadership of the sort exposed by Watergate and Iran-Contra.

In this way, Christian right popular culture makes its adherents more comfortable with the general situation faced by all Americans: a crisis of democratic accountability, traceable in key ways to the advent of the post-Fordist structure of capital accumulation and state organization, that is far advanced in electoral and legislative institutions yet remains unaddressed in an ideological climate dominated by the politics of personalistic populism. Apostolidis's essay thus not only sheds light on the clash between the Christian right and Clinton; it also uses "scandal stories" to uncover the narrative conditions of pseudo-democratic leadership under post-Fordism more generally, as well as the potential for mobilizing counternarratives of leadership that stress the dependence of political equality and citizen power on economic justice.

George Shulman advances the discussion of the right's rhetoric in the Clinton scandal by contemplating the ways conservatives deployed jeremiadic discourses about race and the sixties in their attempt to bring Clinton down. In addition, moving beyond Rothman's analysis of a much earlier era, Shulman shows that today it is still the case that racial meanings are never far beneath the surface (if indeed they are hidden at all) when ideological work must be done to shore up the dominant norm of American individualism. For Shulman, according to the conservative ideal of possessive individualism, the American male's abilities to wisely manage private property and political freedom are vouchsafed by his sexual self-control. Ambivalence about such self-restraint, however, has traditionally led to the displacement of sexual longings onto people of color, especially African Americans. Thus, Shulman argues, attempts from the political right to reinvigorate possessive individualism have usually been accompanied by renewed calls for sexual puritanism and fortified racial oppression. The new right's long-term project of reversing the social, sexual, and racial progressivism of the sixties has proceeded exactly along these lines. This provides a major reason Republicans found Clinton's pursuit of sexual pleasure outside the bounds of procreation, marriage, and convention to be such an abomination. It also yields a key insight into the racial subtext of Clinton's impeachment. Shulman believes that certain of Clinton's defenders—in particular, Toni Morrison, who famously called on liberals and African Americans to close ranks behind "our first black president"—too uncritically reproduced both the right's "blacking up" of Clinton and its strategy of narrating nationhood through invocations of racial identity. He still finds room for hope, however, that articulations of a national "we" can be performed that can include both negative, "counternational testimonies" (like those for which Morrison herself is known) and appeals to common democratic aspirations.

Like Shulman, Anna Marie Smith criticizes the tendency in the attempt to defend Clinton against the right's onslaught to gloss over or rationalize certain elements of his policy legacy that were far from progressive. Whereas Shulman points out the dissonance between Clinton's record on racial issues and his imputed status as the country's "first black president," Smith explores the political and rhetorical strategies Clinton and his handlers employed to promote the image of himself as pro-woman. Smith identifies an "ironic logic of two juxtapositions." First, she finds that Clinton was able to define himself as a pro-woman president despite his spotty record of commitment to public policies promoting women's interests. This became possible, she argues, by virtue of the symbolic power of his marriage to a capable, empowered, and professionally successful woman. Second, Smith observes that Clinton's trysts with Lewinsky occurred during a period when the scrutiny of space and presidential access in the White House was at its most intense because of the government shutdown of 1995 and the Clinton staff's efforts to enhance its professionalism. Why should the physical logistics of the president's liaisons with Lewinsky matter to feminists? Because, Smith contends, they underscore the fact that "one of the most infamous extramarital affairs of the century was conducted in a workplace." They thus furnish feminists with an opportunity to stress the difference between sexual harassment and consensual sex, against strenuous conservative efforts to muddy this distinction, and despite receiving no help in this regard from Clinton. They further enable activists to address sexual harassment through strategies that collectively empower workers to confront a wide range of harmful practices by employers and supervisors, in lieu of what Smith calls a "one-size-fits-all prohibition of sex in the workplace" that saddles feminists with the unsavory task of policing sexual behavior. Working insistently at the intersection of class- and gender-based power relations, Smith thus caps off the demonstration in Part Two of the overlapping—and contestable—dynamics of class, race, and gender in the current conservative hegemonic order, which the Clinton scandal both underscored and opened to challenge.

While the essays in Part Two share the assumption that the Clinton scandal reveals important aspects of social power relations and calls for active engagement in (feminist, anti-racist, working-class) politics, the authors in Part Three more pointedly interrogate the conditions of public engagement as such in the United States today, as well as publicity's relation to a nonpublic zone. Juliet A. Williams notes that in the wake of the Starr probe, there is evidence of a growing popular movement to revive and restore privacy, not just as a legal right but as a cultural norm. Williams is critical of this trend, and issues a series of warnings about the dangers of a renewed commitment to privacy doctrine. "Privacy in the (Too Much) Information Age" begins with a study of the logic and history of privacy doctrine in U.S. law. Although the right to privacy is commonly understood to protect individual autonomy, Williams contends that the law of privacy has been elaborated by the courts in a way that promotes socially sanctioned lifestyles while enabling the regulation of those who reject dominant moral ideals. Instead of confronting the limitations of privacy doctrine, however, Williams notes a pervasive tendency to dismiss critics of the privacy ideal, especially those feminist theorists and activists who have insisted that "the personal is political." Rather than defending the embattled privacy ideal, Williams encourages us to move beyond the rigidly conceived dichotomy between the spheres of public and private. Though the idea of inviolable privacy rights has obvious appeal, especially after the at times excruciating ordeal of the Clinton-Lewinsky-Starr affair, the complexities and ambiguities of the contemporary social world demand new imaginings of social space and relationships within it.

While Williams thus recommends a new, ideologically creative form of political involvement, beyond the defense of privacy, Jeremy Varon raises the sobering question of just how possible this may be in the age of spectacle. He thereby shifts the methodological focus from hermeneutical strategies of unpacking the discourses circulated through the scandal to the forms in which the scandal was experienced. The "society of the spectacle," classically theorized by Guy Debord, still defines our social experience, Varon argues, and the Clinton-Lewinsky-Starr affair epitomized this condition. Viewing the spectacular unfolding of the scandal's events as such served as the crucial means by which Americans organized collective and private memory, created shared vocabularies, and affirmed a sense of their Americanness. In this, the Clinton scandal rehearsed similar rituals of watching enacted previously by the O. J. Simpson chase and trial, the Clarence Thomas confirmation hearings, the coverage of Princess Diana's death and funeral . . . and the list goes on. Emphasizing Debord's critical, not just descriptive, intent, Varon ponders the dimensions of the political real that elude Americans' collective consciousness and capacities for agency under the reign of the spectacle, dimensions whose contours may have been suggested in an appalling and shocking way by the events of September 11, 2001.

Jodi Dean helps us define the problem even more acutely and specifically: How can Americans disengage from the spectacle and carry out rational-critical debate over "real" political issues when, as the Clinton scandal illustrated, the media themselves now routinely use self-evaluations (and self-flagellations) regarding their own failure to meet the ideal of critical publicity as a technique for padding their audiences? Dean's answer, in a spirit contrasting with both Williams' and Varon's interventions, is to throw open the very concept of the public sphere for radical critique and ultimately to reject it in the name of democracy. For Dean, the elements of spectacle and media-driven consumerism that attended the Clinton-Lewinsky affair did not thwart the democratic aspirations of the public sphere because the Habermasian binary between consumer culture and a democratic public sphere itself should be questioned. The consumerist spectacle as such is not the enemy of democracy, Dean insists, because the development of a "global technoculture" has dramatically increased the inclusiveness and participatory qualities of mediated spaces in terms of race, sex, and class. It is rather the ideal of rational-critical publicity, turned into a fetish, that operates ideologically today by constituting the public as the compulsive discussants of revealed secrets (whose need for the disclosure of further secret knowledge grows ever greater) rather than as an active citizenry.

Both commonalities and divergences, in methodology and interpretation alike, thus criss-cross the essays in this collection. Our hope, ultimately, is that *Public Affairs* productively raises and specifies a number of controversies for democratic politics in the United States in the age of sex scandals. Do sex scandals reinforce the power of existing economic, cultural, and political institutions, or hasten their debilitation? Can sex scandals generate real opportunities for citizens committed to feminist and antiracist politics to engage in the battle over the construction of public discourses and the meanings of the key words that prominently circulate through these discourses ("our first black president," "a pro-woman president," "the personal is political"), even while they induce some left-oriented scholar-activists to reinscribe racist and/or sexist understandings of American nationhood and political subjectivity—and even under the conditions of the Debordian spectacle? How far is the transformative power of feminist, antiracist, and class-egalitarian discursive interventions limited by the tendencies of sex scandals to revalidate uncritically the moral authority of core social and political institutions, to hasten the corrosion of party-based mechanisms for ensuring democratic accountability, to generate consent to a post-Fordist political economy marked by deep contradictions, to realize the ideal of the deliberative public sphere as nothing but ideology, and to dissolve all public communication into spellbound fascination with the consumerist spectacle? Does the recent proliferation of sex scandals suggest the need to rekindle public commitment to traditional principles of U.S. governance and modern political theory, or to revitalize modernist-redemptive critiques of the institutions that draw on earlier Marxist and feminist traditions and precedent struggles for racial equality, or to take up the postmodernist (anti)project of becoming active citizens within spectacular technoculture?

While we mean to open all these questions for discussion, there is still a general sense characterizing almost all of the pieces here that the tendencies of sex scandals to reinforce patterns of domination do not and cannot determine the politics of sex scandals in a pure and simple manner. Rather than merely eliciting ripples of ashamed, self-indulgent, and voyeuristic twittering, sex scandals send profound tremors through the discursive tectonics of politics in the United States. For citizens, the primary task is to take the measure of these shocks and quakes and amplify their magnitude in ways that maximally expose and begin to address the faultlines rending U.S. democracy.

Notes

1 Dana D. Nelson and Tyler Curtain, "The Symbolics of Presidentialism: Sex and Democratic Identification," in *Our Monica, Ourselves: The Clinton Affair and the National Interest*, ed. Lauren Berlant and Lisa Duggan (New York: New York University Press, 2001), 34–52; Anne Cvetkovich, "Sexuality's Archive: The Evidence of the Starr Report," in Berlant and Duggan, 268–82.

2 We are grateful to an anonymous reader for the insightful suggestion that in cases in which the alleged perpetrator of a scandalous act tries to cover up a misdeed, there may in fact be a triple boundary crossing: a transgression of a social norm (such as having sex outside of marriage or stealing public funds); the publicization of the transgression; and revelations of efforts at a cover-up. All three of these stages unfolded, for example, in the Clinton, Nixon, and Oliver North scandals.

3 For example, see Robin Gaster, "Sex, Spies, and Scandal: The Pro-

fumo Affair and British Politics," in Andrei S. Markovits and Mark Silverstein, eds., *The Politics of Scandal: Power and Process in Liberal Democracies* (New York: Holmes and Meier, 1988), 62–88; Anthony King, "Sex, Money, and Power," in *Politics in Britain and the United States: Comparative Perspectives*, ed. Richard Hodder-Williams and James Ceaser (Durham, NC: Duke University Press, 1986).

4 William E. Scheuerman, "Kenneth Starr's Rule of Law—and Ours," *Constellations* 6.2 (June 1999): 137–41.

5 Andrew Arato, "Impeachment or Revision of the Constitution?" *Constellations* 6.2 (June 1999): 145–56.

6 Bill Kovach and Tom Rosenstiel, *Warp Speed: America in the Age of Mixed Media* (New York: Century Foundation Press, 1999), 1–9.

7 Molly W. Andolina and Clyde Wilcox, "Public Opinion: The Paradoxes of Clinton's Popularity," in Mark J. Rozell and Clyde Wilcox, *The Clinton Scandal and the Future of American Government* (Washington: Georgetown University Press, 2000), 171–94.

8 Sasha Torres, "Sex of a Kind: On Graphic Language and the Modesty of Television News," in Berlant and Duggan, 102–15.

9 Eric O. Clarke, "Sex and Civility," in Berlant and Duggan, 285–90.

10 See Gwendolyn Mink, *The Wages of Motherhood: Inequality in the Welfare State* (Ithaca: Cornell University Press, 1995); Michael Rogin, *Ronald Reagan: The Movie* (Berkeley: University of California Press, 1987), 245.

11 Lauren Berlant, *The Queen of America Goes to Washington City: Essays on Sex and Citizenship* (Durham, NC: Duke University Press, 1997), 1–4.

12 See Micki McElya, "Trashing the Presidency: Race, Class, and the Clinton/Lewinsky Affair," in Berlant and Duggan, 156–74.

13 On this logic of "presidentialism" as the defining form of American citizenship, see Nelson and Curtain, "The Symbolics of Presidentialism: Sex and Democratic Identification," 34–52.

14 Berlant, *The Queen of America Goes to Washington City*, 50–51.

15 Ibid., 51–52.

16 Hence, for example, the (self-)scripting of Clarence Thomas as the victim of Anita Hill's imputed sexual predations made it difficult for this scandal to inspire either a new interest in the sexual mistreatment of African American women as an important public concern, or a new critical awareness of stereotypes blaming black women themselves (specifically, their supposedly outlandish bodily desires and alleged character flaws, matters by definition "private") for the rape and harassment they have endured. As Berlant puts it, invocations of the sexualized citizen-victim tend to "dilute oppositional discourses" by assimilating more specific questions of justice into the narrow confines of this formula. See Berlant, *The Queen of America Goes to Washington*

City, 2; Homi K. Bhabha, "A Good Judge of Character: Men, Metaphors, and the Common Culture," in Toni Morrison, ed., *Race-ing Justice, En-gendering Power: Essays on Anita Hill, Clarence Thomas, and the Construction of Social Reality* (New York: Pantheon, 1992), 232–50; Claudia Brodsky Lacour, "Doing Things with Words: 'Racism' as Speech Act and the Undoing of Justice," in Morrison, 127–58; Nell Irvin Painter, "Hill, Thomas, and the Use of Racial Stereotype," in Morrison, 200–214.

17 Berlant, *The Queen of America Goes to Washington City*, 2.

18 See Bhabha, "A Good Judge of Character"; Painter, "Hill, Thomas, and the Use of Racial Stereotype"; and Gayle Pemberton, "A Sentimental Journey: James Baldwin and the Thomas-Hill Hearings," in Morrison, 172–99.

19 See Bhabha, "A Good Judge of Character"; Painter, "Hill, Thomas, and the Use of Racial Stereotype"; and Gayle Pemberton, "A Sentimental Journey: James Baldwin and the Thomas-Hill Hearings."

20 Martin Plot, "Deliberative Scenes and Democratic Politics in the Lewinsky Case," *Constellations* 6.2 (June 1999): 167, 172–73.

21 A recent collection of essays on the Clinton scandal edited by Mark J. Rozell and Clyde Wilcox, *The Clinton Scandal*, featuring the work of mainstream political scientists, offers a good example of this sort of interpretive framework. The pieces in this volume reflect thoughtfully and critically on the institutional origins and implications of the Clinton scandal, mainly within the sphere of government. Some especially provocative pieces here provide insights into the ways the independent counsel statute and various court decisions have channeled and circumscribed the agency of presidents and congressional leaders. Throughout the book, however, the citizenry appears only as the source for polled information about public opinion and as an electorate.

22 A more sophisticated and critical approach to analyzing scandal along these lines contends that the politics of scandals emanates more from scandals' formal-practical than their substantive narrative characteristics. In this collection, Jeremy Varon takes precisely this tack, revealing how the Clinton scandal was driven by and reproduced the logic of the spectacle, in Guy Debord's terms.

23 Judith Butler, *Bodies That Matter: On the Discursive Limits of "Sex"* (New York: Routledge, 1993), 10.

24 Kovach and Rosenstiel, *Warp Speed*, 1–9.

1

Sex Scandals in U.S. Politics: Theoretical, Social, and Historical Contexts

Normal Sins

Sex Scandal Narratives as
Institutional Morality Tales

I n the past two decades alone, national politicians have been accused of affairs with female and male prostitutes and pages, fon-
dling or groping others and exposing themselves, attending drugs
and-sex parties, having intercourse with minors, and allowing sex rings
to operate from their apartments. Entertainers have been revealed to
have masturbated in movie theaters, solicited transvestite prostitutes,
made sex videos of themselves, and simulated lesbian sex for photog-
raphers. Religious leaders have been accused of homosexual orgies
with young Brazilian men, liaisons with church secretaries, and wife
swapping, and similar charges have erupted in the military and in the
academy.

Sex scandals, in which sexual activities (demonstrated or alleged)
of public figures are widely broadcast, with an ensuing public discussion of these activities as "transgressions of certain values, norms, or
moral codes," have a long history in Anglo-American culture.[1] Historians have provided rich accounts of scandals in Victorian Britain and
nineteenth-century United States, joined by occasional analytical accounts of individual twentieth-century sex scandals and nonscholarly
books surveying the territory.[2] Yet popular accounts of sex scandals
tend to treat "each new case as if it sprung up *sui generis*"[3] and sociologists have been remarkably reluctant to confront sex scandal stories
as significant cultural phenomena. This is especially odd given that, as
a small body of theoretical literature on the subject has noted, scandals
constitute a cultural genre that is quite distinct and by now familiar:[4]
as outlined by William Cohen, the narrative is built "on the tripartite
juridical model of plaintiff, defendant, and jury," in which "an accuser
exposes an indiscretion or iniquity in the life of an accused and broadcasts that secret for public consumption, and the accused responds

with denial."[5] One can discern, both in others' accounts of sex scandals and in the cases considered in what follows, an increasingly common set of moments in mass-mediated sex scandals following a common scandal script: accusation or revelation, broadcast, denial and/or confession, and, frequently, a comeback or attempted comeback. Just how that script is constructed, and what it might be doing, remains understudied.

Perhaps the sparse sociological consideration of sex scandals can be attributed to their apparent transparency: they appear to be simply barometers of sexual moralities, moments in which a society reminds itself what is and is not acceptable sexual behavior by punishing, with public humiliation and the risk of status loss, those highly visible people caught doing the unacceptable stuff. Such a perspective is not exactly wrong. Behavior can easily be irritating roguery in one generation or country and sexual harassment in another, something people do in public in one century and something seen as behind-closed-doors activity in another, shocking and immoral in one decade and merely a bit unseemly a few decades later or earlier.

Yet, although sex scandal narratives are, generally speaking, carriers of social attitudes toward sexual morality, treating them exclusively as such can keep hidden their more puzzling and revealing aspects. To begin with, the actual *sex* they consider is strikingly banal. As Michael Schudson has argued, and as I will further demonstrate, "The scandalous act rarely involves anything exotic," and "of all the elements of a sex scandal, the scandalous act itself may be the least important."[6] Historically, moreover, sexual conservatism (or, for that matter, sexual liberalism) and the prevalence of sex scandals do not line up consistently.[7]

Even more tellingly, when one looks at nationally publicized sex scandals across institutional settings in the same time period, as does the current study, holding the national sexual culture roughly constant, it is hard to retain the notion that sex scandals are simply snapshots of societywide sexual values or values conflicts. When it comes to sex scandal narratives, a quick historical check suggests that the emergence of a scandal story is tightly tied to its institutional location. As John Summers has shown, even as the sexual activities of movie stars and sports heroes were being "relentlessly probed and devoured" in early twentieth-century mass culture's "agitation against Victorian values" — with Charlie Chaplin and Fatty Arbuckle embroiled in high-profile sex scandals, for instance — politicians were exempted from scrutiny, pursuing "illicit sexual pleasures . . . evidently unafraid that a demand for accountability might lead to opprobrium."[8] And amid all the strange, juicy details of contemporary sex scandals—the cigars as sex toys, the biting and the toe sucking, the steamed-up car windows, and so on—are the noteworthy facts that behavior that is scandalous in one institutional environment barely gets a mention in another. Indeed, what is underplayed in both the limited scholarly work and the voluminous popular commentary on scandal is the simple recognition that the scandal script unfolds, as Gary Alan Fine has asserted, "within an institutional structure (e.g., politics, business, the media) and, more significantly, must be said to characterize that structure."[9]

Institutions matter in another way. Put simply, sex scandal stories are selected and conveyed by media professionals and, as scholars have routinely shown,[10] this institutional mediation—the specific ways reporting is organized, the structure of social relations between media workers and those in other institutional worlds (religious, political, entertainment, etc.)—affects the storytelling. Again, historical evidence offers an anchor. When, for example, a period of regular public exposure about the sexual lives of politicians (e.g., in the 1884 presidential campaign, Grover Cleveland was subjected to accusations of "habitual immoralities with women" and of fathering an illegitimate child) gave way to "reticence and insulation" by the end of the nineteenth century (e.g., while Warren Harding's extramarital affairs were an open secret among politicians and journalists, "neither journalists nor rival Democrats disclosed his philandering to the voting public"), it gave way in large part thanks to the professionalization of journalism.[11] The "promise of reticence," Summers suggests, "permitted elite reporters to get closer to the instruments of government power," offering "an expedient means by which reporters could establish themselves as experts in an increasingly segmented, hierarchical society."[12] Although my focus is on scandal storytelling rather than on the selection or suppression of scandals, the lesson is useful: what is revealed in sex scandal discourse is not simply societal norms—sexual or other, institution-specific or not—but also the institutional operations and relations of news media.

Taking the institutional context of scandals into account requires, then, documenting and analyzing how sex scandal discourse varies from one institutional location to another, and to what degree and in what ways the stories told concern institutions themselves; it further requires a consideration of how media institutional practices shape sex scandal scripts.[13] In this comparative "instrumental case study,"[14] I therefore examine the media coverage of three different U.S. sex scandals that received major national attention during an eight-year time span, each alleging the same behavior (sexual relations between a man and a female prostitute), each involving men who were public figures before the scandal and women who were not, and each set in a different institutional environment: in the realm of religion, televangelist Jimmy Swaggart's encounter with prostitute Debra Murphree in 1988; in the entertainment arena, actor Hugh Grant's encounter with prostitute Divine Brown in 1995; and in the political sphere, presidential advisor Dick Morris's encounter with prostitute Sherry Rowlands in 1996. I rebuild and analyze these media-processed scandal stories based on all full-text coverage available through the online databases Academic Universe and Academic Search, including newspapers, magazines, and television transcripts, all of which are from mainstream regional and national publications, wire services, or programs. After duplicates and items of fewer than one hundred words were eliminated, this yielded a total of 59 documents for the Swaggart case, 69 for the Grant case, and 95 for the Morris case.[15] (These documents were supplemented by coverage of the scandals in "men's magazines" such as *Penthouse*, in which the women of scandal often eventually appear.)[16] Data analysis proceeded through an inductive coding process much like that of "grounded theory."[17] My search was for the limited number of dominant frames— "schemata of intepretation," in the language of media discourse analysts[18]—contained in the media telling of and commentary on each story, and a chronological account of the movement from one theme to another over the course of the scandal's career. The documentary paper trail I follow and use is most accurately understood as stories told by one set of institutional elites (journalists, editors, etc.) about members of other institutional elites (people at the center of religious, political, and entertainment "industries"), with an eye toward those consuming the media product.

The findings dramatically bear out the significance of both institutional location and mediation. On the one hand, within the same overarching scandal narrative, quite different themes come to the fore: in one case, the relationship with a prostitute gives rise to a story primarily focused on hypocrisy; in another, to a story focused mainly on risk taking; in the last, to a story focused mainly on disloyalty. On the other hand, in each case, discussions of sexual "misbehavior" kick the story into gear and are then mostly sidelined, edged aside by discussions of the possibility that hypocrisy, risk, or disloyalty are actually facilitated by the institutional environment in which the scandalous man operates. Sex scandal stories, far from being lessons about individual sexual transgression, morph into *institutional morality tales.* This shared feature of sex scandal narratives is best understood, I argue, through an analysis of media behaviors: it results from pronounced needs on the part of mainstream media organizations to both mimic and distinguish themselves from tabloid media and from journalists' interest in transforming "soft" into "hard" news stories. Given the well-known tendency in U.S. culture toward individualist and away from structural frames and the well-known tendency in sociology to interpret tales of "sin" as reminders of the normative order, such a dynamic is especially striking. While drawing on and buttressing "cultural givens" about masculine sexuality, these scandal stories offer a theoretically challenging twist: an unexpected cultural reversal, in which sexual "sins" reveal not individual but institutional pathologies, not a normative order but institutional decay.

Jimmy Swaggart: Normal Hypocrisy Undoubtedly the most famous image from the 1988 scandal over televangelist Jimmy Swaggart's visits to a New Orleans prostitute was his sobbing, televised "I have sinned!" confession at Swaggart's own World Faith Center in Baton Rouge. Although a spokesman for the Assemblies of God, the parent church that was then investigating the charges of sexual misconduct against Swaggart and considering various punishments, suggested that the preacher had shown "true humility and repentance,"[19] most secular commentators were less impressed. "The sin for which Swaggart has been forgiven is the sexual transgression for which he has apologized," columnist Richard Cohen wrote in the *Washington Post.* "The sin of hypocrisy is a different matter. For that we hear no contrition and no apology from Swaggart."[20] The dominant media frame through which the Swaggart story was typically told was much less about the exposure of scandalous sexual behavior per se than about the exposure of *hypocrisy*—and along with it, a *turf war,* in which feuding preachers use scandal as a weapon in their fight for a share of the religion market. Indeed, as the story progressed, these two frames, joined later by discussions of religious theatricality, overshadowed considerations of sexual norms, focusing attention instead on the workings of market-centered religious institutions.

Of course, sex was an excellent trigger for and carrier of the hypocrisy tale. It is no secret that news organizations perceive sexual stories as attention grabbers, and for the two weeks after the story broke, in late February 1988, reporters regularly took the opportunity to describe the prostitution world to which Swaggart regularly traveled, Arline Highway, "a seedy strip of no-tell motels, their neon lights flashing adult movies, water beds and rooms by the hour," where Debra Murphree said she "performed obscene acts" for the "sex-crazed" preacher.[21] But whereas early reports noted that the investigation by the Assemblies of God focused on "sexual morals charges" and "adultery," the morality of prostitution, and of married men visiting prostitutes, or even of extramarital sex, was almost never the frame of mainstream media stories and commentary.[22]

Instead, what animated the stories was the dramatic contrast between Swaggart's own routine holier-than-thou lashings of other preachers' sexual immorality and the photographs of him in a sweat suit in the Arline Highway parking lot. It was Swaggart who had urged the investigation of Jim Bakker on charges of adulterous and bisexual behavior, news stories reminded readers, and who had preached against false prophets, "pompadoured pretty-boys with their hair done and their nails done who call themselves preachers"; it was he who warned readers of his book *Straight Answers to Tough Questions*, the *Los Angeles Times* pointed out, against sexually corrupting activities such as dancing, mixed swimming, movies, masturbation, and pornography.[23] "Many of Swaggart's holier-then-thou pieties could come back to haunt him now that the worm has turned," *Newsweek* reported early on.[24] Prostitute visits were scandalous not so much because of sexual immorality as because of the hypocrisy they revealed.

If sexual revelations were the means through which a story of hypocrisy was initially carried—the story of a heavy-handed moralist foiled by the very sexual activities he chastised in others—the sexual aspects were rarely the primary subject of nationally publicized discussion, and, except for a gloating, self-justifying *Penthouse* spread, they mostly disappeared.[25] (Swaggart himself never specified his "sins," though Murphree emerged early on with her claim that he had paid her to pose in various positions culled from pornographic magazines while he masturbated.) As the story progressed, news coverage quickly focused not on Swaggart as a renegade hypocrite, but on what the scandal revealed about the *profession and institution of televangelism*.

As soon as it erupted, in fact, the scandal began to be placed in a context that made hypocrisy seem a rather unsurprising part of Swaggart's world, in which public moralizing was routine, performance was part of the job, financial stakes were high, and rivalries were numerous. The hypocrisy-revealed frame was quickly joined by a second major frame, that of a larger "holy war," as *Newsweek* called it,[26] in which the Swaggart investigation was one battle. In this frame, Swaggart and his fall were taken as representative of televangelism's workings, its product rather than its exception. "The turmoil in [Swaggart's] ministry in this year of wild upheaval in the television evangelism," a *New York Times* report suggested, "may be the most telling indicator to date of the tensions that threaten to transform the billion-dollar world of the electronic church."[27]

Many accounts told the story of a religious "industry," "wealthy spiritual empires" that "nurture gold-plated lifestyles," composed of money- and-power-hungry backstabbers.[28] Swaggart sat at the head of a "$156 million-a-year global television empire," the *Washington Post* reported in its first article on the scandal, living, the *New York Times* reported, in "a $2.4 million house with security fence, electronic sensors, and columned whirlpool bath fed by a faucet in the form of a golden swan."[29] In the "holy war" frame, the fight for control of such riches is exactly what triggered the scandal in the first place: "a rival evangelist," Marvin Gorman, who had filed a 1987 lawsuit against Swaggart for spreading rumors about Gorman's own sexual misconduct, effectively ending Gorman's ministry, went in search of the "sweet taste of vengeance," the *Washington Post* suggested, and found it on Arline Highway.[30] Others in this competitive marketplace, most notably Rev. Jerry Falwell, quickly staked claims in the "turf war" by calling for further investigations.[31]

If high-stakes rivalry characterized coverage of the moment of revelation, the moment of confession was characterized by discussions of theatricality—like rivalry, presented as a typical feature of evangelical religious institutions. While Swaggart emphasized personal responsibility ("I have no one but myself to blame," "I am not going to whitewash my sin," etc.),[32] mainstream media assessments tended to treat his confession as a demonstration of Pentecostal evangelism's constant stream of performances, this one distinguished only by its extravagance. "Swaggart should have been nominated for an Oscar in the best actor category this year," said commentator Andy Rooney, for instance.[33] In a typical passage, a *San Diego Union-Tribune* writer also described the confession as a performance "truly worthy of an Oscar":

> Rolling his eyes toward heaven and proclaiming with all the fire and brimstone of a modern day Elmer Gantry, Swaggart confessed that he had sinned. . . . As the cameras zoomed in for a closeup of Swaggart's

tear-soaked, distorted face, he was careful not to wipe even one of those tears away. His voice was a mere whisper as he begged his family's and his Lord's forgiveness. In the picture was his dutiful wife Frances, nodding her pardon, and their son mouthing a tearful "I love you." In the background were white-robed choir members shaking and sobbing. And as the camera panned the congregation, it revealed that many had fallen to their knees in prayer. When it was over, the audience gave the fallen minister a standing ovation.[34]

In this narration, Swaggart's confessions and apologies demonstrate not moral recovery but snake-oil evangelist doing shtick for a paying audience.

When, several months later, the comeback-attempt phase of Swaggart's scandal arrived—he returned to the pulpit against the orders of the Assemblies of God—it was widely reported as another theatrical attempt to "salvage his crippled $150 million empire from the wages of his confessed sin."[35] On the pulpit, in the *Washington Post* account, he was "defrocked but defiant," dancing around the stage in "a natty blue suit," exhorting Satan and "declaring that Jesus had not just washed away his, but all sin."[36] In a strikingly similar *Los Angeles Times* report, "The golden-haired preacher in the sharp black suit wept, shouted Scripture, spoke in tongues, sang, danced, groveled on his knees, played piano, wept, hugged his weeping wife and told in whispers of dark, prophetic dreams and desperate, late-night conversations with the Lord," launched "into a long sermon about guilt, and why he should no longer feel it," and also "asked for money more than once," concerned with "removing the paralysis that has clutched his $150-million-a-year ministry."[37]

Just as the story of Swaggart's sexual transgressions quickly became one of hypocrisy, the hypocrisy revealed became, as the scandal narrative unfolded, an emblematic feature of evangelical institutions: given the financial stakes, media storytelling suggested, televangelists routinely gave performances of morality rather than lived by it. Institutional logic, in fact, made it hard to tell whether you were looking at "holy man or huckster," as *Larry King Live* put it.[38] As the *New York Times* summed it up, "The Spirit-filled passions that brought men like Mr. Swaggart or Jim Bakker to the top are the very things that could spell their downfall in a competitive world in which too many preachers may be chasing too few dollars."[39] In the end, the mass-mediated scandal story became one not of an individual's sexual transgressions but of an institutional environment that encouraged inauthenticity and thus hypocrisy: a competitive, cutthroat televangelist marketplace in which morally conservative rhetoric and theatricality are rewarded with earthly delights.[40] In the evangelical religious world revealed in these scandal stories, the gaps between public face and private action, so succinctly and salaciously revealed in Swaggart's Arline Highway visits, are shown to be *expected* rather than shocking. In this media telling, only the naïve ought to be scandalized by a clergyman who does not practice what he preaches.

Hugh Grant: Pure Hollywood As with Jimmy Swaggart, movie actor Hugh Grant's televised 1995 confession to sexual indiscretions with a prostitute became the summary moment of his sex scandal. "What the hell were you thinking?" asked Jay Leno on the *Tonight Show*. "I did a bad thing," Grant said of his arrest at 1:30 A.M. for "lewd conduct" (oral sex, it turned out) with prostitute Divine Brown while parked in his BMW near Hollywood's Sunset Strip. "And there you have it." It was, he said the day after his arrest, "something completely insane."[41]

Yet, if for Swaggart visiting a prostitute triggered a discussion of hypocrisy, Grant's encounter elicited not a whisper of such moral outrage. Prostitution and prostitute visits themselves, moreover, were only rarely subject to moral evaluation; one lone-wolf editorial, for example, complained that media coverage of Grant ignored "the real problems of prostitution," which is both "morally repugnant" and "unhealthy."[42] In fact, reports referred only obliquely to the actual sex, referring to the "lewd conduct" charge or generically to "a sex act" or "dallying," except for a brief moment, when Divine Brown sold her story to a British tabloid (including comments about his penis, his fantasies of sleeping with a black woman, and the oral sex she provided).[43] The sexual encounter instead took its place in the storytelling in one of two frameworks: in celebrity gossip discussions of Grant's relationship troubles with Elizabeth Hurley, as evidence of personal disloyalty; and, in the even stronger *image-as-commodity* frame, as evidence of the gap between a "nice" public image and a "naughty" boy's private self.

In both versions of the storytelling, media coverage began with a bemused puzzlement over risk and motivation. "Why did he do it?" asked CBS, CNN, the *San Francisco Chronicle*, the *Toronto Star, Los Angeles Times*, the *Minneapolis Star Tribune, People* magazine, Larry King, and many others.[44] "Why does a dashing guy like Grant . . . pick up a Sunset Boulevard hooker? Why does a guy who could crook his little finger and have half the female population at his disposal opt for a quickie in the front seat?" asked the *Washington Post*.[45] *USA Today* put it in even simpler terms: "Why would a heartthrob turn to a street hooker?"[46]

Various explanations were initially offered: sexual compulsion, the desire for uncomplicated sex, male piggishness, British innocence, the lures of the Hollywood playground, the pressures of fame.[47] ("Hollywood is predicated on bad behavior. It's almost a job requirement," wrote a *Washington Post* reporter, beginning a transformation of Grant from an unusual risk taker to a creature of his Hollywood environment.)[48] Interestingly, however, speculations about why he might have turned to a prostitute quickly gave way (in part preempted by Grant's next-day move to the confessional phase) to questions of impact, as the story took two simultaneous directions: the story of a relationship in trouble, and the story of a career in trouble. It is through the second, in particular, that Grant's story became emblematic of the Hollywood entertainment industry.

Told mainly by entertainment reporters and gossip columnists, one frame considered the Grant-Brown encounter as a trigger for a saga of betrayal and forgiveness. In the soap-operatic tones characteristic of most entertainment celebrity reporting, reporters speculated on whether girlfriend Elizabeth Hurley would leave Grant, asking readers whether they think she should leave him, culminating in an interview given by Hurley to Barbara Walters, who asked, "Can she forgive and forget?"[49]

Yet even within the framework of betrayal and forgiveness were hints of the stronger frame through which this scandal story developed in the mainstream media: of a crisis in image management. Hurley herself was, for instance, regularly portrayed as performing, rather than living, the role of hurt girlfriend. "It may be the performance of actress-model Elizabeth Hurley's career," the *Phoenix Gazette* reported. "Since her boyfriend Hugh Grant was arrested with a Hollywood hooker . . . Hurley has convincingly portrayed the beautiful, betrayed girlfriend to an audience far bigger than any of her previous performances."[50] Brown, too, was absorbed into the framework of scandal as celebrity-business opportunity: "peddling panties" in a thirty-second Brazilian TV commercial for $30,000 and appearing in a spoof of the milk mustache advertisements in *Esquire*, she was "using up her fifteen minutes of fame."[51]

From the beginning, in fact, Grant's sexual act was brought into view primarily as a demonstration of the difficulty of keeping a private self in line with a saleable public image. The image of Grant, derived mostly from his film roles, as a "handsome leading man, best known for playing a shy romantic," "the suave, boyish-looking English star" with "the bashful grin" and "sparkling GQ persona," was consistently compared against his arrest "with his black pants pulled down to his knees" in "a sleazy section of Sunset Boulevard."[52] What made Grant's act so extraordinary was not the sexual impropriety but the undercutting of a valuable image, the way the "bizarre arrest," as *People*'s Grant-adorned cover put it, "tarnishes the image of Hollywood's most charming leading man."[53] "On his field trip into the Sunset night," *Time* magazine claimed, "Grant went *out of character*, played disastrously *against type*, punctured a *popular illusion*. As many moviegoers saw it, he didn't cheat on Hurley so much as he cheated on them."[54] If Swaggart was the huckster-hypocrite showing his true colors, Grant was the fate-tempting movie star, playing fast and loose with his primary commodity, his publicly available persona.

Thus, the persistent focus from the day after Grant's arrest was on the impact of the scandal on his career as actor and celebrity, which depended on intricate management of image. An online poll showed that "Hugh Grant's awfully big misadventure on the streets of LA may actually help his career"; *USA Today* wondered about the "effects of the scandal . . . on Grant's squeaky-clean career"; *Newsweek* suggested that "the hooker episode could actually improve his image, giving him a bit of a dark side—and quelling rumors that he might be gay"; and the *Los Angeles Times* added that "the consensus in Hollywood is that the damage, if any, will be minimal," because "Grant finds himself at the curious juncture of contemporary celebrityhood where reward and punishment merge."[55] Indeed, even the Will they stay together? story line was often melted into that of image management, as in this *Atlanta Journal and Constitution* column: "What if the issue [of Hurley and Grant's future together] hangs in the balance for a few weeks? Say, until . . . 'Nine Months' is scheduled to open. During that time, Oprah, Montel, Geraldo, and every local media outlet imaginable conduct a public debate: Should she forgive him? . . . Finally, at the premiere of 'Nine Months,' Hurley and Grant appear together magically. All is forgiven. All is sunshine and lollipops. His charm intact, his virility enhanced, Grant's career skyrockets. . . . Everyone lives happily—and wealthily—ever after."[56] In the entertainment business, relationships are performances; scandal, managed properly as a publicity tool, is good show business, "a career move," as *Time* proposed.[57]

Indeed, the moments of confession and apology were covered as pure, brilliant spin—and such brilliant spin that the scandal's confession and comeback phases collapsed into one another. In a striking parallel to the Swaggart coverage, Grant's clothes, mannerisms, words, even his hair were scrutinized and interpreted as public relations maneuvers. The *San Francisco Chronicle* described the apology as "Hugh-mility, show biz style," in which Grant, "perhaps trying to erase the image of his police booking photo in a striped pullover," wore a "dark blue pinstriped suit" and a "checked pink" tie, "smiled a lot and was fidgety," his hair flopping "all over the place."[58] The day after Grant's *Tonight Show* apology, CBS *This Morning* gathered a couple of entertainment reporters to answer the question How did he do? ("He seemed very contrite," said one; "the obligatory amount of squirming," said the other) and the *Los Angeles Times* reported that Grant, with his "pained hang-dog look" and "the embarrassed face that everyone wanted to see," had "been appropriately remorseful."[59] This was, the *New York Times* asserted, "the World Series of Damage Control." The *Times* called in the city's leading publicists for their postgame assessments. "A great success," said one. "*He stayed in character.*" Another publicist concurred: "He was properly, impishly contrite."[60] "Hugh Grant's post-prostitute PR sweep seems to be working like a charm," *USA Today* reported; others praised Grant's "miraculous save of his career," his "skillful handling of the media," and his publicist, who earned "high praise for her deft touch in handling the affair (Grant's penitent appearances on TV)."[61] As Grant moved through "television's stations of the cross," a *New York Times* commentary claimed, he became more and more a creature of his environment: "A recognizably human leading man had metamorphosed into the bland Hollywood commodity ready to be plugged into the assembly-line."[62] Grant became, that is, a better performer, a more typical Hollywood product, through the sex scandal.

The Hugh Grant sex scandal was never a story in which sexual norms per se were much at stake. Mainstream media discourse, in treating the scandal as a story of an image-commodity risked and recuperated, transformed Grant into a symbol of Hollywood's celebrity system; the story of a relationship-risking sexual act was overshadowed by the story of an institution's public image pressures. In a manner that, despite their different forms, resembles Swaggart's story, Grant's behavior became gradually normalized: the focus shifted rapidly from sex to image, the sin from breaking sexual norms to breaking character, the lessons from individual to institutional. A consistency between image and reality, this scandal discourse proposed, was both required and confounded by the entertainment industry; in that kind of institutional environment, the story goes, where an image crisis is always hiding in wait, an actor who is not what he seems to be is expected, and the revelation of the public/private gap through scandal comes to be routine. "Another summer," as one pair of reporters sighed, "another Hollywood scandal."[63]

Dick Morris: Political Prostitution In August 1996, in the midst of the Democratic Convention, the tabloid *Star* broke the news that top Clinton advisor Dick Morris had been seeing a prostitute named Sherry Rowlands, who reported not only that Morris liked "sucking toes and being dominated," but also that he had bad-mouthed the president ("the Monster") and first lady ("the Twister"), let her listen on the phone while he spoke with the president, told her of the NASA discovery of life on Mars before it was announced to the public, and let her read a Hillary Rodham Clinton speech before it was delivered.[64] Discussing Morris's resignation on *Larry King Live* the next day, the *Star* reporter who investigated and wrote the piece argued that "this is not just a story of somebody who is having an illicit affair. It's not a story of him betraying the trust of his wife, embarrassing his wife. The story is that he was betraying and embarrassing the president."[65] The Morris scandal unfolded, in fact, as one in which the central relationship was between Morris and Clinton— "the president and the sleazeball," in one commentator's phrasing—and the relationship between Morris and his wife, Eileen McGann, was secondary.[66] "If the Dick Morris scandal were only a story about a presidential adviser who'd been caught in an immoral or embarrassing lapse, it would not have been so unique," an ABC report tellingly asserted. "There have been plenty of such Washington lapses over the years. No, this is a story that many people see as one of betrayal, not only of Morris' wife, but betrayal of the president as well."[67] As in the stories from religion and entertainment, as the media coverage progressed, Morris's "fall" was normalized, taking its place as a demonstration not of a bad apple spoiling the bunch, but of a U.S. political environment in which good apples, not bad ones, ought to be the surprise.

As with Swaggart and Grant, there was nothing particularly shocking about Morris's sexual behavior itself, even if it was, as in the other media tales, the source of some fun copy and late-night talk show punchlines. While tabloid papers and television shows kept the "kinky sex, including toe-sucking and dominance" details alive,[68] neither tabloid nor mainstream coverage focused much attention on the morality of prostitute visits or extramarital sex, at least not as discrete or remarkable normative violations.[69] CNN's lead into the story, for instance, first mentioned allegations "that Dick Morris allowed a woman to listen in on conversations he had with the White House, and also allowed her to read an advance copy of the speech given by Hillary Clinton," only later mentioning that the woman in question was a prostitute; even then, the "big question" concerned not sexuality or sexual norms but "how all of this will affect the president, how it will affect his campaign."[70] As told primarily by political reporters, the sexual behavior instead initiated a story of *disloyalty and hubris*, positioned with the larger institutional framework of *politics as a game*, in which spin trumps belief. Whatever the outcome, media reports implied and asserted, this scandal revealed politics as usual.

Like much political campaign reporting, which tends to focus, horse-race-style, on how one event or another affects a candidate's odds,[71] media coverage focused immediately on the impact on Clinton's campaign. The "timing was incredibly bad," overshadowing the president and "tossing a big blob of mud on what should have been the shining climax to Clinton's nominating convention," perhaps "a set-up" "carefully orchestrated to embarrass the president," but certainly "a major distraction," a "bombshell for the campaign," and a "public relations disaster" that detracted from "an otherwise successful effort to capture favorable publicity."[72] And it could not help that "the central force behind the emphasis on family values" was caught with a call girl, providing a "counterpoint to the convention's focus on cherishing children and strengthening families—a Morris-drafted script."[73] (Interestingly, the hypocrisy theme was weaker than in Swaggart's case, and the related public/private gap theme weaker than in Grant's, suggesting perhaps that expectations of integrity are weaker among journalists covering politics.)

In this framework, it was the revival of the "questions about Clinton's own personal behavior that have dogged him"—the "character issue"—that threatened the campaign.[74] Morris "revived the enduring question about whether Clinton stands for what he stands for," *Time* suggested.[75] He did so, according to most media storytelling, in part by echoing Clinton's alleged sexual pursuits with his own, but even more so by revealing not just sexual but ideological and political promiscuity. From the day the story broke, Morris was routinely characterized as an "unprincipled hired gun," an "amoral creep" selling himself to the highest bidder, a "switch-hitting consultant" with "a devotion to tactics and the game that seemed to be unmoored to ideology or party," a "chameleon . . . known to blend in his political coloration with the color of his paycheck," a "brilliant and sometimes arrogant strategist with little partisan loyalty," a "political mercenary," "a man with no compass or beliefs," an "opportunist who had no compunction about switching back and forth between the Democratic and Republican parties."[76] "As far as I'm concerned," author Larry Sabato summed it up for *People* magazine, "there were two whores in that [Jefferson] hotel room."[77]

Clinton's "character," the reports repeated, was being judged at least in part by the company he chose to keep, and that company was unprincipled, disloyal, amoral. "A lot of people are going to say," suggested CNN's Bobbie Battista, " 'How can the president have hired a man like that?' "[78] "The problem is that [Clinton] knew exactly who Morris was and still chose to rely on him," a *US News & World Report* columnist argued.[79] "The problem," the *Wall Street Journal*'s Paul Gigot suggested on PBS, "raises questions about political judgment and political sincerity. The judgment is about who a president, any president, any candidate, surrounds himself with."[80] Within this frame, the fact of a married man visiting a prostitute was just one small piece of evidence of rottenness, and reports repeatedly underlined this through the assertion that the transgression was not sexual immorality but the telling of White House secrets.

If the revelations of Morris's loose sexual ethics, and even more of his willingness to breach White House rules to impress a woman, demonstrated his amoral character, his postrevelation behaviors were brought in as final proof. Having first refused to "dignify" the "sadistic vitriol of yellow journalism," Morris resigned, in what appeared to be a quick, steep fall, and issued a public apology to his wife.[81] Within days, however, the comeback phase of his scandal story had begun: he was on the cover of *Time* magazine for the second week in a row, albeit for a less flattering article than that of the prior week, and signed a lucrative book deal. "How the fallen have risen," said the *New York Times* two weeks after Morris's resignation.[82] "Dick Morris's term as a political pariah," the *Washington Post* reported, "seems to have lasted about an hour and a half."[83] This "comeback"—the first of two—became further evidence in the story of Morris's disloyalty and shamelessness, the "blab-book deal Morris negotiated for Random House" another "obvious betrayal," "the payoff to this immorality tale," its prepublication another "Morris-style machination," its contents a violation of "the minimum moral requirements of loyalty."[84]

Most revealingly, in a parallel to Swaggart and Grant, the story had become even more firmly focused on those traits not only as individual character flaws but as role behaviors rewarded by political institutions, and particularly of politics guided by teams of "consultants." Morris became, through the revelation and especially through the comeback phase, the quintessential political consultant, a symbol of politics-as-game. Now, instead of consulting for the president, he was consulting for himself, becoming, as the *New York Times* characterized it, "his own client."[85] "The day after he was forced to resign from Clinton's inner council because of a sex scandal," *USA Today* reported, "he was spinning his story to a news magazine"; soon after, we see him turning "a political-science classroom at New York University into a major political event in his campaign to rehabilitate his image."[86] Although the tone was different—less exoticizing than the Swaggart coverage, less jokey than the Grant coverage—this theme of Morris's comeback-as-performance closely resembles the narration of the other two scandals. Morris was, as the story was told, "engineering another comeback: his own," using his well-honed manipulation skills to "save himself" and "keeping his name in lights," "trying to mastermind his own resurrection, even as others proclaim him finished."[87] CNN's *Inside Politics* even awarded Morris its capstone Political Play of the Week for "masterminding his own comeback."[88]

Morris, argued writer David Brooks, was "thoroughly politicized": he "turned his own marriage into a grotesquerie in order to save his political skin," posing for a " 'homey' dinner table picture in *Time* with his wife," who herself offered a statement that sounded like "a focus-group-tested paean to adulterers." How, Brooks asked, "could a totally politicized consultant in this atmosphere not devolve into an unnatural creature, beyond shame and plausibility?"[89] As Morris's "amoral" behavior came to be seen as a feature of politics-by-consulting, even the secret-spilling, president-eavesdropping, toe-sucking visits to a prostitute became, in retrospect, similarly emblematic of the institution of politics. Adultery and prostitution visits were objectionable not so much as sexually immoral acts, but as reminders that U.S. politics rewards amorality and untrustworthiness. Morris's "train wreck," wrote a *Time* columnist, "compounded by his ideological promiscuity, adds to the widespread public suspicion that it takes an unwholesome personality—a professional liar or a power fetishist—to go into politics in the first place."[90] To be "politicized" may encourage amorality, this dominant frame suggested; in politics, it may be normal to be an "unnatural creature," and Morris's story summarized that lesson. Although it began with the tabloid-driven sex story, in the hands of mainstream political reporting it became a story of politics as usual. The scandal was not how unusual a character was Dick Morris, but how representative he was of U.S. politics.

Sex Scandal Narratives: Sexuality, Institutional Moralities, and Media Behaviors The three cases recounted and analyzed here do not, of course, tell us finally about all media-conveyed sex scandal discourse, but they do provide fresh illumination. They suggest, first of all, that the reinforcement of sexual norms and ideologies, though certainly a contribution of sex scandals, is not their primary one. It would be overstating the case to suggest that sex scandal narratives are not really about sex; it is, after all, sexual behaviors and not, say, unusual eating or parenting behaviors that so regularly stir scandal. Sex scandal narratives certainly do, on a general level, reveal sexual values directly, and even more so indirectly, through the "cultural givens"[91] regarding sexual behavior their storytellers take for granted. For instance, despite their differences, the three cases here take for granted and reproduce a relatively cavalier, if conflicted, attitude toward prostitution, proceeding with the background assumption that the purchase of sexual services by men is both shameful and understandable; they take for granted, that is, a familiar gendered sexual order. The women whose sexuality was for rent were dismissed or further objectified in the storytelling (largely erased from the mainstream media stories, Murphree, Brown, and Rowlands were relegated to tabloid and pornographic press), while the men who purchased sexual services were located in a masculine world in which prostitute visits were often narrated as demonstrations of manhood.[92] Within the larger discourse of masculine sexuality assumed in the storytelling, men were sexual subjects, the relationships between men were central, and manhood was reaffirmed by naughty-boy transgression: Morris was "Bill's Bad Boy";[93] Grant, aided by a ribbing Jay Leno, put to rest rumors of sissyhood and homosexuality; Swaggart and Gorman competed for wealth and power, their sexual relationships with women one tool in their warrior arsenal.[94]

Still, although scandal stories rely on and reproduce assumptions about gendered sexuality, there are excellent reasons to doubt that the communication of sexual values is their distinct and primary cultural contribution. As it does in other public discussions, sexuality takes its place in these morality tales more as symbol and vehicle than as topic.[95] To begin with, the same sexual action yielded not a singular narrative of sexual morality, but narratives whose themes and characters—hypocrisy, recklessness, and amorality; the charlatan, the daredevil, the mercenary—both varied according to different institutional settings and extended far beyond the morality of commercial or "adulterous" sex, suggesting a process more complex than the transmission of collective sentiments about appropriate sexual behavior. Even the sexual act that gave rise to each case received strikingly little attention as a transgression of sexual morality per se and dropped out of discussion rather quickly. If a character was common to all of them, in fact, it was less the sexual cad than the confidence man, a longstanding cultural figure who, as one nineteenth-century advice manual put it, was found "putting on false appearances," his "language and conduct" proceeding not from "fixed principle and open hearted sincerity but from a spirit of duplicity and management."[96] If a theme united them, it had less to do with sex than with inauthenticity: revelations of stark contrasts to the professed persona, confessions that were staged performances rather than cleansing repentances, comebacks achieved through effective spin rather than forgiveness. Sexual transgression was hardly the central drama here.

The surprising element of these scandals is not just the relative quiet of sexual themes nor their common distrust of public faces, but the theme of institutional decay that got louder as the media storytelling progressed. Sexual stories were edged out by stories of public institutions: of how evangelical institutions work, how the entertainment industry operates, how political games are played. These institutional frames were geared toward making sense of the lack of integrity demonstrated in scandal: they suggested that *personal* behavior at first presented as "shocking"—the hypocrisy or recklessness or disloyalty revealed in the encounter with a prostitute—may be quite typical of those in the institutional *role*, that the individual *nonconformity* to sexual norms may actually reveal a sort of *conformity* to institutional norms. Public institutions, each story's dominant frame suggested, demand and reward performances that they make difficult to maintain, encouraging inauthentic role playing and increasing the chances that public personae will turn out to contradict private selves. Given how religion, entertainment, and politics *really* work, these stories suggest, scandal is always already there, waiting to show itself.

Given the well-documented penchant in U.S. culture, and especially in U.S. media, for individualist rather than structural frames and personal rather than institutional storytelling,[97] and given the overdetermined status of sexuality as "personal," such a narrative dynamic is especially striking. Why, in these cases, do we find this unusual narrative reversal? Although there is certainly evidence that American cynicism about institutions has increased, especially in the post-Watergate years—and scandals certainly circulate and emphasize such cynicism—it seems unlikely that what we are witnessing in these cases is a sudden eschewing of both individualism and sexual content by U.S. citizens. The dynamics encountered here—the interest in and then backing off from sexual discussion, the focus on the common falsity of public images, and especially the rapid movement toward the framework of institutional pathology—are best understood, I propose, through an analysis of media organizational interests and behaviors. The institutional frame solves quite a few problems for mainstream media organizations, especially their simultaneous need for both sensationalism and legitimacy, and serves reporters' interests in getting their story prominent placement as "hard" rather than "soft" news.

Sexual stories present both an opportunity and a challenge for mainstream news organizations: an opportune shortcut to larger audiences that poses threats to legitimacy. Sex, among other forms of sensationalism, is widely acknowledged among commercial media producers to be a means to attract readers and viewers, and news organizations of all kinds therefore have an obvious competitive interest in telling sexual stories.[98] Yet mainstream news organizations also rely for their survival on the perception that they are not simply purveyors of sexy sensation but of credible, reliable, and necessary information.[99] As, in recent years, market forces have pushed mainstream news organizations toward the topics and presentation strategies of tabloid publications and tabloid television,[100] this tension has become even more pronounced, as mainstream media organizations increasingly court the charge that they are more like tabloids than unlike them. It is in this context that contemporary sex scandal stories are told, and that steers the storytelling away from sexual details and toward news frames that focus on institutions. The degree of institutional critique may be tempered by social proximity, as in the case of entertainment, in which reporters and industry workers are tightly aligned,[101] or heightened by social distance, as in the case of religion, in which reporters and religious institutions have historically stood in tension.[102] But across the different settings, by framing the sex scandal as an institutional morality tale, the news organization retains both credibility and, literally, sex appeal, offering audiences "public service" (instructions on how and why public images are not to be trusted) that justifies the appeal to sex, and a social significance (the moral failings of institutions) that marks these stories as legitimate and newsworthy.

The institutional framework is pushed along by internal media organizational processes as well. Its logic dovetails with reporters' pursuit, long since routinized into practice, of professional legitimacy. The division of news into a hierarchy from hard to soft, human-interest stories[103] and the correspondence of those categories to particular news beats generates a struggle for professional status, in which prestige is derived from a story that is both long-lasting and hard.[104] (A study of religion reporters, for instance, found that "placement in sections outside the identified religion section . . . or placement in the news section of the paper, is the most sought-after.")[105] Some journalists are better positioned in that struggle than others: the politics beat produces mostly hard news by definition, and both entertainment and religion tend to be considered soft beats.[106] It is no accident, for instance, that the case with the least institutional focus (Hugh Grant) was also the one least successful at moving from its more limited, lower-status placement (entertainment sections of newspapers, magazines, and television programs) to a position of greater stature—and also no accident that the attempt to lend the case significance through an institutional framing was nonetheless pursued. The narrative push toward institutions is one strategy for hardening and lengthening what is, on the face of it, a soft, short-lived, and lower-status story.

The resulting distancing of sexual discussion, and intensified attention to the institutional roots of individual pathologies, is a striking exception to the usual U.S. media habit of individualist reasoning. It is also, in a broader sociological sense, theoretically provocative. Drawing on Durkheim, sociologists are accustomed to thinking of public stories of transgression, sin, or deviance as reminders about society-wide norms for individual action.[107] Indeed, the small body of theoretical literature approaching scandals sees them mostly as stories of "individuals who privilege their personal desires over the rules of society," which thereby provide "the most extreme example of how, in practice, individuals are held to an imagined, idealized standard of social conduct."[108] These scandals move far past the narrative of the individual sinner, whose normative violation is painted as atypical and underlines what must not be breached; here, it is the institution's moral universe, as much or more than the individual's character, that is revealed to be rotten. Structured largely by media organizational interests, they remind their witnesses not of normative order but of disorder, not of what they believe but of what cannot be believed. As such, they provide an unusual addition to understanding how norms circulate culturally: rather than proving the normal with the deviant, they show the perversions of U.S. institutional habitats, which, in the end, seem to make the sinner more normal than not.

Notes

I am grateful for thoughtful comments on earlier drafts of this paper from William Gamson, Wendy Griswold, Abigail Saguy, John Summers, and several excellent *Social Problems* reviewers.

1 John B. Thompson, "Scandal and Social Theory," in *Media Scandals*, ed. James Lull and Stephen Hinerman (New York: Columbia University Press, 1997), 39.

2 See William A. Cohen, *Sex Scandal: The Private Parts of Victorian Fiction* (Durham, NC: Duke University Press, 1996); Trevor Fisher, *Scandal: The Sexual Politics of Late Victorian Britain* (Phoenix Mill, England: Alan Sutton Publishing, 1995); Kali Israel, "French Vices and British Liberties: Gender, Class, and Narrative Competition in a Late Victorian Sex Scandal," *Social History* 22 (1997): 1–26; Norma Basch, "Marriage, Morals, and Politics in the Election of 1828," *Journal of American History* 80 (1993): 890–918; Richard Wightman Fox, *Trials of Intimacy: Love and Loss in the Beecher-Tilton Scandal* (Chicago: University of Chicago Press, 1999); John F. Marszalek, *The Petticoat Affair* (New York: Free Press, 1997); Michael Schudson, "Sex Scandals," in *Our National Passion: 200 Years of Sex in America*, ed. Sally Banes, Sheldon Frank, and Tom Horwitz (Chicago: Follett, 1976), 41–57; Laura Castor, "Did She or Didn't She: The Discourse of Scandal in the 1988 U.S. Presidential Campaign," *Genders* 12 (1991): 62–76; John Nguyet Erni, "Queer Figurations in the Media: Critical Reflections on the Michael Jackson Sex Scandal," *Critical Studies in Mass Communication* 15 (1998): 158–80; Gary Alan Fine, "Scandal, Social Conditions, and the Creation of Public Attention: Fatty Arbuckle and the 'Problem of Hollywood,'" *Social Problems* 44.3 (August 1997): 297–321; Laura Stoker, "Judging Presidential Character: The Demise of Gary Hart," *Political Behavior* 15.2 (1993): 193–223; Kenneth Anger, *Hollywood Babylon* (New York: Dell, 1975); Gail Collins, *Scorpion Tongues: Gossip, Celebrity, and American Politics* (New York: William Morrow, 1998).

3 Cohen, *Sex Scandal*, 2.

4 See James Lull and Stephen Hinerman, "The Search for Scandal," in Lull and Hinerman, 1–33; Sally Engle Merry, "Rethinking Gossip and Scandal," in *Toward a General Theory of Social Control*, ed. Donald Black (Orlando, FL: Academic Press, 1984), 271–301;

Thompson, "Scandal and Social Theory." At a general level, Lull and Hinerman (11–13) suggest major criteria for delineating scandal from nonscandal: "Social norms reflecting the dominant morality must be transgressed," and those transgressions must be carried out by specific persons in an exercise of their own desires or interests; the perpetrators must be identified and shown to have acted intentionally or recklessly, and to be held responsible for their actions, which then have "differential consequences" for those involved; the revelations must be widely circulated by communications media and "effectively narrativized into a story which . . . inspires widespread interest and discussion."

5 Cohen, *Sex Scandal*, 7–8.

6 Schudson, "Sex Scandals," 51.

7 John Summers, "What Happened to Sex Scandals? Politics and Pecadilloes, Jefferson to Kennedy," *Journal of American History* (December 2000): 1–33.

8 Ibid., 11. See Anger, *Hollywood Babylon*; Fine, "Scandal, Social Conditions, and the Creation of Public Attention."

9 Fine, "Scandal, Social Conditions, and the Creation of Public Attention," 297; see also Mark D. Jacobs, "Scandals as Normal Crises of Political Culture," paper presented at the annual meeting of the American Sociological Association, San Francisco, 1998.

10 See, for instance, W. Lance Bennett, *News: The Politics of Illusion*, 3d ed. (White Plains, NY: Longman, 1996); Todd Gitlin, *Inside Prime Time* (New York: Pantheon, 1983).

11 See Summers, "What Happened to Sex Scandals?"

12 Ibid., 18, 20.

13 In a more general sense, I am here following the lead of sociologists of culture who insist on specifying links between institutional and discursive analyses of cultural phenomena, calling attention to the mutual influence of institutional environments and cultural scripts, "the ways in which enduring social institutions are explicitly constructed out of a complex process of negotiation and contestation over cultural meanings" (John W. Mohr, "Measuring Meaning Structures," *Annual Review of Sociology* 24 [1998]: 350), and the ways those institutions themselves shape cultural meanings.

14 Robert E. Stake, "Case Studies," in *Handbook of Qualitative Research*, ed. Norman K. Denzin and Yvonna S. Lincoln (Thousand Oaks, CA: Sage, 2000), 437. As Diane Vaughan has recently noted, qualitative case comparison "of similar events, activities, or phenomena that occur in distinctly different social settings" is a promising means towards theorizing that links cultural and structural levels of analysis. See Diane Vaughan, "Signals and Interpretive Work: The Role of Culture in a Theory of Practical Action," paper presented at

Towards a Sociology of Culture and Cognition, Rutgers University, November 12, 1999. Like any such comparison, this one is necessarily loose, because every sex scandal has its own idiosyncratic cast of characters and particular history. Still, one can safely assume that both the professional workings of and cultural attitudes toward prostitution did not make great shifts and that the operation of news media did not change dramatically in this brief time period.

15 Most of the documents were from newspapers and magazines, although the sample also included television transcripts (4 in the Swaggart case, 9 in the Grant case, and 11 in the Morris case). Most were reports, but the sample also included a small number of interviews (1 in the Swaggart case, 3 in the Grant case, and 8 in the Morris case), and a significant number of commentary documents (7 in the Swaggart case, 22 in the Grant case, and 25 in the Morris case); because I take the story to be framed through both reporting and commentary, I do not separate the two in the analysis. Although these data provide quite a comprehensive picture of mainstream media framing of the sex scandals, their limitations should also be noted. They do not provide elaborate information about how tabloid press covers these scandals (though the "legitimate" press often reports on, and laments, tabloid coverage), or how media serving particular communities (e.g., African American press, Christian press) cover them. A comparison across these different types of outlets, although beyond the scope of this paper, would be extremely useful.

16 See Joshua Gamson, "Jessica Hahn, Media Whore: Sex Scandal Icons and Female Publicity," *Critical Studies in Media Communication* (June 2001): 157–73.

17 See Kathy Charmaz, "Grounded Theory," in Denzin and Lincoln, 509–35; Barney Glaser and Anselm Strauss, *The Discovery of Grounded Theory* (Chicago: Aldine, 1967); Gery W. Ryan and H. Russell Bernard, "Data Management and Analysis Methods," in Denzin and Lincoln, 769–802.

18 See Amy Binder, "Constructing Racial Rhetoric: Media Depictions of Harm in Heavy Metal and Rap Music," *American Sociological Review* 58 (December 1993): 753–67; David Snow et al., "Frame Alignment Processes, Mobilization, and Movement Participation," *American Sociological Review* 51 (1986): 464–81.

19 Wayne King, "Swaggart Says He Has Sinned," *New York Times*, 22 February 1988, A1.

20 Richard Cohen, "Swaggart and That Other Sin," *Washington Post*, 26 February 1988, A23.

21 Art Harris, "Jimmy Swaggart and the Snare of Sin," *Washington Post*, 24 February 1988, C1; "Swaggart Led Sex-Crazed Secret Life, Prostitute Claims," *San Diego Union-Tribune*, 25 February 1988, A1.

22 Michael Isikoff and Art Harris, "Swaggart Is Focus of Adultery Investigation," *Washington Post*, 20 February 1988, A11. Sexual morality may in fact have been a more frequent theme in the religious press (see, e.g., Laura Sessions Stepp, "Swaggart Falls Spur Discussion of Sex," *Washington Post*, 11 April 1988, A3), and sexual behavior was a primary focus in the few interviews conducted with Murphree herself (see "More on the Jimmy Swaggart Scandal," *Larry King Live*, CNN, 27 June 1991).

23 "The Human Comedy," *Los Angeles Times*, 23 February 1988, part 2, p. 6; Isikoff and Harris, "Swaggart Is Focus"; Peter H. King, " 'What's Past Is Past,' " *Los Angeles Times*, 23 May 1988, A1; John Dart, "Swaggart Steps Down after Public Confession," *Los Angeles Times*, 22 February 1988, A1; John Dart, "A Twist of Fate," *Los Angeles Times*, 5 March 1988, B6.

24 George Hackett, "A Sex Scandal Breaks over Jimmy Swaggart," *Newsweek*, 29 February 1988, 30.

25 In fact, even in a *Penthouse* article and photo spread featuring Debra Murphree, the "siren of New Orleans's seedy Arline Highway," in which sex was of course central, sexuality was featured in the service of a hypocrisy narrative. The article, which recounts the rivalry between Swaggart and Gorman and includes the explicit, pornography-derived sexual requests from Swaggart to Murphree ("He wanted me to have a dress on, and I'd pretend that he's not there, and then he'd come sneak up and peek up my dress"; "He'd ask me if I'd ever let anyone screw my daughter"; etc.), begins with a passage from Matthew warning against "false prophets, which come to you in sheep's clothing, but inwardly they are ravening wolves." Art Harris and Jason Berry, "Jimmy Swaggart's Secret Sex Life," *Penthouse* (July 1988): 104–06, 123–26, 138–42, 176. That the priority is on driving home hypocrisy rather than eliciting sexual fantasy is accentuated by the "Debbie Does Swaggart" pictorial, which contrasts sharply with the soft-focus, full-color, lacy Pet-of-the-Month centerfold layout just before it: a somewhat chunky Murphree poses, in large tinted sunglasses and little makeup, in stark black-and-white photos that recreate the positions for which Swaggart paid. The pictorial begins by counterposing two quotes: "Pornography titillates and captivates the sickest of the sick and makes them slaves to their own consuming lusts," says the first, from Swaggart's *Rape of a Nation*. The second is allegedly from Swaggart to Murphree: "Pull down your panties. . . . Pull your panties up your crack, like a magazine I've seen. . . . Get on your hands and knees with your ass in the air." "Debbie Does Swaggart," pictorial, *Penthouse* (July 1988): 107–22. (One of the writers of this story, Art Harris, also covered the scandal for the *Washington Post* and later for CNN.)

26 Hackett, "A Sex Scandal Breaks over Jimmy Swaggart." See also Whitney Mandel, "Swaggart Deserves an Oscar," *San Diego Union-Tribune*, 12 March 1988, B15.

27 Peter Applebome, "Swaggart's Troubles Show Tension of Passion and Power in TV Evangelism," *New York Times*, 28 February 1988, A30.

28 Lynn Rosellini, "Why Did Jimmy Swaggart Yield to Temptation," *U.S. News & World Report*, 7 March 1988, 62.

29 Isikoff and Harris, "Swaggart Is Focus"; see also Rosellini, "Why Did Jimmy Swaggart Yield to Temptation"; Dart, "Swaggart Steps Down"; Wayne King, "Church Orders 2-Year Rehabilitation for Swaggart," *New York Times*, 23 February 1988, A20.

30 W. King, "Swaggart Says He Has Sinned"; Hackett, "A Sex Scandal Breaks over Jimmy Swaggart"; Harris, "Jimmy Swaggart and the Snare of Sin"; see also Art Harris, "The P.I. on Swaggart's Trail," *Washington Post*, 13 April 1988, B1.

31 Mandel, "Swaggart Deserves an Oscar."

32 Dart, "A Twist of Fate."

33 Andy Rooney, "Most Television Evangelists Are Con Men," *San Diego Tribune*, 4 March 1988, B8.

34 Mandel, "Swaggart Deserves an Oscar."

35 Art Harris, "Swaggart's Spirited Return," *Washington Post*, 23 May 1988, C1.

36 Ibid.

37 W. King, "Church Orders 2-Year Rehabilitation for Swaggart."

38 "More on the Jimmy Swaggart Scandal," *Larry King Live*.

39 Applebome, "Swaggart's Troubles Show Tension."

40 In 1991, the Gorman lawsuit came to trial, Swaggart was found with another prostitute in California (Carol Castaneda, "Evangelist Swaggart Teeters in Scandal," *USA Today*, 15 October 1991, 4A), and new photographs of Swaggart with Murphree were released, and there was a brief revisiting of the scandal. As with the original, the replay largely was a "sordid feud" (Judy Keen, "Swaggart vs. Gorman," *USA Today*, 8 July 1991, 2A) and considered "whether Swaggart cared more about morality or market share" (*CNN Specials*, CNN, 27 June 1991).

41 Jeff Leeds and William Touhy, "Another Summer, Another Sex Scandal," *Houston Chronicle*, 28 June 1995, A4.

42 "Hugh Grant's Unfunny Crime," *Tampa Tribune*, 13 July 1995, 10.

43 "Prostitute Tells of Tryst with Actor," *Atlanta Journal and Constitution*, 2 July 1995, 6D.; "Hugh Grant Arrested for Lewd Conduct with a Prostitute," *CBS News*, 28 June 1995; "Negative Opinions of Hugh Grant's Personal Character Affect the Opinions of His First Hollywood Movie," *CBS News*, 19 July 1995; Richard Roeper, "Hugh Grant Fallout Turns to Stardust," *Chicago Sun-Times*, 9 August 1995, 11.

44 Susan Ager, "Hugh Grant Just Looking for a Quick Fix," *Toronto*

Star, 6 July 1995, C6; Anita Chaudhuri, "Making Sense of Hugh Grant's Misadventure," *Star Tribune*, 30 June 1995, 3E; "Hugh Grant Returns to England Amid Sex Scandal," *Showbiz Today*, CNN, 30 June 1995; "Hugh Grant Talks about His Arrest," *Larry King Live*, CNN, 12 July 1995; Michael Colton and Dennis Romero, "Grant's Arrest Leaves Many Wondering 'Why?' " *Los Angeles Times*, 30 June 1995, EI; "Hugh Grant Arrested for Lewd Conduct with a Prostitute," CBS *News*; Karen S. Schneider, "A Night to Remember," *People Weekly*, 10 July 1995, 50–54; Ruthe Stein, "The Big Question: 'Why Did You Do It, Hugh?' " *San Francisco Chronicle*, 28 June 1995, EI.

45 Roxanne Roberts, "What's the Matter with Hugh?" *Washington Post*, 28 June 1995, CI; see also Jean Seligmann and Jeanne Gordon, "A Drive-by Scandal," *Newsweek*, 10 July 1995, 54.

46 Karen Thomas and Kitty Bean Yancey, "Hugh Grant Faces Lewd Conduct Charge," *USA Today*, 28 June 1995, 1D.

47 Ager, "Hugh Grant Just Looking for a Quick Fix"; Colton and Romero, "Grant's Arrest Leaves Many Wondering 'Why?' "; Matthew Gilbert, " 'Four Weddings' but No Funeral for Lewd Hugh," *Boston Globe*, 29 June 1995, 65; Judy Mann, "Getting to the Top by Reaching Bottom," *Washington Post*, 30 June 1995, E3; Stephanie Mansfield, "Scandal? In Hollywood, It's Show Biz as Usual," *Washington Post*, 17 July 1995, B1; Roberts, "What's the Matter with Hugh?"; Stein, "The Big Question."

48 Mansfield, "Scandal?"

49 See Joshua Gamson, *Claims to Fame: Celebrity in Contemporary America* (Berkeley: University of California Press, 1994); Dan Ehrlich and Rob Kappstatter, "Take It for Granted, She Walks Out on Hugh," *Daily News*, 3 July 1995, 3; Orla Healy, "Liz Tells Pal Her Night with Hugh Was 'Hellish,' " *Daily News*, 13 July 1995, 3; "Hugh's Moral Lapse Sets Off Some Howls of Outrage, but Just a Few Say 'Tut-tut,' " *Detroit News*, 8 July 1995; Geoffrey Kula, "Readers to Supermodel: Dump Grant," *Boston Herald*, 12 July 1995, 39; "Questions for Elizabeth," *20/20*, ABC, 4 August 1995.

50 "A Career Performance," *Phoenix Gazette*, 4 July 1995, A2; see also Roeper, "Hugh Grant Fallout."

51 Helen Kennedy, "You Can Look Divine, Keep Man Hooked: Ad," *Daily News*, 1 August 1995, 25; Catherine Stengel, "Brown Enjoying Her Fleeting Fame," *Tampa Tribune*, 27 August 1995, 3; see also Kitty Bean Yancey, " 'Esquire' Milks Brown in a 'Dubious' Spoof," *USA Today*, 14 December 1995, 2D.

52 Gilbert, " 'Four Weddings' but No Funeral"; Paul Sullivan, "Hugh Caught with His Pants Down," *Boston Herald*, 28 June 1995, 1; Bernard Weinraub, "What's the Hollywood Topic? Hugh Grant's Future, Mainly," *New York Times*, 29 June 1995, C16.

53 Schneider, "A Night to Remember."

54 Richard Corliss, "Two Weeks after His Arrest, Grant Takes to the Talk Shows and the Multiplexes," *Time*, 24 July 1995, 58–59 (emphasis added); see also Mark Steyn, "Hugh Embarrassment," *American Spectator* (September 1995): 38–39.

55 Gilbert, " 'Four Weddings' but No Funeral"; Karen Thomas, "Hugh Charged," *USA Today*, 30 June 1995, 2D; Seligmann and Gordon, "A Drive-by Scandal"; Michael Walker, "The Hughman Factor," *Los Angeles Times*, 10 July 1995, F1.

56 Eleanor Ringel, "Take Nothing for Grant-ed in a Scandal in Movieland," *Atlanta Journal and Constitution*, 3 July 1995, 7C; see also Beth Teitell, "Spin Doctors Offer Cures for Hugh Grant's Image," *Boston Herald*, 29 June 1995, 37. This cynical statement was actually quite prescient. The week after it was written, in the midst of Should she forgive him? stories, Grant went on his apologetic publicity tour. Grant and Hurley appeared together at the premiere of *Nine Months*. Although her story never became a TV movie, Divine Brown (whose real name is Stella Thompson) was reportedly paid $150,000 to tell her story to the British *News of the World* and received two commercial deals (Roeper, "Hugh Grant Fallout").

57 Corliss, "Two Weeks after His Arrest."

58 John Carman, "Hugh Grant Eats Crow on 'The Tonight Show,' " *San Francisco Chronicle*, 11 July 1995, E1.

59 "Michael Fleming and Jess Cagle Discuss Actor Hugh Grant," *CBS News*, 11 July 1995; Carla Hall, "Hugh Grant Gets Fine, Probation on Misdemeanor," *Los Angeles Times*, 12 July 1995, B1; Chris Riemenschneider, "Actor Hugh Grant 'Fesses Up to Leno on 'Tonight Show,' " *Los Angeles Times*, 11 July 1995, B1.

60 Robin Pogrebin, "The World Series of Damage Control," *New York Times*, 16 July 1995, 4.

61 Sue Facter, "Hollywood Grants Hugh Forgiveness," *USA Today*, 13 July 1995, 2D; Roeper, "Hugh Grant Fallout"; "Hugh Grant Spin Control Works Wonders at Box Office," *Showbiz Today*, CNN, 17 July 1995; Mansfield, "Scandal?"

62 Frank Rich, "Scandal for Profit," *New York Times*, 26 July 1995, A19.

63 Leeds and Touhy, "Another Summer, Another Sex Scandal."

64 Gayle Fee and Laura Raposa, "Call Girl Says Clinton Top Aide a Strange Bedfellow," *Boston Herald*, 29 August 1996, 6; David Maraniss and Peter Baker, "President's Chief Political Adviser Quits," *Washington Post*, 30 August 1996, A1.

65 "Dick Morris Resigns over Alleged Call-Girl Scandal," *Larry King Live*, CNN, 29 September 1996.

66 David Brooks, "Dick Morris: Alive and Well in the Solipsism Zone," *Weekly Standard*, 16 September 1996, 27.

67 "Dick Morris Interview," *ABC News*, 16 January 1997.

68 "Top Strategist Quits Campaign amid Reported Sex Scandal," *Detroit News*, 30 August 1996, A1.

69 It is revealing, in fact, that in an attempt to manage the scandal, the Clinton campaign reasserted a narrow sexual morality frame, saying, "The president is obviously against the crime of prostitution" (George Lardner and John Harris, "Dick Morris May Testify on FBI Files," *Washington Post*, 7 September 1996, A6), a frame that never took. On *Larry King Live* in September, *Star* editor Dick Gooding complained that Clinton advisor James Carville "wants to make this *just a sex story*" ("Dick Morris Resigns").

70 "Democratic Strategist Discounts Effect of Morris Story," CNN, 29 August 1996.

71 See Bennett, *News: The Politics of Illusion*; Thomas Littlewood, *Calling Elections: The History of Horse-Race Journalism* (South Bend, IN: University of Notre Dame Press, 1999).

72 Bill Lambrecht, "Morris Fallout Expected to Have Little Effect on Clinton," *St. Louis Post-Dispatch*, 30 August 1996, 14A; Karen Ball, "Aide Quits in Sex Flap Tale of Trysting," *Daily News*, 30 August 1996, 5; "President Clinton's Key Political Strategist Dick Morris Resigns," *CBS News*, 29 August 1996; "Campaign Shake-up, Sex & Politics," *MacNeil/Lehrer News Hour*, PBS, 29 August 1996; "Clinton Administration Forced into Damage Control Mode," CNN, 29 August 1996; "Nightline Speaks to Democrats amid Morris Scandal," *Nightline*, ABC, 29 August 1996; Sara Fritz, "Clinton Strategist Resigns in Flap," *Los Angeles Times*, 30 August 1996, A1.

73 Richard L. Berke, "The Democrats: The Resignation," *New York Times*, 30 August 1996, A1; Susan Page and Bill Nichols, "Morris Flap Angers President," *USA Today*, 30 August 1996, 1A.

74 Page and Nichols, "Morris Flap."

75 Richard Lacayo, "Skunk at the Family Picnic," *Time*, 9 September 1996, 24–30, 32–33; Richard Cohen, "A Betrayal of Confidence," *Washington Post*, 5 September 1996, A23.

76 Lambrecht, "Morris Fallout"; R. Cohen, "A Betrayal of Confidence"; Ball, "Aide Quits"; Alison Mitchell, "The Consultant," *New York Times*, 2 September 1996, A10; Adrianne Flynn, "Clinton Aide Leaves amid Sex Scandal," *Arizona Republic*, 30 August 1996, A1; Amy Bayer, "Sex Scandal Rocks Campaign," *San Diego Union-Tribune*, 30 August 1996, A1; "Nightline Speaks to Democrats," *Nightline*; Gloria Borger, "The Company He Keeps," *U.S. News & World Report*, 9 September 1996, 20; Fritz, "Clinton Strategist Resigns."

77 Larry Sabato, quoted in Rob Howe, "Man on the Spot," *People Weekly*, 16 September 1996, 207.

78 "Democratic Strategist Discounts Effect of Morris Story," CNN.

79 Borger, "The Company He Keeps."

80 "Campaign Shake-up," *MacNeil/Lehrer News Hour*; see also R. Cohen, "A Betrayal of Confidence."

81 Berke, "The Democrats."

82 James Bennet, "For Fallen Clinton Aide, Forum for Ethics Lecture," *New York Times*, September 13, 1996, A22.

83 David Streitfeld, "Publishing: Dick Morris Signs Deal for Book on Clinton Race," *Washington Post*, 5 September 1996, C1. Revising the usual sequence, Morris saved his more elaborate mea culpa phase for a series of talk show appearances months later, coinciding with the release of his book. "Dick Morris Tells All," *Larry King Live*, CNN, 16 January 1997; "Dick Morris Interview," *ABC News*; "Interview with Former Clinton Advisor Dick Morris," *Prime Time Live*, ABC, 15 January 1997. The story he told was, not surprisingly, quite different from that told about him at the height of the scandal: of individual failings and sexual addiction. "I had a fundamental flaw in my character," he told ABC's *Good Morning America*. He led a double life, one of "the daytime," and the other the "hidden life . . . of sexual promiscuity" ("Dick Morris Interview," *ABC News*). His book was published to mixed reviews in 1997, and Morris has continued a successful career as a writer and political pundit. Martha Moore, "One-time Clinton Power Broker Emerges Unbroken," *USA Today*, 16 August 2000: 6A.

84 Thomas Oliphant, "The Rise and Fall of the Morris Myth," *Boston Globe*, 8 September 1996, D7; Marc Peyser, "A Strategist of His Own Fall," *Newsweek (Special Edition)*, November 1996, 12; Todd Purdum, "Fallen Adviser Says He Is Still Welcomed by White House," *New York Times*, 11 January 1997, A7; Gloria Borger, "Singing a Song of Himself," *U.S. News & World Report*, 16 September 1996, 62.

85 Mitchell, "The Consultant."

86 Susan Page, "Now, Morris Wants to Be the Comeback Kid," *USA Today*, 11 December 1996, 8A; Susan Estrich, " 'Comeback Kid' for Real," *Los Angeles Times*, 15 December 1996, M2.

87 Page, "Now, Morris Wants to Be the Comeback Kid"; Estrich, " 'Comeback Kid' for Real"; R. Cohen, "A Betrayal of Confidence"; Mitchell, "The Consultant."

88 "Morris' Brashness Earns Him Play of the Week," *Inside Politics*, CNN, 6 September 1996.

89 Brooks, "Dick Morris."

90 Lance Morrow, "Does the Morris Thing Matter?" *Time*, 9 September 1996, 78.

91 See Binder, "Constructing Racial Rhetoric"; Michael Schudson, "The Sociology of News Production," *Media, Culture, and Society* 11 (1989): 263–82.

92 Gamson, "Jessica Hahn."

93 Bayer, "Sex Scandal Rocks Campaign."
94 It seems unlikely, for instance, that the same sort of scandal script operated in narratives featuring nonmasculine men such as George Michael, Pee Wee Herman, and Michael Jackson. In those cases, where assumptions about the relationship between masculinity and sexuality were disrupted, the scandal was likely more directly focused on sexual norms and less on institutional expectations.
95 See Joshua Gamson, "Taking the Talk Show Challenge: Television, Emotion, and Public Spheres," *Constellations* Vol.6, no.2, June (1999); Gayle Rubin, "Thinking Sex: Notes for a Radical Theory of the Politics of Sexuality," in *The Lesbian and Gay Studies Reader*, ed. Henry Abelove, Michele Aina Barale, and David Halperin (1984; New York: Routledge, 1993,), 3–44.
96 Qtd. in Karen Halttunen, *Confidence Men and Painted Women* (New Haven: Yale University Press, 1982), 33.
97 See Bennett, *News: The Politics of Illusion*; Robert Bellah et al., *Habits of the Heart* (Berkeley: University of California Press, 1985).
98 Bennett, *News: The Politics of Illusion*.
99 Herbert Gans, *Deciding What's News* (New York: Vintage, 1979).
100 Joshua Gamson, "Incredible News," *American Prospect*, no. 19 (1994): 28–35.
101 See Gamson, *Claims to Fame*.
102 Mark Silk, *Unsecular Media: Making News of Religion in America* (Urbana: University of Illinois Press, 1995).
103 Gaye Tuchman, *Making News* (New York: Free Press, 1978), 47–48.
104 Gans, *Deciding What's News*.
105 Qtd. in Stewart M. Hoover, *Religion in the News* (Thousand Oaks, CA: Sage, 1998), 73.
106 See Gamson, *Claims to Fame*; Hoover, *Religion in the News*.
107 See Emile Durkheim, *The Rules of Sociological Method* (1895; New York: Free Press, 1982); Kai Erikson, *Wayward Puritans* (Boston: Allyn and Bacon, 1968).
108 Lull and Hinerman, "The Search for Scandal," 29, 5.

Power and Corruption
Political Competition and the Scandal Market

For fifty years, between 1872 and 1923, when Americans heard scandal, they thought Crédit Mobilier, because this scandal was followed by no national scandal of equal magnitude. After 1924, when Americans heard scandal, they thought Teapot Dome, because no other scandal of equal scale and scope followed it—until it was overshadowed by the very special set of scandals of 1949–1954, which dominated the scandal discourse until Watergate.

During the years intervening in those four outstanding episodes of scandal, the United States was not a nation without sin. In fact, in the last decades of the nineteenth century U.S. politics was considered virtually synonymous with corruption. Now, after Watergate, though no one can say U.S. politics is more corrupt than ever before, recent decades have been chronicled as an era not only of unprecedented numbers of scandals but one during which "the incidence of scandal has risen exponentially . . . even though the number of federal employees has remained stable . . . [In] the early 1980s, federal prosecution of public officials grew by a factor of ten."[1] Moreover, this can be considered a conservative estimate, because it does not give appropriate weight to the unprecedentedly large number of the highest levels of the political elite involved in scandal, including three speakers of the House of Representatives, several other senators and House figures, cabinet and other high-ranking public figures, one president (Clinton), and nearly a second one (Reagan).

Some would attribute the extended era of large and spreading scandal to the creation of the Office of the Independent Counsel, which provided an opportunity in which more and more players have "increasingly sought to make use of these mechanisms to discredit their opponents. When scores of investigators, accountants, and lawyers are deployed to scrutinize the conduct of a Bill Clinton or a Newt Gingrich, it is all but certain that something questionable will be found."[2] This argument has some merit, but the converse is even more tantalizing: that the independent counsel and all of its mechanisms, discretion, and generous budget are altogether more a symptom than a cause.

These contrasting and contradictory patterns evoke some important questions worthy of the most serious reflection. In particular: Why, in the most corrupt late nineteenth century, were there so few memorable scandals? And why have there been so many of note in our time? Does all this mean that we are suddenly a more corrupt society? Or have we suddenly become more moral and therefore less willing to tolerate corruption and more eager to expose it and root it out? Finally, why do the two concepts, corruption and scandal, arise together? Are they synonymous?

The last question comes first, and it will get us directly to the other two. The *Oxford English Dictionary* defines corruption as a pattern of private conduct contrary to conscience. It implies derangement of judgment, inability to make good decisions, moral insensitivity. Scandal is defined as the public exposure of a corrupt act, the revelation of guilty knowledge. Thus, although the two concepts are closely related—so close that it is hard to suppress one as the other is uttered—they are not synonymous.

My conclusion from this etymological excursion is that corruption is a constant and scandal is a variable. The level of corruption in politics is culturally and socially determined. One does not expect the overall level of corruption to fluctuate, except over decades or generations, not by the year or the quadrennium. Scandal, in contrast, tends to fluctuate in much shorter terms. In politics, scandal is, in fact, a commodity, and as a commodity it has market value. It exists as guilty knowledge that has a certain value to its possessor, and its release is, like any traded commodity, a calculated risk. These are calculated risks shaped by the political environment, just as risky business decisions are shaped by estimates of probability of success conditioned by the general economic environment. And, as with the economic marketplace, the political marketplace fluctuates, even if not in a regular cyclical pattern. Who are the customers? The most important customers are probably the allies and potential allies of the political players who possess the guilty knowledge, release of which may help mobilize their party for electoral campaign or legislative vote. Sometimes it is the opposition who are the best customers, for whom the guilty knowledge may end up demoralizing their party or weakening valuable leaders about whom the guilty knowledge is concerned. For example, the guilty knowledge on Bill Clinton released by Independent Counsel Kenneth Starr was not consumed by as many Democrats or Republicans as the Republican leadership had hoped and expected; in contrast, the guilty knowledge released in the Watergate affair was consumed voraciously by the Democrats and as a necessary prerogative by a number of important Republicans.

There is indeed a scandal market, and, as with the economic market, the scale of the scandal market expands with advances in the technology of information research, retrieval, and communication. However, although market scale may expand continuously, market values should be expected to fluctuate, expanding and contracting as demand fluctuates. This fluctuation gives us genuine bull markets and bear markets. This is not a metaphor: scandal is a real commodity with a real market, and it should be studied accordingly. It may call for a new subdiscipline of political science, which some have entitled *scandology*.[3] Here we have an opportunity to tease out some insights into the vitality and the weaknesses of U.S. political institutions, particularly in the context of political competition through political parties and their relation to the electorate. If the incidence of scandal is cyclical and the level of corruption is more or less constant, then it is not possible to explain changes in the rate of scandal by changes in the level of corruption. First of all, this would involve an attempt to explain the specific with the general, which ends up being merely altruistic or knee-jerk moralist. Second, explaining scandal by corruption is not desirable, because such a theory would imply that true reform requires human perfectibility. Thus, a good theory of political scandal must deal with observable aspects of public life, and strategic exposures of these corrupt acts must be dealt with on their own terms, from within the context of political institutions, practices, and rules rather than from some personal perspective on the morality of the players.

A Brief History of the American National Scandal Market

THE PREMODERN ERA: GRANT AND THE GREAT BULL MARKET, 1865-1880

This account begins with a great bull market on the eve of the modern era, roughly 1865–1880. President Grant entered the period as a hero but ended his two terms (1869–1877) in disgrace. Although there is no evidence that Grant was directly involved, many Republicans close to him were. Crédit Mobilier was the spectacular scandal involving a series of exposures during the electoral campaign of 1872 in which thirteen Republican members of Congress plus other prominent Republicans were exposed as having received shares of Crédit Mobilier stock for their support. Several other exposés followed, implicating Grant's secretary of war, a number of post office officials, tax collectors, and others. Grant's own private secretary was implicated.

The national politics of this era has to be categorized as dominated by a one-party system. The South had been readmitted but on a limited basis, under military occupation, and the Democratic Party was a presence in Congress but under the hegemony of the Lincoln-Grant Republican Party that had saved the Union. As is so often the case in democracies, one-party dominance tends eventually to be faction-ridden. Republicans lost the House of Representatives briefly to Democrats in the 1874 election, and the Democrats proceeded to conduct the investigations of the Grant administration that contributed to the bull market in scandal. The electoral crisis involving the 1876 election contributed to the conditions favorable to the scandal, largely because the two major factions, Grant and Hayes, were held together by personal rather than party loyalties. Factional strife was intensified in the next and last administration of this era, led by still another Republican, James Garfield. Intraparty strife became so extremely personalized that the major factions took on war-like names: Stalwarts versus Halfbreeds.[4]

It is very important to note here, for more serious comment later, that during the late nineteenth century the party system had changed to virtually a revolutionary extent, from a one-party hegemonic, albeit faction-ridden, system to a nationally competitive — a closely competitive — two-party system. But at the same time, *there was no concomitant, commensurate change in state development*. If Rip Van Winkle had fallen asleep in 1850 and awakened in 1880 (or 1890 or 1900), he would have had hardly any intimation that we had endured the worst war in history up to that time and had been governed by virtual martial law for nearly four years. We were the same "state of courts and parties," as Skowronek puts it, and the same patronage state, as I put it, with virtually no appreciable change in our national institutions or in our dual federalism, despite President Lincoln and despite adoption of the three great Constitutional Amendments (Thirteenth, Fourteenth, and Fifteenth) for which the war was fought.[5]

The post–Civil War era ended abruptly following the longest presidential election crisis in U.S. history (including the Bush-Gore crisis). The "Compromise of 1877" gave Hayes the election over Tilden, but it was made possible by the agreement to end Reconstruction, to withdraw federal troops from the former Confederate states, and to restore "home rule" and thus the all-white Democratic Party to the southern states. Because a good bit of federal patronage in internal improvements and at least a few federal jobs went with the compromise, the southern Democratic Party quickly became the second wing that would enable the national Democratic Party to fly. And during the decade of the 1880s, the Democratic Party was able to restore the Union to two-party rule.[6]

However, and strange as it may seem, the great bull market of the previous era, which had already been declining, virtually disappeared as two-party competition was restoring itself. Parties remained the same patronage parties they had been. Civil Service reform had established itself and was advancing, but it had not made serious inroads as yet. In fact, many would argue that we had taken the legendary one step forward and two steps back by allowing Democratic and Republican administrations to "cover in" existing appointees, thus protecting them from "rotation outward," as new administrations came to office. (State parties and local political machines were pursuing the same pattern of reform.) Parties thus remained organizationally strong and also tied to the same practices that so systematically associated them (partly in reality and partly in myth) with corruption. Nevertheless, though the level of corruption remained the same, the bull market was replaced by a bear market that would last until well into the Harding administration.

Although the Republican Party was hegemonic from the Civil War until the Depression, its internal factional strife gave Democrats two victories with Grover Cleveland (separated by four years) and two successive victories with Woodrow Wilson, enough to maintain genuine competitiveness between the two parties. However, once the Republicans could dispose of TR, they would return in 1920 with sufficient unity to put the Democrats back in the deep minority position they occupied in the electorate. The Democratic defeat in 1920 was not only a decisive national electoral defeat but revealed that they had become nothing but a southern party, having carried the electoral votes of eleven states, all southern. This set the stage for the next bull market.

President Harding was very much like President Grant, staffing his administration with a few members of great distinction and many of no account. Harding was having jolly good fun with the bully pulpit of the presidency, which he called "bloviating," and was known among elites of both parties to be enjoying "sexual satisfaction from women other than his austere and matronly wife, whom he called 'Duchess.' The general public, however, remained unaware of Harding's self-indulgent and weak character."[7] His happy national goal of "return to normalcy" (also his word) turned sour in 1923, with a stream of revelations of illegal and unethical conduct of high-ranking members of his party and his administration. The scandal bull market of 1923 got its name from the most sensational of the events, Teapot Dome, a conspiracy centered on the secretary of the interior and the secretary of the navy turning over control of valuable naval oil reserves in the Teapot Dome Reserve of Wyoming, along with the other reserves in California, to corporate energy interests. The conspirators ended up in Leavenworth Federal Penitentiary. Although Harding himself was not implicated, the revelations surely reached him. At the height of the scandal, he left for a tour of the Alaska territory, on the way becoming ill with what was reported to be food poisoning, and died in San Francisco. His death was received with national mourning, but revelations of corrupt acts continued, many of them going well beyond the confines of naval oil reserves.

Although the Teapot Dome scandal was essentially over in 1924, the scandal bull market continued. Attorney General Harry Daugherty, who had been the engineer of the famous "smoke-filled room" nomination of Harding for president, was implicated in illegal sales of liquor permits and pardons, leading to his removal after Harding's death, a trial, and a bare escape from conviction, thanks to two hung juries. His brother, Mally Daugherty, was also implicated but gained his fame largely from his refusal to testify before Senate committees, leading to a contempt of Congress case that went clear to the Supreme Court.[8] The director of the Veterans' Bureau was sentenced to a term in the federal pen for corrupt sale of government property and access. Lesser scandals, without prominent names attached, flowed, driven largely by House and Senate investigations, whose constitutional power of subpoena was to be validated in 1927 in *McGrain v. Daugherty*. Although Republicans controlled the House and the Senate, the revelations were driven by the efforts of Democratic Senators Thomas Walsh and Burton K. Wheeler of Montana — with the support of Republican progressives who had recently rejoined the party after the Theodore Roosevelt insurgency and were not to remain happy campers in the Republican fold. One historian of the Senate was moved to write in 1938, "At no other period in its history had the Senate been so engrossed with investigations as during the six months [of the] first session of the 68th Congress [December 3, 1923–June 7, 1924]."⁹

The bull market in Harding scandals slowly petered out, with one revelation after another paraded before congressional committees, some reaching the courts. Interestingly, some of Harding's sexual adventures also came to light, but very little was made of them.

President Coolidge helped bring the bull market to an end by seizing the initiative with the assignment of two Justice Department lawyers of the most sterling reputation to prosecute these cases — as a sort of preemptive strike against further efforts at scandal revelation by the Democrats. V. O. Key suspected that disarray within the Democratic Party reduced the ability of its leaders to seek further advantage in exposés: "So weak was the spirit of protest that the country paid little heed to the Teapot Dome scandals. The Democratic party, rent by internecine struggle, did little to encourage the public in the belief that it had the capacity to govern. Its 1924 national convention was a savage bout beautiful to behold."¹⁰ Credible as that may appear, it is a bit too broad and subjective to provide a satisfactory explanation, and it overlooks one point of greater explanatory value: the sudden death of the relatively popular President Harding, coupled with the deaths by suicide of two of the more serious offenders.

The bull market popularly remembered as Teapot Dome was, in any case, over. What followed was possibly the longest bear market ever, lasting at least through the 1940s. The factors underlying this long bear market are so obvious that little more is needed than a quick and brief inventory: depression, mobilization, war, and the death of one of America's most important and beloved presidents. The only source of scandal would have been produced by Senator Harry Truman, whose rise to prominence came from his senatorial investigations of unethical and illegal war profiteering. But Truman was a Democrat investigating the dealings of Democrats, and this brought him to the 1944 nomination to run as vice president on the ticket with Franklin Delano Roosevelt. Reward for good work, or co-optation of possible insurgency: either way, world war was no time for adversaries to try to make hay with any guilty knowledge they might have possessed.

It is difficult to give a precise date for the onset of this bull market, because it arose out of the 1946 election, which not only returned Congress to Republican control after sixteen years but gave Republicans every expectation that the election of 1948 would give them control of the entire national government. If Great Britain could turn Churchill out, the United States would surely have done the same to all the Democrats in 1946, if only our rigid constitutional principle had not ordained that 1944 be followed inexorably by 1948. The loss in 1948, especially to a party led by even less a figure than Britain's Clement Atlee, had a tremendous influence on the Republican Party, leaving its leadership and the public at large to wonder if the party had an electoral future at all. In that context, the power game would have to be played by "politics by other means," to use that felicitous phrase of Benjamin Ginsberg and Martin Shefter.[11]

Indeed, there was ordinary corruption in the Democratic Party that would spread inevitably out of lax and casual restraints during war and by such a long period of control of the government, which would give rise to suspicions that "power corrupts." Government-by-crony and cronyism were virtually invented to fit the type of corruption associated with an old party hack like Harry Truman. The most prominent of the Truman cronies was White House military aide General Harry Vaughn, who took a $500 deep freeze as a gratuity for a kindly intervention, typical of the many efforts he had made to help friends expedite their interests in various government agencies. The first revelation of Vaughn's antics was in mid-1949, when a Senate investigating committee revealed that he had used his influence to help friends. This became part of a series of disclosures of "influence peddling," generated by congressional Republicans, even though by then they had lost majority control of the House and Senate, thanks to the 1948 election. But such exposés of influence peddlers and "five-percenters" did not seem to get the Republicans anywhere, either by weakening their adversaries or by mobilizing public support for themselves. One factor in their failure to gain from these exposés was, in effect, an accidental preemptive strike in 1950–1951 by Senator Estes Kefauver's investigation of organized crime. This was the first use of TV for exposure, and the public did warm up to the Kefauver revelations, diverting public attention and appetite away from national politics altogether.

No, the real bull market was not in the ordinary type of corrupt activity. The real bull market was composed of a very special form of scandal, not experienced since the Alien and Sedition fiasco of 1800. The scandals that gave us the real bull market beginning in the late 1940s gave that market a very special name because it was a very special kind of scandal: *McCarthyism.*

McCarthyism was born in postwar anxiety generally and the Alger Hiss case in particular. The movement to investigate and expose communist subversion had already begun in earnest with the FBI as early as 1945. Their investigations, however, failed to produce the public mobilization that FBI Director J. Edgar Hoover had sought, until the movement was joined by the House Un-American Activities Committee after the Republicans took over Congress in 1947. Investigations were proceeding in earnest, but it was the investigatory persistence by young member of Congress Richard Nixon and his crafty cross-examination that produced contradictions in the testimony of Alger Hiss and Whittaker Chambers—and the rest is history, or prehistory. The exposés became a frenzy, especially after Hiss was accused, indicted, and convicted of perjury (never of subversion or treason), so that by the end of 1949, when Republicans had lost the 1948 presidential election as well as the control of Congress they had enjoyed for a mere two years, the momentum was beginning to carry itself. Soon, "moderate" Republicans were engaging in "Red smears," and, most important, communist sympathy had been redefined as corruption, a prima facie case of deranged judgment and moral insensitivity.[12]

Once association of any kind with communism was defined as a form of corruption, all the makings of a historic scandal bull market were in place—perhaps the greatest of bull markets, as measured by its breadth, its depth, and especially by the height of its reach: two secretaries of state, a number of top military brass, high-ranking diplomats, top scholars and clergy, and luminaries in entertainment and the media. And we should never overlook the fact that McCarthyism was a political movement, not a cultural movement, not an identity movement, not a psychological phenomenon. It was a crass use of scandal to supplement or indeed substitute for electoral power. The spread of the scandal market to social, educational, and culture elites was a by-product. McCarthyism was not McCarthy alone, of course; it was vigorously supported not only by Nixon and many other members of the Republican right wing, but also, albeit surreptitiously, by the mainstream of the Republican Party, including presidential candidate Eisenhower himself, "Mr. Republican" Robert Taft, and many other respectable Republicans who had reaped the benefits without paying the cost of their oft-repeated proviso "I don't like some of McCarthy's methods but his goal is good."[13] Nelson Polsby's careful study of McCarthyism and its tactics in state campaigns definitively confirms that McCarthyism was Republican Party strategy.[14]

The McCarthyism bull market petered out after roughly four fat years and three lean. McCarthy was discredited by censure in the summer of 1955 by a vote of 67–22 in a Senate that had returned to Democratic control after the 1954 election, but it was a decisive bipartisan vote in a Senate that "had produced exactly one anti-McCarthy vote, Fulbright's, the previous January."[15] Its most appropriate political obituary was a brief one by Eric Goldman: "Flailing away at the descending oblivion, [McCarthy] summoned a press conference and 'apologized' for having supported Eisenhower in 1952. The President smiled and the nation yawned."[16] Richard Nixon inherited the McCarthy mantle as chief Republican campaigner and "ax-man" and used McCarthyist anticommunist tactics in 1956.

THE WATERGATE BULL MARKET

The long bear market was abruptly interrupted by the work of several Republican underlings who attempted to burglarize the Democratic National Committee headquarters in the Watergate apartment complex in Washington in mid-1972. Except for the minor trespass itself, there wasn't anything very extraordinary about the Watergate break-in. Political espionage is just as familiar as industrial espionage and therefore would hardly be a piece of news so potent that it could cause a revolution in party strategy. But this was going to be different, because, by 1973, factors favoring the politics of scandal were going to trump the factors that encourage continuance of electoral politics.

First and foremost, Nixon was not a paranoid but had well-justified fears of enemies, going all the way back to the McCarthy period. He was not going to go down without a fight, and this meant that he would do anything to prevent information from the executive branch and the Republican National Committee from getting into the hands of investigators. The list of his efforts to plug the leaks and cover up the conduct is too familiar to recount here. But the phenomenon of the cover-up is such an important feature of all scandal that it deserves a brief digression.

Every scandal tends to go through a metamorphosis of three stages, and each helps explain the true value of scandal as a political commodity. As advertisers used to claim of the original long-playing record in the late 1940s, scandal is "the gift that keeps on giving." The first phase is obviously the exposure. The second phase is the denial; when the denial is not entirely truthful, it is referred to as the nondenial denial, which enhances the value of the emerging scandal not only to the journalist but also to the exposer. The third phase is the investigation. Investigation is an end in itself, because it is sustained, institutionalized, or formalized exposure that can shrink power without assassination. Investigation may become prosecution, but that is obviously not necessary, because even without it, the commodity value of scandal is immensely enhanced, with a kind of multiplier effect, by the guarantee that each scandal will produce at least three stories.

For purposes of analysis, these three phases can be broken down into two dimensions: the substantive and the procedural. Exposure, the revelatory first phase, is the making public of the actual scandal: the breach of a moral code or norm, such as taking the money, giving the inside information, meeting the girl, trading forbidden military goods for strategic advantage. Once the substantively corrupt conduct has been revealed and while it is still in the realm of accusation, interpretation, and denial but prior to incontrovertible proof, the original scandal can be extended, because it then enters the procedural dimension. For a great, perhaps the largest number of scandals, the cover-up or procedural dimension can be more devastating than the substantive scandal itself.

This was certainly true in the Watergate situation, because, as earlier observed, the original conduct was nothing more than campaign espionage with a bit of trespass thrown in. If the trespassers and their handlers had owned up immediately, they probably would have gotten off with suspended sentences, as none of them had a record of chronic criminal conduct. The momentary embarrassment of such confessions would certainly have had little impact on Nixon's prospects for a second term. (The same is almost certainly true of the factors that led directly to Bill Clinton's impeachment. The ultimate procedural event was the nondenial denial, "It all depends on what your definition of 'is' is.")

The Nixon cover-up surely deserves ranking as the richest and most extensive mine of cover-up data in the history of scandal, at least in U.S. history. The procedural dimension, in other words, produced virtually all of the scandalous items that gave us the brief but probably the most important bull market in our history. There is no need to itemize the scandals here. Many of them were simply embarrassing; a number of them were criminal, and some officials actually served time in prison for them; others reached the profound constitutional level of abuse of power and misuse of presidential prerogative, putting us on the edge of collapse of the national regime altogether.

It is quite possible that the imminence of collapse and constitutional crisis contributed to the shortness of the Watergate bull market, because it ended less than two years after it began. The transition from Richard Nixon to Gerald Ford provided not only a legitimate succession but served to clear the arena and the atmosphere. Prominent journalists and many public intellectuals were quick to remark on the genius of U.S. politics, which was deemed confirmed by its ability to purge itself and heal its wounds. There was, of course, a heavy dose of rationalization in those claims—a telling of one of Plato's Noble Lies to bring about that which was being praised. But even the most cynical of witnesses to the Noble Lie would have to recognize that in the months that followed the Nixon resignation, a bear market in scandal was replacing the intense two-year bull market, and that bear market would last through the Ford and Carter administrations and into the first four years of the Reagan administration.

But there is more to the bear than the scare. Carter, a most unlikely candidate, had put the Democrats back on the electoral track; it was perhaps an unfair fight between a disabled Democrat and a wounded Republican, but Carter and Ford led their parties in a conventional electoral competition, and their administrations, as well as Reagan's first, were scandal-free. We know now they were not corruption-free, but no one can doubt that they brought us through a twelve-year bear market. The contribution of the ordeal of Watergate to the bear market of 1974–1986 was helped by the fact that President Carter's was a unified government and Reagan's a half-unified government (with control of the presidency and the House, but not the Senate). But the pattern of oscillating control from Nixon to Ford to Carter to Reagan was, in my opinion, the trump that favored electoral over alternative forms of political competition in that twelve-year period. Meanwhile, although the Watergate explosion may have contributed to a prompt end of the bull market and the onset of the bear market, it can also be credited in a more positive way with the laying of the foundation of what was to become a permanent bull market, or the *institutionalization of scandal*.

A cartoon accompanying a review essay by Nicholas Lemann in the *New Yorker* presents caricature sketches of Ford, Carter, Reagan, Bush the elder, and Clinton, with a shadowy Nixon enveloping them in the background. The caption is: "The Post-Watergate Presidency: An Ever-Increasing Engagement in Prosecution Management."[17] We can take "prosecution management" as a synonym for institutionalization of scandal. In brief, Watergate produced a number of serious and potentially important reforms, each of which can be appreciated as a more efficient and effective means of exposure of corrupt actions and therefore the promotion of bull markets. For example:

1. Campaign finance reforms of 1973–1974 set much more stringent requirements on collecting, reporting, and spending money by political parties. And those reforms created the conditions that gave rise both to the criminalization of more political acts as well as to the tremendous expansion of PACs to avoid criminalization.

2. The War Powers Act (WPA) required presidential consultation with Congress prior to any act of international hostility. This was a definite blow aimed at the "imperial presidency," an appropriate title for the growing tendency of presidents to consider themselves above the law, especially in all matters that concerned international relations and national security.

3. The Hughes-Ryan Amendment of 1974 strengthened the WPA by requiring the president to keep eight different congressional committees informed of any clandestine operations. (This was reduced to two committees in 1980.)

4. The Budget and Impoundment Act of 1974 created, among other things, a Congressional Budget Office to provide Congress with much greater ability to contest and combat presidential spending commitments and to reveal any use of presidential discretion to divert budgeted funds or to refuse, by "impoundment," to spend the budgeted funds.

5. Congress created the Office of the Independent Counsel in 1978, an action triggered by the difficulties encountered by the special prosecutor in the Justice Department charged with criminal investigation of the Watergate cases.[18]

It must be emphasized once again that these reforms were by-products of the Watergate bull market and, above all, were intended to create an atmosphere of political morality more than actually to produce one. But these laws could be as real as Congress and hostile investigators could make them. There is no question that these mechanisms made far more likely the institutionalization of scandal.

Two Bull Markets Become One: From Iran-Contra to Impeachment
This brings us to the final era in our history of scandal, or I should say, the final two bull markets that can be better understood as one long bull market. In early November 1986, two defining events took place: on November 3, 1986, a Lebanese newspaper, *Al-Shiraa*, published a report revealing that the United States had been selling arms to Iran for the purpose of exchanging them for the release of U.S. hostages; a

few days later, the 1986 election returned control of the Senate to the Democrats after six years.

Attorney General Meese, heading for a speech at West Point, changed his text on the way and made it an occasion for a preemptive strike by officially admitting that the Reagan administration had indeed been selling arms to Iran for at least a year, using Israel as the go-between, in hopes of making an exchange for U.S. hostages.

The fears of the Reagan administration leading up to the preemptive strike were realized almost immediately. The Democratic-controlled House Intelligence Committee was now joined by the newly elected Democratic Senate to dedicate separate investigations of the affair. Five days later, President Reagan named a three-member commission to investigate the role of the National Security Council and its staff, under the direction of former senator John Tower (R-TX). In December, a fourth investigation was set in motion by the judiciary's appointment of Lawrence Walsh to begin a separate and independent investigation under the authority of the Independent Counsel Act and the 1978 Ethics in Government Act.[19] The arms sales to Iran were contrary to the Reagan administration's own oft-repeated policy against any such negotiations and bribes. And the diversion of the funds from those sales to the Contras, which by then had been revealed by the Reagan administration, violated a series of laws explicitly prohibiting use of funds to aid the overthrow of the government of Nicaragua. These prohibitions were embodied in the well-known Boland Amendments to annual appropriations bills between 1982 and 1986, each being more explicit and authoritative than the previous ones.[20]

Thanks to the preemptive strike of Attorney General Meese, the procedural dimension of the Iran-Contra scandal was not nearly as important as it might have been. But, in terms of the substantive dimension, the actions exposed in the affair were more numerous and far more serious than those of Watergate or Teapot Dome. First, they were patently illegal, not merely by some broad statutory interpretation but by laws adopted precisely for the purpose of prohibiting the very actions taken by the NSC staff members, their conspirators in the private sector, their conspirators in Israel and Nicaragua, and their high-level operators in and around the White House, namely Colonel Oliver North, Admiral John Poindexter, Secretary of Defense Caspar Weiberger, and CIA Director William Casey. Second, the key actions and their authorizations came far closer to the "high crimes and misdemeanors" of which impeachments are made. From the standpoint of one's moral code, murder, rape, and incest may be considered examples of the most profound corruption; from the moral standpoint of the body politic, criminal intrusions into national security would seem to me far more corrupt. Nevertheless, they still must be treated as commodities in the market for scandal.

Even though the case against Reagan for impeachment was much stronger than that against Nixon (or, I might add, against Clinton), the Democrats were probably loath to force still another Republican president prematurely out of office. But we do not need to be concerned with their private motivations. The fact is that all the Democrats needed to do was weaken Reagan and diminish his power and that of his party. This will return again with Clinton, whose conviction and removal were sought only by the radical Republicans, not by the Republican elite. This is the scandal game and the scandal market: assassination is truly radical, patently destructive of the procedural niceties that make democracy and representative government possible. Reagan's actions were censured by the Tower Commission and by the congressional investigating committees; a number of top staffers were discredited and forced to resign, and others were thrown into early retirement. In return for dropping all the more serious charges, President Reagan agreed to accept a public rebuke for bad management and disregard for established procedures.

The long bull market continued. In February 2001, a *Washington Post* columnist led off his column as follows:

A lameduck president grants a slew of controversial pardons, 11th-hour Get Out of Jail Free Cards for the politically well-connected.

His pardon list includes: a former cabinet official who could have been in a position to implicate the president himself in federal crimes. An assistant secretary of state who withheld information from Congress and a CIA official who lied to it. And a Pakistani who was caught smuggling $1.5 million worth of heroin into the United States and had 47 years left on his sentence.

Outrage billows. Editorials thunder. "The pardon," says a prominent prosecutor, "undermines the principle that no man is above the law." . . . The president was George H. W. Bush . . . Christmas Eve 1992.[21]

And the bull market continued. When Clinton took office in January 1993, Lawrence Walsh was just finishing up his investigation of the 1986 Iran-Contra scandal. Joseph diGenova was just beginning what was to be a three-year stint as independent counsel on the 1992 Passportgate scandal involving President Bush's rummaging through records of Clinton's 1960s visit to Moscow. Kenneth Starr was merely more of the same, only more so. The grant of authority he received from his appointment as independent counsel placed virtually no limit on the discretion he could use in his pursuit of Clinton's behavior, and there was also no time limit and no explicit budgetary limit on his office. Thus, the institutionalization of scandal has been advanced by the reaction produced by the very presence of the Independent Counsel: "Defense lawyers relentlessly expanded their jurisdiction over what Clinton says in public and how he spends his time. The basic weekly rhythm has been set to an amazing extent by legal proceedings, press inquiries, and congressional hearings on official misconduct." [22]

Two factors give the impression that the Clinton bull market was exceptional: sex and impeachment. Both can be set aside, however, leaving Clinton's ordeal ordinary but, as with everything about Clinton, more spectacular. As for the first, sex has never been important in the history of U.S. political scandal. I leave to others the task of speculation about why, but I insist that Clinton's case be included in their examination, because Clinton's troubles had very little to do with sex. Monica Lewinsky became a factor only as a part of Paula Jones's civil rights case against Clinton for sexual harassment and sexual discrimination. The actual sexual relations Clinton had with Lewinsky, whatever they were, have about the same moral/political weight as the original Watergate trespass: substantially inconsequential, procedurally dynamite. Because Lewinsky's encounters with Clinton were entirely consensual, with no hint of sexual harassment or sexual discrimination, Clinton at first denied the relationship to protect his own stature and his family relationships. His denial became a cover-up of tremendous procedural consequence only when the Jones case put him in a situation where he was making the very same denials *but under oath*. This he should have seen, or his legal advisors should surely have seen, as a trap. But the point here is, once again, that, like Watergate, the original scandal was a bit of trespass that, in and of itself, would have had no bearing on Clinton's political fate.

Scandology: A Political Theory of Corruption and Scandal It is time to turn away from bull and bear, to try to pull together some kind of explanation—not a formal, causal theory but a rationale, an argument that makes sense of the pattern and can link it to an assessment that has a chance of improving our democracy. The two most readily available arguments consider corruption and the media. The third, my own, does not reject the other two but rather subsumes them in an approach that aims to feed the imagination and demand speculation about politics and democracy.

The first approach to an explanation, introduced and, by implication, rejected at the outset, is corruption itself as the primary independent variable: Can fluctuations in the incidence of scandal be explained by changes in the level of corruption, or of general public morality? Here I respond by repeating two points already made, points that take on greater power in the context of the history of scandal. First, we can reject this theory on purely scientific grounds without denying that corruption exists and without denying that corruption provides the raw material, as it were, for scandal. It cannot serve as an explanation because it requires us to reason from the very general to the very particular, and the level of societal or general political corruption changes too slowly and too infrequently to serve as a variable in the scientific sense. Thus, to invoke corruption to explain each scandal or each phase in the incidence of scandal merely begs the question. Second, corruption should be rejected for normative reasons because not only is it too distant from the "dependent variable," but the mechanism of its influence rests entirely on human character and leaves no room for consideration of improvement by reform of political institutions. The clergy can go on preaching about human perfection as though "men [can be] angels," and their preaching may do some good without doing any great harm to the body politic. But in the Madisonian spirit, political scientists ought to deal with actual governments within which *homo politicus* operates. The demand for reform through human perfectibility is the beginning of totalitarianism, with "the new socialist man" and all that.

The second approach to explanation is "the media." I put this in quotes because this factor is usually invoked holistically, as though media were a singular noun possessing a spirit or inner will capable of specific efficacy, as in "the weather" or "the sun" or, indeed, "information technology." We have had "mass media" of some sort for virtually the entire period covered by the history of scandal in this essay. The mass circulation newspaper, "yellow journalism," can surely be considered one of the causes of the Spanish-American War, and the mass circulation newspaper dominated communication until it was joined by another mass medium, radio. The rest is history. But, much like corruption, the various media, from print to electronic, are, as a whole, far too general and much too close to linear or serial development to be useful in explaining particular fluctuations in the scandal market.

Still another truth about the news media seriously weakens the media as a key explanatory variable: few scandals, if any, are actually produced by the media in general or one medium in particular. Every medium of communication has its reporters, and those reporters are pawns of power holders in a power game, with guilty knowledge as its most valued resource. The sensitive ears of these reporters dramatize the scenario laid out earlier, with each political player asking, When does it serve my purpose to expose an adversary with the guilty knowledge that I have in my possession? When a reporter is trusted or favored by a political player, a scoop is made to order. But there are very few truly investigative reporters who independently produce a genuine exposé when those who hold the guilty knowledge do not want it to be exposed. In a true exposé, the value to the possessor of the guilty knowledge would be wasted, or could in fact be counterproductive if the revelation came at the wrong time; meanwhile, the reporter who independently manufactured the exposé wins a Pulitzer prize. The normal situation is one in which reporters spend their time (1) being present on their beat; (2) cultivating the familiarity, friendship, and trust that render them capable and dependable pawns of key power players; and (3) maintaining ignorance of what game is being played or of the purpose the leak is to serve for the leakers. Deep Throat is the most notable example, and it is quite probable that Deep Throat was not one but several informants. All of this underscores the contention that the media, jointly and severally, are precisely that: channels of communication. The medium may influence the message, but the medium is always the messenger and rarely the message.

Theoretical effort number three is to be commended not because it is adequate in itself but because it is a genuinely political, indeed political science, effort. By that I mean it seeks explanation in the participants and their institutions, thus in phenomena very close to the relevant actions themselves and within institutions that we sometimes have the wit and the power to improve. In my humble opinion, this includes "the media." Whether we call it collectively the Fourth Branch or not, the media, collectively speaking, is a political institution that can be reformed.

This third approach is not only political; it is party-centered. As this has been intimated throughout the essay, the main job here will be to summarize and highlight. And because my focus is on national politics, it seems useful to initiate the conclusion with a classic story that takes place at the local level.

As the national or presidential parties were emerging in the late nineteenth century, local political organizations were also coming into their own. The most famous or notorious case is that of Tammany Hall, the fraternal name of the Democratic Party of New York County, the island of Manhattan. The man most often given credit for Tammany Hall, William Marcy Tweed, held the top post for quite a while but ultimately became victim of a number of scandals that terminated his career, in 1871, and his life, in jail. Tweed, like his predecessors, operated in the era of what Martin Shefter has called "rapacious individualism"; he did consolidate many of the loose elements of the precincts and assembly districts but was unable to maintain party discipline with "only the bribe and the pay-off."[23] Thus, Tammany Hall did not achieve full consolidation until several years later, under Tweed's successor, John Kelley.

Kelley is the one who should be credited with having earned for his Democratic Party the title of "machine": "[Kelley] led the party in Tweed's wake [and] pioneered both the institutionalization of intraparty discipline and the accommodation with reformers. The first was a prerequisite both to party rule of the city government and to negotiation; the latter was an agreement to maintain the city government's fiscal soundness. The accommodation of boss and reformer with one another was not without its coercive element. Those in the financial community could abort the worst disasters by threatening to make city bonds unmarketable. Bosses could coerce (or woo) men of wealth by adjusting tax assessments and the like."[24]

This accommodation of the "dangerous classes" with the "respectable element" produced relative peace between the machine and its enemies and genuine competition between the city Democratic Party and the state Republican Party (under the leadership of Mark Hanna). Peace led to the consolidation of the "Greater City of New York" in 1898 and a stretch of relatively scandal-free New York City governments until a local bull market of scandal produced the removal of the colorful Mayor Jimmy Walker just as the Great Depression was getting under way.

My version of the moral of the Tammany story is that consolidation of two kinds produced machine politics and also produced a fairly long local bear market in scandal. Consolidation type 1 was Kelley's consolidation within the party by controlling, precinct by precinct, the nominating process and the electoral process—and the true acid test of organization strength is control of the nominating process. Consolidation type 2 was the working out of peace treaties between Tammany and the major economic interests, to the substantial benefit of both sides. This gives a clear picture of political parties as a channel for the sublimation of ambition and greed into constructive purposes. As Adam Smith wrote in a book that sold better in America in 1776 than in Great Britain, "It is not from benevolence of the butcher, the brewer, or the baker, that we expect our dinner, but from their regard to their own interest. We address ourselves, not to their humanity but to their self-love."[25] From here I follow Madison, who appears to base his theory of politics on exactly this same principle: "Ambition must be made to counteract ambition."[26] A proper interpretation of this is that ambition is to political rationality what greed is to economic rationality. To carry this further, it seems to mean that human beings—by nature, by original sin, or by social environment—are corruptible but under certain conditions can be elevated, not rendered virtuous, certainly not beautified, but still made capable of virtuous, public-regarding acts. It all depends on the more proximate political conditions, the *constitution* that provides the context for improving the probability of elevated use of ambition. For Madison and associates, a good constitution built on the separation and counterpoise of power would, through competition, be the antidote for the ultimate corruption: tyranny. At the risk of appearing to be moving from the sublime to the ridiculous, I suggest that the political party, *properly understood*, made itself, during two centuries, part of such a favorable context or constitution.

However, the history of scandal markets reveals that not all competition is equal. The cases of Reagan and Clinton may best illustrate the point. Both were carried to the heights of scandal bull markets and to the historic depths of disgrace, including jeopardy of impeachment and downright conviction, which would have been unprecedented. In both instances, the adversaries, who were in fact in control, backed off, letting both presidents hang out to dry but not quite to die.

Backing off from the radical approach to scandal—assassination—confirms the functional validity of the relationship between scandal and political competition. In return for dropping the more serious charges, President Reagan agreed to accept a public rebuke, leading to serious shrinkage in his position. President Clinton, in return for his ultimate confession of guilt in the matter of perjury and obstruction of justice, kept the Republicans from moving successfully out of the impeachment in the House to almost certain conviction in the Senate. And the radicals were punished rather severely for having tried to push all the way to assassination when the tacit bargain was the shrinkage of Clinton's power and his neutralization in the 2000 election. Because Clinton could not succeed himself, premature removal would have brought on "Mr. Clean" Gore to complete the term as president of the United States, to receive a virtually free ticket to the nomination and a high road to victory. However, although the strategy of scandal to diminish without assassinating worked constructively in both the Reagan and the Clinton cases, scandal has to be considered a form of political competition that is inferior to electoral competition. Scandal should be understood as a bona fide and potentially constructive form of politics but an inferior alternative, a suboptimizing, pathological form of political participation. It is not directly incompatible with electoral competition but ultimately corrosive to it and to democracy itself.

This may be why we have tended to get bull markets in scandal mainly when one party has reached a pessimistic assessment of its electoral prospects. Because the primordial purpose of political parties is to win elections, there must be considerable derangement of organization and perspective before or during a commitment to pursue the suboptimal, *incremental* course of weakening the opposition party one person at a time. In fact, a bull market violates the fundamental principle of party democracy: the principle of numbers as the real and proper basis of party as well as democracy.

The grip of capitalism on the economy and on the Republican Party in Albany made Tammany Hall's electoral dominance a sham—like Casey at bat, all power and no prowess. Tammany had to learn from Tweed the power of the new money and began to use its electoral power to equalize the plutocratic. And it worked, giving New York City better government than it had had, while saving post-Tweed Tammany leaders from disgrace and jail.

Meanwhile, nationally, the Democrats were in far worse shape. Their long-running minority status in the shadow of a sixty-year Republican hegemony had been masked during the Wilson administration, whose two elections were attributable mostly to *intra*party insurgency and defection of Theodore Roosevelt's progressives. As Republicans plastered their party back together with Harding, the Democrats required forty-four ballots to nominate an obscure James Cox (another Ohio state politician), thus failing the acid test of party: control of the nominating party.[27] The still greater ignominy was revelation later in the 1920 election that the Democratic Party had become merely a southern party, having won the electoral votes of only eleven states, all southern. Harding's vulnerability need not have been (and probably was not) any deeper than that of his typical predecessor. But the need of the Democratic Party for an alternative to election after 1920 was close to unprecedented.

I have already put the next great bull market, McCarthyism, thoroughly into the party matrix. Nelson Polsby's results confirm that McCarthyism was not only a party strategy but an incremental one that was aimed at spoiling the Democratic Party by discrediting its leaders one by one. They could be liberals, such as Senator Brien McMahon of Connecticut, or archconservatives such as Senator Joseph Tydings of Maryland, but above all, they were Democratic leaders.

Reelection of a Republican president in 1956 proved that the Republicans were not necessarily a minority party any longer, thus increasing incentives to rededicate the party to electoral politics and reducing incentives to resort to exposés that would weaken the majority party one power holder at a time.

Commitment to electoral politics was vastly reinforced by the 1960 election, one of the closest national elections in U.S. history—so close, in fact, that a recount in one state alone (Illinois) could have reversed the national result. It was also one of the most partisan campaigns. Although Richard Nixon was crown prince of McCarthyism, he brought to the 1960 campaign an intensity of partisanship the United States had almost forgotten. The "new Nixon" was now leading a partisanship that was much more one of party versus party, to win "the whole enchilada" by mobilizing majorities, whether they were silent majorities or vocal ones.

It is my contention, therefore, that the very long bear market that followed McCarthyism is attributable, more than anything else, to the revival of partisanship and genuine electoral politics. This bear market includes even the first four years of the Nixon administration, despite the fact that these were four Republican years, with the power of investigation resting entirely with a Democratic-controlled Congress.

Divided government's return with Nixon in 1969 would thus lead to an expectation of another bull market, given the amount of intraparty strife in the Democratic Party, especially with Nixon's Southern Strategy fanning the flames. Many serious observers were in fact wondering if the tables had not now been turned, with the Democratic Party's future in doubt. Divided government can be a factor in scandal bull markets, and would turn out to be so in the next two bull markets. But not yet, because the other party factor, electoral competition, trumps it and was very much present in 1969. It is true that Democrats held Congress and would soon use the investigative powers of Congress to produce the Watergate bull market; nevertheless, in 1969–1973, Democrats were still the hegemonic party, and their policy productivity during the first Nixon administration was equal if not superior to the first four years of FDR. What killed the electoral orientation and lit the fire once more under the scandal incentive was, of course, the 1972 Democratic loss—not only losing the election but losing such a chunk of the party that the key words for post-1973 were decomposition and de-alignment, coupled with "the new Republican majority."

For the Democrats, the situation in 1973 was not unlike the position of the Republicans in 1948. Watergate, *the cover-up*, would provide them with an inexhaustible supply of usable scandal. For the 1948 Republicans, Democratic Party policies were buying up all the sources of electoral opposition; to Republican leaders there seemed to be no means or resources to combat the "state party" or the "party state" that the Democrats would become after what was now going to be twenty years. Comparably, the 1972 Democratic Party leaders genuinely had lost control of their own nominating process, their party rules and regulations, and had lost most of their traditional southern core. A mainstream Muskie couldn't beat an insurgent McGovern. If Democrats had no Joe McCarthy, they would have to invent one—and they did: the mythical Deep Throat. Enterprising journalists Bob Woodward and Carl Bernstein were going to feed the body politic a rich diet of scandal that would eliminate, one by one, an entire Republican administration.

During the post-Watergate bear market, a lot was happening that would derange even the healthiest and best-organized political party. These developments would weaken the parties to such an extent that a large-scale debate broke out over whether "the party's over."[28] The following are the highlights of this antiparty development:

1. The binding primaries were taking away party control of the presidential nominating process.
2. The rise of the PACs was undermining party control of finance. Even in many instances where PAC money was given to the parties, that kind of finance was actually converting the parties into what I have called "taxation parties," where a party's organization may collect and spend a lot of money without being able to take advantage of it to maintain the strength of the party as an institution.
3. Added to these strictly "party reform" developments were, of course, the Independent Counsel Office and related developments referred to earlier.

The debate over the fate of the parties and the party system was settled, at least for a while, by Reagan's 1980 election and the formation of a national Republican coalition worthy of succeeding the New Deal coalition after nearly a decade of national wandering in the wilderness without a national coalition at all. However, the reelection of Reagan in 1984 so weakened the Democratic Party and rendered its outlook so pessimistic that, surely, the incentive to engage in scandal strategies was growing more and more attractive. It was the awareness of such incentives, coupled with the Democratic recapture of the Senate in 1986, that led to the Republicans' preemptive strike of Attorney General Meese's speech at West Point immediately following the Lebanese publication of the story of Iran arms sales.

We can see all the more clearly through Iran-Contra a confirmation of my party-centered theory. But here it takes on special character because, from 1986 through 2001 (and counting), *both* parties have joined the war of exposure, whereas in the past, the scandal strategy was preferred by the weaker, more deranged party. We now have "politics by other means" with a vengeance.

Two developments have contributed most toward this new bipartisan agreement not to compete through elections. First is the effect of the governmental reforms identified earlier, especially the independent counsel. Second is divided government. Between 1946 and 2000, thirty-four of the fifty-four years (62.9 percent) were years in which one of the parties controlled the presidency while the other party controlled Congress. When first recognized, divided government didn't seem to matter very much, because presidents continued to turn out proposals and Congress continued to pass important legislation.[29] But a closer look at the past twenty years reveals another pattern entirely, when it matters a great deal. Between 1980 and 2000, eighteen of the twenty years (90 percent) were years of divided government. This surely means that divided government has become institutionalized, a kind of *separation-of-party* government. Each party is nested in one of the branches and has high expectations that this situation will continue. This is not party government. This is *duopoly government*, comparable to duopoly markets in the economy. With 90 percent-confirmed expectations that each party will control one of the branches, each will tend to operate as a *majority party*. With such a guaranteed position, or market share, there is, as in the economic context, a strong tendency to be risk-averse, to reason that We must be doing something right.

Under such conditions, both parties would tend to de-prioritize any strategies aimed at seriously trying to win the whole enchilada: outright control of both elective branches of the national government. Granted, the candidates of both the major parties seem to have gone "all out" to win the presidency in 2000. But the two national parties continued to stress campaigning for control of Congress only in those states and congressional districts where elections of their candidate were close and in doubt and presidential coattails were neither offered nor sought. But true contests involve only about 20 percent of all candidates for House and Senate, leaving at least 80 percent of the districts certain to reelect the incumbent. Even if the national election for president had not been so close, Congress was going to turn out very equally divided — so close to equal in the Senate that Republicans took control at first only through the tie-breaking vote of the Republican vice president, and soon afterward, they lost control of the Senate by the defection of just one senator, Mr. Jeffords of Vermont. Back, therefore, to divided government.

Still more to the point, the strategies of the two parties have been and are very likely to continue to be incremental: stress bipartisanship in the drafting of policies and continue to try to alter the power of the other side by attrition, one leader at a time. Newt Gingrich is an outstanding case. Beginning with the Speaker of the House of Representatives Jim Wright in 1989 (followed immediately by his deputy, Tony Coelho), Gingrich's spectacular success in gaining control of the House in the 1994 election confirms the strategy, because he built on his 1989 success by the incremental method of recruiting, one by one, new, conservative candidates for Congress and then helping to finance their elections. Here again, he was building on the fact that control of both chambers is so closely balanced that it takes only a few, even in the very large House of Representatives, to alter the party in control. I have already stressed as strongly as I could the fact that the aim of the attack on President Clinton was, except for a few radical Republicans, to weaken, not to remove.

This 1989 Gingrich strategy was reaffirmed by loss of the White House to the Democrats in 1992. In response, President Clinton moved step by step, incrementally, toward the position of the Republican Party on a number of important policy issues. Republicans screamed in full voice in criticism of Clinton's claim that the Welfare Reform Act of 1996 was his own. The Republicans were absolutely correct, but Clinton still got the credit. That was only the most important of a number of Republican projects that Clinton took as his own. For some, this can be praised as bipartisanship. For Clinton, it was his incremental way to protect his own power and at the same time to undermine (quite successfully) Gingrich and then other Republicans as they came forward to do him greater harm. This is a very important reason why the most radical Republican strategy, to remove by impeachment, backfired. What do the elections of 2000 and 2002 contribute to the long bull market in scandal? The extremely close call in the 2000 presidential election coupled with an abortive end of the crisis by Supreme Court intervention (which some consider a great scandal in itself) left us with the two majority parties we already had, only now their permanence is formalized with a Republican majority in the Electoral vote and a Democratic majority in the popular vote. Loss of one defector (Republican Senator Jeffords) and thereby loss of the Senate to the Democrats returned the nation to divided government, reviving incentive to invest soon again in the bull market. Although the stunning election of a solidly *unified* government in 2002 may soften scandal incentives, one converse factor has intervened: 9/11, the continuing war against terrorism, and the development of a unilateral, interventionist, preemptive, virtually Napoleonic presidency. This has demoralized the Democratic Party, reducing its ability to partisanize and electoralize political competition for 2004. With less than two years between Iraq and 2004, it was probably already too late to get a national electoral act together; and with just short of a dozen Democratic candidates for the nomination, the party is already back to the Will Rogers caricature unleashed earlier. Unless the Democratic act can be miraculously pulled together to produce a second one-term Bush president, the incentive to scandalize the wars, especially the post-wars, will be overwhelming. Signs were already looming: No weapons of mass destruction, cooking intelligence data, hiding intelligence data. Capital for scandal was building even before the first missiles were being hurled at Baghdad.[30]

Party government today is still duopoly government, and this has to be understood to possess a dynamic comparable to duopoly in the economy. Business duopolies are risk averse and will compete in any number of ways except on price, because gain in market share would be vitiated by reduced prices. Why not the same mentality in politics—as we have seen in the past? To compete for the "whole enchilada"—a governable majority—would risk the future of the Democratic Party. Even from the perspective of mid-2003, Democrats have a better chance of advancement one seat at a time—strengthening the mentality of the bull market.

We cannot know the post-2004 situation, but it is possible to deal with it on an if/then basis. If the bull market persists and scandal strategy continues to trump electoral strategy, the guilty knowledge involved in this incremental strategy of gaining power will not only continue to have high value but will build upon itself. We had intimations of this already in the expanded use of sex as political scandal in the 1990s—something that was rare up until then. Another intimation is the expanded scandalizing of presidential pardons. Anyone who thinks President Clinton's questionable pardons were unprecedented should go back briefly and review the little game played on Bush in the *Washington Post* reported earlier.[31] Note also that no scandal was made of it then. The same is true of such practices on the part of their predecessors and, more scandalously, the many governors of past and present, about whom such practices were considered hardly worth the effort to expose.

If the demand for scandal remains high and the resources of scandal are readily expandable (as they appear to be), we have to find institutional means of devaluing and discouraging scandal as a strategy by channeling the ambition that generates the stuff of scandal in the first place and, in the second place, sublimating the urge to play the scandal strategy into more productive avenues.

Up to a point, guidance comes once again from Madison, the principal American architect of the struggle against that ultimate form of corruption, tyranny. In *Federalist* No. 48, Madison's conclusion is that "a mere demarcation on parchment of the constitutional limits of the several departments is not a sufficient guard against those encroachments which lead to a tyrannical concentration of all the powers of government in the same hands." This was a necessary but insufficient condition. On top of that, he provides what are to him the sufficient conditions for the institutional solution: *the separation of powers and perspectives as well as institutions.* Again Madison: "Each department should have a will of its own; and consequently should be so constituted that the members of each should have as little agency as possible in the appointment of the members of the others." All this was based on the underlying principle that "ambition must be made to counteract ambition" (*Federalist* No. 51).

But over two hundred years of experience informs us that the separation of powers, though necessary, was, even in its fullest definition, insufficient to put ambitions into competition. Just as it is rare to have the ideal conditions necessary for proper operation of free market competition, it is rare to have conditions ideal for the interbranch competition necessary to the proper working of political competition. The legislature was to be the "first branch." It no longer is. The presidency was to be an office of delegated powers. It no longer is. Something else is needed, and we need no longer be delicate about this: *The Founders were just plain wrong about political parties.*

The institution of the political party made itself an indispensable part of the real U.S. Constitution. It turned out to be the link between the formal Constitution and the democracy of numbers that the Constitution refused to formally incorporate. Schattschneider was courageously correct in his thesis "that the political parties created democracy and that modern democracy is unthinkable save in terms of the parties."[32] But even Schattschneider did not go far enough. The parties made democracy a practical reality by providing a channel for ambition that is about as close as we can possibly get to an arena of public life that comes anywhere near the ideal of the agora. Of all the reasons Lord Bryce gave for "Why Great Men Are Not Chosen Presidents," or, to put it more generally, why the best men of business do not go into politics, he left out the most important, which is that politicians must reveal too much of themselves. It takes only a moment to compare the open book of political lives to the virtually complete privacy enjoyed by corporate leaders. Corporate executives can remain phantoms if they like. But for those who go into politics today, privacy is the first sacrifice. This greatly increases the likelihood of the scandal game.

Democracies must always strive to improve morality in public life by providing the framework for direction and incentive toward some level of public-regarding concern. But because this must be done by distinctly nonmoral, instrumental methods, what it comes down to is *credibility*. The same is true in business, where it is called *credit*. Note well that the two words come from exactly the same origin: *credere*, to believe. In both realms, credibility, or trust, can be maintained only by sublimation or suppression, and in this effort politics confronts the greater difficulty because, at least in liberal democracies, politics is far more transparent than business.

If there is a large and growing "confidence gap" (i.e., loss of credibility) in politics today, we can of course explain it by such things as the rising cost of campaigns and elections, tying the candidates and parties closer and closer to "the interests." But it goes far deeper than that, and it goes much farther back than yesterday. The Tammany Hall story emphasizes that parties always have problematic ties with the corporate world. If political credibility is at critically low levels today, and if political parties are the only proven instrument for channeling private ambition into public-regarding virtue, then we have to ask whether our particular two-party system, with its winner-take-all, single-member district representation, is appropriate for the twenty-first century. I personally think a multiparty system is more appropriate today. But whatever the type of party system, I am all the more confident about the definition of the problem any party system has to face: If the parties today cannot come to terms with private interests in a credible public venue, then it is time to change the parties, not time to impose a morality test on the players.

Incremental parties of today, by virtue of their own divide-and-conquer strategies, are incapable of confronting each other eyeball to eyeball in competition for mass support. And if they cannot do that, they cannot confront the major private interests whose need for governmental welfare can otherwise be satisfied incrementally. Party government is the answer, with one party *as an organization* in control of government on the basis of mass election. The alternative to this is not a mythical pluralism, with a universe of groups competing toward an equilibrium that approaches "the public interest." The real alternative is a government of barons and satraps. If we did not have a party system in some form or another, we would have to invent one. And if we allow the two parties to continue to atrophy by scavenging each other with cascades of petty scandals, then we may be turning into a system that is beyond salvage. If so, it will not only be an unsalvageable party system but an unworkable government system.

Notes

1 Suzanne Garment, *Scandal: The Culture of Mistrust in American Politics* (New York: Anchor-Doubleday, 1991), 3, 5. See also Benjamin Ginsberg and Martin Shefter, *Politics by Other Means*, 2d ed. (New York: Norton, 1999), 26–27; they report on prosecution and indictments of public officials at state and local as well as federal levels.

2 Ginsberg and Shefter, *Politics by Other Means*, 29.

3 Scandology was first proposed as a subdiscipline, partly tongue-in-cheek, by Anthony King, "Sex, Money and Power," in *Politics in Britain and the U.S.: Comparative Perspectives*, ed. Richard Hodder-Williams and James Ceaser (Durham, NC: Duke University Press, 1986). Scandology was picked up and taken more seriously by Andrei S. Markovits and Mark Silverstein, eds., *The Politics of Scandal: Power and Process in Liberal Democracies* (New York: Holmes and Meier, 1988).

4 To indicate the intensity of the strife between the two Republican fac-

tions, it is worthwhile to add that Charles Guiteau, the assassin of President Garfield in July 1891, shouted as he was being carried away by arresting officers, "I am a Stalwart . . . [Chester] Arthur is now president of the United States." And it is true, Arthur was a stalwart Stalwart, a "chief henchman" of Stalwart leader Roscoe Conkling. See George B. Tindall and David Shi, *America: A Narrative History*, 2d ed. (New York: Norton, 2000), 761–62, and Morton Keller, *Affairs of State: Public Life in Late Nineteenth Century America* (Cambridge, MA: Harvard University Press, 1977), 264–68.

5 Stephen Skowronek, *Building A New American State: The Expansion of National Administrative Capacities 1877–1920* (New York: Cambridge University Press, 1982).

6 That is to say, at the national level. After 1896, the United States developed two *one*-party systems, North and South, but still that continued to give us *nationally* a two-party system, albeit, two competing one-party systems, until the 1950s.

7 Tindall and Shi, *America*, 919.

8 *McGrain v. Daugherty*, 273 U.S. 135.

9 George H. Haynes, quoted in David R. Mayhew, *America's Congress: Actions in the Public Sphere, James Madison through Newt Gingrich* (New Haven: Yale University Press, 2000), 85 n. 17. Mayhew goes on to report that at least fifty senators "went at it as 11 committees held public hearings."

10 V. O. Key, *Politics, Parties and Pressure Groups*, 5th ed. (New York: Crowell, 1964), 184.

11 Ginsberg and Shefter, *Politics by Other Means*.

12 For good and readable accounts of McCarthyism, see Eric Goldman, *The Crucial Decade—And After: America, 1945–1960* (New York: Random House, 1960), and William Manchester, *The Glory and the Dream: A Narrative History of America, 1932–1972* (Boston: Little, Brown, 1974), chs. 17, 21. For a good treatment of the Truman administration's perspective on McCarthyism, see Alonzo L. Hanby, *Beyond the New Deal: Harry S. Truman and American Liberalism* (New York: Columbia University Press, 1973), chs. 15, 17.

13 Quoted in Goldman, *The Crucual Decade*, 216.

14 Nelson Polsby, "Towards an Explanation of McCarthyism," *Political Studies* 8 October 1960, 250–71.

15 Manchester, *The Glory and the Dream*, 717–18.

16 Goldman, *The Crucial Decade*, 289.

17 Reprinted in Richard M. Pious, *The Presidency* (Needham Heights, MA: Allyn and Bacon, 1996), 101.

18 I am grateful to Mark Silverstein for his careful inventory of these post-Watergate actions bearing on the power to expose scandals: "Watergate and the American Political System," in Markovits and Silverstein, 30–

33. When Nixon refused to deliver up tape and documents demanded by a court order sought by Special Prosecutor Archibald Cox, he ordered Cox fired in a series of movements and countermovements that came to be called the "Saturday Night Massacre." The independent counsel was set up with far greater independence of presidential discretion.

19 This latter requires that when the attorney general, after an investigation, determines there are "reasonable grounds," he must notify the Special Division of the federal judiciary (created by the Act) to appoint an independent counsel to use grand jury proceedings and other investigative powers to investigate the conduct in question. The independent counsel can be removed only "for cause," subject to review by the Special Division and the Judiciary Committees of the Senate and the House. The constitutionality of this Act was reviewed and granted by the Supreme Court in *Morrison v. Olson*, 108 S.Ct. 2597 (1988).

20 A good account of the events and context can be found in Gordon Silverstein, *Imbalance of Powers: Constitutional Interpretation and the Making of American Foreign Policy* (New York: Oxford University Press, 1997), 146–51.

21 Quoted in Michael Powell, "President Extended Trail of Questionable Pardons," *Washington Post*, quoted in the *Ithaca Journal*, 28 February 2001, 2B.

22 Nicholas Lemann, "Scandalizers-in-Chief—Five Presidents and How They Shrank," *The New Yorker*, 5 January 1999, 77–80.

23 Quoted in Amy Bridges, *A City in the Republic: Antebellum New York and the Origins of Machine Politics* (Ithaca: Cornell University Press, 1984), 152.

24 Ibid., 153.

25 Adam Smith, *Wealth of Nations* (New York: Oxford University Press, 1981), 1: 26–27.

26 *The Federalist*, No. 51.

27 Granted, the Democrats still had the two-thirds rule for delegate votes to nominate, but still, 44 ballots in 1920 followed by 103 ballots to nominate John W. Davis in 1924 are decisive evidence of a party in disarray. As Will Rogers put it at the time, "I am a member of no organized political party. I'm a Democrat" (qtd. in Tindall and Shi, *America*, 25–26).

28 David Broder, *The Party's Over* (New York: Harper and Row, 1972). For a good review and evaluation of that debate, see John Aldrich, *Why Parties?* (Chicago: University of Chicago Press, 1995), ch. 1. For the other side, see Xandra Kayden and Eddie Maye, *The Party Goes On* (New York: Basic Books, 1985).

29 David Mayhew, *Divided We Govern: Party Control, Law Making, and Investigations, 1946–1990* (New Haven: Yale University Press, 1991); Morris Fiorina, *Divided Government*, 2d ed. (Boston: Allyn and Bacon, 1996).

30 See, for example, Robert Dreyfuss, "The Pentagon Muzzles the CIA—Divising Bad Intelligence to Promote Bad Policy," Cover Story, *The American Prospect*, 16 December 2002, 26–29.

31 See note 21.

32 E. E. Schattschneider, *Party Government* (New York: Holt, Rinehart and Winston, 1942), 1.

JOSHUA D. ROTHMAN

Hardly Sallygate

Thomas Jefferson, Sally Hemings,
and the Sex Scandal That Wasn't

O n November 1, 1998, newspapers across the country reported
the impending release by *Nature* magazine of DNA test results
giving scientific substance to the two-hundred-year-old story
of Thomas Jefferson's sexual relationship with an enslaved woman
he owned named Sally Hemings.[1] Scholars have only just begun assessing the significance of the scientific findings for their historical
understandings of Jefferson specifically, and of race and slavery in the
United States generally.[2] The news reports about the *Nature* article,
however, appeared just two days before midterm elections considered
by many to be a referendum on the possible impeachment of a president named, of all things, William Jefferson Clinton, for denying the
truth about an illicit sexual relationship of his own.

Such a coincidence was too obvious for some observers to resist
comparing the two men and their respective scandals. In their commentary accompanying the *Nature* bombshell, for example, biologist
Eric S. Lander and historian Joseph J. Ellis noted that the revelations
about Jefferson and Hemings would almost certainly play some role
in President Clinton's impeachment hearings. Lander and Ellis wisely
and carefully noted that "there is a world of difference between a slave
and master at the close of the eighteenth century, and a White House
intern and a married man at the end of the twentieth." Still, they concluded that Thomas Jefferson's involvement with Sally Hemings ought
to remind us that "our heroes—and especially presidents—are not
gods or saints, but flesh-and-blood humans, with all of the frailties and
imperfections that this entails."[3]

On reading the comments of Lander and Ellis, *New York Times* editorialist William Safire detected a whiff of conspiracy. In a column

entitled "Sallygate," Safire aired his suspicions that a cabal he sarcastically labeled "Lefty Historians to Save Clinton" played some unspecified role in orchestrating the timing of the release of the DNA evidence relating to Jefferson and Hemings so as to influence American voters to overlook President Clinton's indiscretions. Safire suggested that notwithstanding the efforts of Lander, Ellis, and other scholars, it was inapt to draw a parallel between the third president, who never directly addressed the matter of his relationship with Sally Hemings in public, and the forty-second, who lied about his relationship with Monica Lewinsky while under oath.[4]

To what extent we might compare the ethical behavior of Thomas Jefferson and Bill Clinton regarding their sexual activities is debatable. Examining how a presidential sex scandal played out in the public sphere of the early republic, however, suggests a stark contrast between our own political environment and that in which Jefferson functioned, because in his own era, Jefferson's involvement with Hemings was hardly a scandal at all. When journalist James Callender wrote a series of articles for the Richmond *Recorder* in the fall of 1802 detailing the rumors about Jefferson and Hemings, he hoped readers would be so revolted and so scandalized by the revelation of Jefferson's private immorality that it would ultimately destroy Jefferson's political career. He could not have been more wrong.

Jefferson's Federalist political opponents had a great deal of fun at the president's expense in the months after Callender's articles first appeared. In editorials, poems, and cartoons, they branded Jefferson a hypocrite for having a sexual relationship with Hemings despite his publicly expressed opposition to sex across the color line. One of the most widely distributed lampoons of Jefferson, for example, was James Akin's cartoon portraying Jefferson as a rooster and Hemings as a hen. Given the title "A Philosophic Cock," the drawing was ironically captioned "Tis not a set of features or complexion or tincture of a skin that I admire."

Yet even most Federalists did not intimate that Jefferson's sexual involvement with Hemings had or ought to have any impact on his ability to act as president, and they largely dropped the matter after just a few months, by which point voters had bolstered Jeffersonian Republican congressional majorities.[5] By the presidential election of 1804, Callender was dead and published references to Hemings were practically nonexistent. Jefferson was reelected in a landslide, and Jeffersonians retained control of the presidency until 1824. Far from being remembered primarily for his involvement in personal scandal, Jefferson became one of the most influential and iconic figures in U.S. history, a sentiment most famously expressed by his biographer James Parton, who maintained in 1874 that "if Jefferson was wrong, America is wrong. If America is right, Jefferson was right."[6]

The dearth of political fallout for Jefferson from the Hemings revelations was not for want of obsession with the character of politicians or of ferocious partisan politics. The first few decades after the ratification of the Constitution, in fact, were probably the most politically divisive in U.S. history. The experiment of republican government was extraordinarily fragile and its very structural framework still unsettled. Republicans and Federalists saw in one another not merely the political opposition, but men of compromised integrity who would lead the fledgling nation to tyranny in the form of mob rule or monarchy, respectively. Because American politicians felt so much was at stake and so much depended on the character of American leadership, vicious personal attacks were part and parcel of political discourse in the early republic, and sometimes even spilled over into physical violence. Perhaps no incident better represents the personalized nature of U.S. politics and the failure of politicians to separate entirely their ideological differences from their individual distaste for one another than the 1804 death of Alexander Hamilton during a duel at the hands of his personal and political enemy (and then vice president) Aaron Burr.[7] Still, that the Hemings matter failed to become a full-scale political debacle for Jefferson suggests that in the early republic, the relationship between the moral character and the political stature of an individual was somewhat indeterminate.

In an era filled with editors who specialized in what the catchphrase-inclined today might call "the politics of personal destruction," James Callender was a master of the art. An angry, bitter, and cynical man who made a career out of invective and character assassination, Callender ruthlessly and often crudely savaged anyone unfortunate enough to be caught in his journalistic sights. Many of his contemporaries, especially those he attacked and their supporters, tried to dismiss him as nothing but a libelous scandalmonger. Scholars largely followed suit and used Callender's reputation to bolster their own assertions that the sexual relationship between Jefferson and Hemings never existed. Historian John Chester Miller, for example, denigrated Callender's very claims to practicing his profession legitimately, writing, "Callender made his charges against Jefferson without fear and without research. . . . He never made the slightest effort to verify the 'facts' he so stridently proclaimed. It was 'journalism' at its most reckless, wildly irresponsible, and scurrilous. Callender was not an investigative journalist; he never bothered to investigate anything."[8]

A closer examination of Callender's articles on Jefferson and Hemings, however, reveals that not only were they prototypical products of a public world where attacks on private behavior were deemed legitimate means of expressing political hostility, but, despite being pieced together largely from gossip and rumor, the reports were essentially accurate. It is clear that Callender researched the Jefferson-Hemings matter and that he talked to numerous people about it, primarily from Jefferson's own county and class. These sources could not have known every detail about life at Monticello, but they did have a great deal of reliable information, and they gave it to Callender. Callender was purposefully sensationalistic, but with respect to the facts he presented, his tone was cautious and variable. He used strong, definitive language when he believed in the reliability of his sources, but he also sometimes corrected inaccurate information, and when he printed stories he felt were of questionable veracity he noted that they were merely rumors. Callender was a lot of things, but he was not usually a liar. He knew Jefferson's supporters would deny the Hemings story. But if the story was to have the catastrophic consequences for Jefferson's political career that he desired, Callender also realized he had to be absolutely sure that they could not refute it, and he repeatedly dared them to do so. They never did.

That Callender's articles failed to have the impact he hoped for had only little to do with his own established pattern of journalistic scurrility. Under slavery, sex across the color line was both ubiquitous and notorious. Usually, interracial sexual relationships (using the word in its broadest sense) entailed rape of enslaved women by their owners. Even when they occupied ambiguous positions between coercive and consensual, sexual relationships between blacks and whites generally and masters and slaves specifically were supposed to be carried out discreetly. Such an ethic restrained public discussion of the normalization of racialized sexual assault in the South, but it hardly made interracial sex a well-kept secret. Most people who lived in the small communities that composed much of the southern landscape knew precisely who was engaged in such illicit sexual conduct, and they gossiped among themselves accordingly. Jefferson and Hemings were no exception, a reality Callender understood and exploited to his advantage.[9]

Callender overestimated the injury revelations of interracial sex would do to Jefferson's political standing because he fundamentally misread the sentiments of white Virginians toward sex between masters and enslaved women. No matter how much they may have personally disapproved of his sexual behavior, as far as most white Virginians were concerned, Jefferson acted with propriety in his relationship with Hemings both publicly and in front of his white family, and what he did behind closed doors with his own slave property was largely his prerogative. Similarly, no matter how much they might have gossiped privately, few would have ever considered exposing and criticizing Jefferson publicly, given the implicit challenge such an action would entail both to Jefferson's honor and to the systematic racial (and, when it came to black women, sexual) domination that constituted slavery itself. If Callender had thoroughly understood these kinds of unwritten cultural rules, he might have realized that the biggest scandal his articles would produce was not that the president of the United States had children by one of his own slaves, but his own distasteful decision to put that fact in the newspaper for widespread public consumption.

To make this argument is not to say that Americans saw no connection between the private virtue and the public conduct of their leaders. They very much did, which is precisely why newspapers and politicians devoted so much energy to circulating rumors about the moral failings of public officials. Gossip was politics, and Jefferson was hardly the only political giant of his era to be implicated in a sexual scandal. Just a partial list of others accused of sexual malfeasance would include George Washington, Benjamin Franklin, Alexander Hamilton, and John Marshall. In a political environment where personal enmity was integral to and inseparable from partisan warfare and where the line between private and public realms was blurry, it is unsurprising that Callender thought releasing a story about the president's personal life would inflict the maximum damage to Jefferson's political career.[10]

But Callender did more than simply fail to grasp the subtleties of southern attitudes toward interracial sex. In a broader sense, he also did not seem to realize that although revelations of a public figure's moral hypocrisy might be extraordinarily embarrassing and might provide a source of great mirth for a man's enemies and great prurience for a journalist's readers, humiliation did not *necessarily* translate into political disgrace. Such was especially the case if, as was true of Jefferson's involvement with Hemings, the private actions in question seemed to bear no direct relevance to the performance of public duties. Safire drew an important distinction between the actions of Clinton and those of Jefferson when he noted that President Clinton lied about his affair with Monica Lewinsky to a federal grand jury. What he did not point out is that it is difficult to conceive a scenario in which Jefferson would have been answering questions under oath about Hemings in the first place.

The Vendetta, the Story, and the Sources James Callender emigrated to the United States from his native Scotland in 1793, fleeing British authorities he feared would charge him with treason for his 1792 publication of *The Political Progress of Britain*, a pamphlet in which he attacked British political institutions and advocated Scottish independence. Callender was a radical egalitarian who detested the pretension and condescension he saw in wealthy and powerful men. Once in the United States he was drawn to Jeffersonian Republican politics for their antielitist, anticorruption, and anti-English overtones, and he began working for the Philadelphia *Gazette*, reporting the proceedings of Congress. Most leaders of the Republican Party were ambivalent about Callender from the outset of his U.S. career. Some found his journalistic style unpalatable; others feared the extremism of his advocacy. But the Republicans of the 1790s were a party struggling desperately to get into power, and, in the words of his biographer, Callender "could be guaranteed to diminish the public stature of his opponents."[11]

Thus, even after the editor of the *Gazette* fired him in 1796, party officials clandestinely continued to feed Callender information with which to attack prominent Federalists. Callender struck his sharpest blow in 1797, when his *History of the United States for 1796* forced Alexander Hamilton to reveal publicly an adulterous affair with a woman named Maria Reynolds in order to counter allegations of his complicity with Reynolds's husband in an illegal speculation scheme using government funds. Callender was thrilled with his own efforts, writing to Jefferson in September 1797 that Hamilton's embarrassing written reply to the *History of 1796* was "worth all that fifty of the best pens in America have said against him."[12]

Jefferson and Callender probably first met in June or July 1797 in the office of a Philadelphia printer where Jefferson, then the vice president, gave Callender $15.14 for copies of his *History of 1796*.[13] Callender thereafter repeatedly turned to Jefferson for financial support and assistance, and Jefferson responded by giving him over $200 from his personal accounts during the nearly four years following their initial meeting, more than he gave to any other Republican journalist.[14] Jefferson rarely wrote to Callender personally, but he solicited others to subscribe to Callender's publications, and when he did write he indicated that he appreciated Callender's efforts and encouraged the journalist to continue writing and publishing. In October 1799, for example, after seeing some advance pages of Callender's soon-to-be-published *The Prospect Before Us*, a relentless political and personal attack on President John Adams, Jefferson sent his congratulations and his assurance that "such papers cannot fail to produce the best effect. They inform the thinking part of the nation."[15]

In 1798, a Federalist-dominated Congress passed the Sedition Act to stifle Republican newspaper criticism of Adams and his administration by using the threat of imprisonment against anyone publishing sentiments deemed hostile to the government, Congress, or the president. Afraid of being arrested and prosecuted under the new law and uncertain that even his fellow Republicans would stand behind him, Callender promptly fled Philadelphia and ended up in Richmond. He became increasingly hostile to most Republicans in 1798 and 1799, perceiving quite accurately that they looked down their noses at him, used him when he served their interests, and left him to confront Federalist hostility alone when his work got him into trouble.[16] Even as his anger toward the Republican Party grew, however, he became increasingly attached to Jefferson, the one man who seemed to offer the support and respect that he felt he deserved. In letters to Jefferson during 1799 and 1800, Callender began to use the pronouns *us, we,* and *our* when discussing Jefferson's chances of winning the presidential election of 1800.[17]

In June 1800, Callender's fears came to pass. He was tried under the Sedition Act, primarily for his excoriation of Adams in *The Prospect Before Us*. Found guilty, he was fined $200 and sentenced to nine months in prison. Republicans turned him into a political martyr, publishing the minutes of his trial as a campaign document for Jefferson. Having to pay his fine mostly out of his own pocket nearly forced Callender into bankruptcy. Jefferson won the election of 1800, a victory in which Callender, not unfairly, believed he had played an important role. By the time he got out of jail in March 1801, he had already made entreaties to Jefferson about a remission of his fine and about a job as a postmaster in the new administration.[18]

But by the time Callender had served his sentence, Jefferson no longer needed him. Callender's antagonistic and provocative style was highly effective for an opposition party, but for a party in power it might prove more a liability than an asset. In addition, there was always the risk that his extremism would turn him into a critic rather than a supporter of the party, most of whose members he distrusted anyhow. On assuming the presidency, Jefferson pardoned all Republican journalists who had served time in jail under the Sedition Act, including Callender, and he promised to remit any fines paid as a consequence of the convictions. But he had no intention of offering Callender a patronage position. Callender had already sensed while in prison that Jefferson might be freezing him out, and when the remission of his fine got delayed and he still heard nothing from the president, he quickly became impatient.[19] Desperate for money and still suffering from an illness contracted in prison, he wrote a hostile letter to Jefferson in April 1801. He expressed his disgust that Jefferson had failed to help him retrieve his fine or give him any reward on taking office, both of which he took as personal slights. He denounced the Republicans for having abandoned him once he had helped them achieve victory, and regretted that he had ever devoted himself to any single cause when all he received in return was betrayal.[20]

Several weeks later, with Jefferson continuing to ignore him, Callender appealed instead to James Madison, the secretary of state and Jefferson's closest political ally. Subtlety, never Callender's strong point, had now left his writing entirely. He utterly failed to understand how Jefferson, who "repeatedly said that my services were considerable," could cast him out after winning the presidency, although he also claimed that he had always suspected Jefferson might turn on him. Callender also threatened the president in his missive to Madison, warning that he would reveal to the Federalists what he believed to be Jefferson's duplicity respecting the fine. More ominously, he hinted that he had items of greater significance to bring to light. "I am not the man," Callender suggested, "who is either to be oppressed or plundered with impunity."[21]

Jefferson, who surely heard about Callender's threats from Madison, would not submit to the journalist's intimidation. But he also knew that Callender relished tearing apart public figures in print and did not wish to antagonize the man further. Accordingly, in the hope that it would give Callender some immediate satisfaction and contain his temper, Jefferson asked his personal secretary, Meriwether Lewis, to call on Callender and give him $50 to tide him over until the rest of the fine could be recovered. Callender replied to Lewis's offer with an even more overt attempt to blackmail Jefferson than that contained in his letter to Madison. According to Jefferson, who described the encounter between Callender and Lewis in a letter to Virginia governor James Monroe, Callender "intimated that he was in possession of things which he could and would make use of in a certain case: that he received the 50. D. not as a charity but a due, in fact as hush money; that I knew what he expected, viz. a certain office, and more to this effect." Appalled at Callender's temerity, Jefferson canceled all financial assistance he had authorized for him and assured Monroe that Callender "knows nothing of me which I am not willing to declare to the world myself."[22] Whether Jefferson suspected that Callender's threats entailed revealing his relationship with Hemings is uncertain, but with such an unequivocal rejection of Callender's blackmail he effectively chose to let whatever information Callender possessed appear in the newspapers.

Considering what he published in the fall of 1802, Callender probably was alluding to the Hemings matter when he told Lewis that he had damaging "things" to write about Jefferson. He almost certainly had heard rumors about the relationship between the president and Hemings by the spring of 1801. Although Callender would be the first editor to put any specifics of the story in print, he was not the proximate source of the information. Jefferson's political enemies hinted at the affair even before the election of 1800, with William Rind, editor of the Virginia *Federalist*, claiming allusively in June of that year that he had "damning proofs" of Jefferson's "depravity."[23] Vulgar poems intimating Jefferson's sexual involvement with black women appeared in newspapers months before Callender ever linked the president to any particular woman.[24] Shortly after Callender published his report of the story, the *Gazette of the United States* announced that it would not print the story without greater corroboration from its own sources, but acknowledged that it had "heard the same subject freely spoken of in Virginia, and by Virginia Gentlemen."[25] That Jefferson and Hemings had some kind of sexual association can hardly be said to have been common knowledge nationally by the time Callender got hold of it, but some people clearly had already ground it in their gossip mill.

Callender detested African Americans and found the notion of sex across the color line repulsive. Once he reported the Jefferson-Hemings story, he described Hemings herself in virulently racist terms, calling her a "wench" and "a slut as common as the pavement," accusing her of having "fifteen, or thirty" different lovers "of *all colours*," and referring to her children as a "yellow litter."[26] When he had held Jefferson in esteem, Callender discounted the rumor. In prison, however, feeling himself falling out of Jefferson's favor, he began to turn against the man he had once admired. After his release he made inquiries of his own, some of which confirmed what he once refused to believe. Now he had ammunition.[27]

Callender's fine was remitted in June 1801, but it was too late to restore his good opinion of the president. He had been run out of one city and served nine months in jail in another. All of his work in the United States had been as a Jefferson supporter, and once Jefferson made it clear that the relationship would not be reciprocal, Callender wanted revenge. In February 1802 he began writing for the Richmond *Recorder*, a nominally Federalist newspaper, but he used the paper less to support Federalist policies than to voice his own hostility toward the Republicans, who taunted him mercilessly in their papers for his misfortunes.

By May 1802 a full-scale newspaper war was underway between Callender at the *Recorder* and his former employer, Meriwether Jones of the Richmond *Examiner*. Jones accused Callender of apostasy for turning against Jefferson and baited him to reveal whatever damaging information he claimed to have on his erstwhile patron.[28] For his part, Callender hurled epithets and accusations of his own at Jones, including the claim that Jones had a black mistress with whom he slept in his home and in his marital bed whenever his wife was away.[29] The personal salvos flew back and forth and escalated in the degree of their vitriol. Editors of newspapers in other major cities got involved. On August 25, 1802, William Duane, editor of the Philadelphia *Aurora*, accused Callender of infecting his wife with venereal disease and of getting drunk in the next room while she languished and died and his children went hungry. This charge was too cruel even for Callender. In the next issue of the *Recorder*, under the heading "The President Again," he wrote that it was "well known that the man, *whom it delighteth the people to honor*, keeps, and for many years past has kept, as his concubine, one of his own slaves. Her name is SALLY."[30]

The crux of the matter as Callender originally reported it was that Jefferson and a house slave named Sally were involved in a sexual relationship; that Sally had gone with Jefferson and his two daughters to France when he was serving there as the American minister; that she and Jefferson had "several" children together, including a ten- or twelve-year-old son named Tom; and that "President Tom," as Callender sarcastically called this boy, closely resembled Jefferson. As he suggested with the accusations leveled at Jones, Callender indicated his belief that Jefferson exacerbated the depravity of his sexual relationship with a black woman by disregarding the feelings of his white family in the process. Hoping his readers would find Jefferson's allowing Hemings's presence alongside his white daughters particularly galling, Callender wrote that "the delicacy of this arrangement must strike every person of common sensibility. What a sublime pattern for an American ambassador to place before the eyes of two young ladies!" Two weeks after the original article, Callender brought specificity to the number of Sally's offspring, writing that she and Jefferson had exactly five children. Again, he insinuated that Jefferson aggravated the contemptibility of his sexual behavior by granting Hemings a position of domestic legitimacy, this time by referring to the president as "Sally's husband."[31]

By presenting so many details, Callender tried to establish from the outset that his charges, far from being concocted, were grounded in verifiable fact. He challenged Jefferson's supporters to refute them, writing, "If the friends of Mr. Jefferson are convinced of *his* innocence, *they* will make an appeal. . . . If they rest in silence, or if they content themselves with resting upon a *general denial*, they cannot hope for credit. . . . We should be glad to hear of its refutation. We give it to the world under the firmest belief that such a refutation *never can be made*."[32]

Callender got most, if not all, of the information for his first round of articles directly from individuals who lived in Albemarle County; he may have made a special trip there after being released from prison, as suggested by a toast made in his honor at Richard Price's Albemarle tavern just over a month after he got out of jail.[33] He certainly implied that people in Jefferson's county were his sources when he claimed there was "not an individual in the neighbourhood of Charlottesville who does not believe the story; and not a few who know it."[34] He correctly reported not only the story's outline, but some significant details. He correctly identified Hemings by her first name, he knew both that she had been in France with Jefferson and that she worked in the house at Monticello, and he knew that she had had exactly five children, including a boy who would have been roughly twelve years old. The accuracy of this information strongly suggests that some of Callender's informants had, or knew people who had, extensive familiarity with domestic life at Monticello over the course of at least a dozen years.[35]

Callender claimed in print to have collected evidence from a large number of people, even asserting in December 1802, in response to repeated denials of the Hemings affair by Republican journalists, that he would happily meet Jefferson in court and "prove, by a dozen witnesses, the family conviction, as to the black wench and her mulatto litter."[36] If he was serious about this challenge, his witnesses would have to have been white. He would have acquired his information from the most likely places to hear local gossip in Albemarle, as in any Virginia county: taverns, markets, the steps of the courthouse, other social gatherings. He probably relied especially on members of the Virginia gentry from Albemarle and counties nearby for what he believed to be his most accurate evidence. These men—and they were almost certainly men, given the significant breach of etiquette it would have been for a woman to discuss sexual matters with a man not her husband— might have overheard their slaves discussing the Hemings story. They also would have been the whites most likely to have visited Jefferson at Monticello, to have been inside the house (and thus to have seen Hemings and perhaps her children), and to have heard the prevalent gossip about Jefferson and Hemings in elite circles. Callender, however, may well have received some reports from other whites who might have been at Monticello only briefly if at all but could see Jefferson or his slaves when they came down from the mountain to town. Some sources were more reliable than others, but anyone who lived near Jefferson was a possible informant. As Henry Randall, an early biographer of Jefferson, wrote in private correspondence in 1856, Callender "was helped by some of Mr. Jefferson's *neighbors*."[37]

For five weeks after the middle of September, Callender added no new information to the Jefferson-Hemings story. The story was an evolving one, however, and once it appeared in print, new sources, possibly but not necessarily from Albemarle, came to Callender in Richmond to feed him new information or to correct errors he had originally published. That Callender changed the number of Hemings's children from "several" to "five" in the two weeks between September 1 and September 15 is likely an example of just such a dynamic. Similarly, on October 20, Callender wrote that a few days after the original article ran, "a gentleman" came into the district court in Richmond and offered to bet anyone present a suit of clothing or any amount of money that the story was true, except for one small detail, namely that Sally Hemings had not actually gone to France with Jefferson, but had joined him later (Jefferson originally left for France in 1784, but Hemings did not arrive until 1787 as a travel escort for Jefferson's daughter Mary).[38] Callender corrected this mistake but used the correction as an opportunity to reassert how reliable his information was, writing, "If we had been mad enough to publish a tale of such enormous . . . ignominy, without a solid foundation, the Recorder, and its editors must have been ruined." He did not identify the man in the district court, but noted that no one would take the bet, because the man was known both to be very wealthy and "to have the best access to family information."[39] Whether or not the courtroom drama actually took place, there is little reason to doubt Callender's description of his source, for the correction the man called for was not only accurate but was such a tiny detail that only someone unusually familiar with the Jefferson family, the events in question having taken place almost two decades earlier, could have known it.

In the first few months after Callender published his original story, people started bringing him as much misinformation and innuendo as fact, some of which he printed. On November 10, for example, he wrote, "It is said, but we do not give it as gospel," that one of Hemings's daughters, presumably fathered by someone other than Jefferson, was a house servant currently working somewhere in Richmond.[40] This story was patently false, for no such daughter ever existed. That Callender printed the story at all indicates that despite all he did know, there were some important things about Hemings he did not, including her age. In 1802, Hemings was just twenty-nine years old, making the possibility of her having a daughter old enough to be a house servant unlikely.

That Callender made this mistake is not to say that he became careless or that he lacked the ability to distinguish fact from fiction. On the contrary, in the same November 10 article he reported that Jefferson had freed Hemings's brother, who had an "infirmity" in one of his arms and had been seen selling fruit in Richmond. Here, Callender was almost certainly referring to her older brother, Robert, who in fact had been freed by Jefferson in 1794 and had subsequently moved to Richmond, where he lost a hand in a shooting accident.[41] Callender did not catch every error he made in reporting the Jefferson-Hemings story, but he was very familiar dealing with personal gossip about public figures, and he had a good sense of when a story might be inaccurate. Hence, he purposefully indicated that the story about Hemings's daughter was only a rumor, whereas he published the story about her brother, for which he must have felt he had more reliable information, without qualification.

Yet it may be no coincidence that although he continued to hammer away at Jefferson for his relationship with Hemings for another month or two, Callender printed no new information about the relationship after November 10. Most important, of course, the midterm elections had passed by then, limiting the utility of continuing to develop the story—not that it had proved especially useful, as Republicans increased their majorities in both houses of Congress on election day. But it is also possible that Callender's sources dried up. There was, after all, probably very little anyone could have added to what he had already published. Similarly, by November he may have suspected that the rumor mill was spinning wildly and that the stories he now heard contained more falsehoods than truths. Before September 1, the story circulated mostly in private among people relatively close to the original sources of information. After September 1, though, so many people in so many places had heard the story that it became impossible to tell where the various pieces of gossip originated anymore. Callender was concerned with accuracy, and when he ran out of useful material, he stopped publishing additions to the story.

It is not surprising that Callender's reports contained some inaccuracies. White informants with the most intimate knowledge based their suppositions not on anything Jefferson told them directly, but at best on deductions and inferences from what they had seen at Monticello or in Charlottesville. Most people who knew the story had probably heard it at least secondhand, meaning Callender's information came to him through at least one other person and more likely through two, three, or four. The more people the story passed through before it got to Callender, the less likely that all the facts would be correct. The detail that Hemings and Jefferson went to France in two different ships a few years apart, for example, could easily have been collapsed into a single ocean voyage or, alternatively, Hemings could have been confused with her brother James, who had in fact been on the same ship as Jefferson when he first left America. We are all aware of rumors with grains of truth that get embellished to the point that they nearly lose their truthfulness altogether. Especially regarding a story of this nature, it is remarkable testimony to the extent and transmission of social knowledge about private interracial sexual affairs in Virginia communities that Callender got so much right.

Why There Was No Scandal: Virginia Not everyone in Albemarle had information for Callender because not everyone had heard the story, but we should not doubt Callender's assertion that nearly everyone in the county he mentioned it to believed it. Given what Virginians already knew about sex and slavery in their society in general, they did not need to have heard the details of Jefferson's relationship with Hemings to believe he might have some kind of sexual relationship with her. Even Meriwether Jones, who tried to defend Jefferson in the pages of the *Examiner* against Callender's charges, acknowledged the regularity with which white men raped enslaved women, noting that "in gentleman's houses every where, we know that the virtue of unfortunate slaves is assailed with impunity."[42] A white man conceding such a reality (not to mention recognizing that enslaved women might possess virtue) in a public forum was rare, but also refreshing if only for its candidness. Not every slave owner was a rapist, and certainly not every slave owner had the kind of ongoing sexual relationship with a slave that Callender accused Jefferson of having, but enough white men did have sex with enslaved women that the allegations about Jefferson would not have been entirely implausible.

Jefferson's particular actions and associations also gave residents of Albemarle County reason to believe the story. People visiting Jefferson had commented on the existence of very light-skinned slaves — the tell-tale sign of sex across the color line—at Monticello since at least the 1790s.[43] In addition, Jefferson's thrice-widowed father-in-law, John Wayles, was also Hemings's father, having had a long-term sexual relationship with Betty Hemings, Sally's mother.[44] The Hemings family filled the most prominent roles in Jefferson's household in 1802, and Jefferson had already freed Hemings's brother. Moreover, Jefferson may have had other close relatives who engaged in interracial sex. In an 1858 letter, Jefferson's granddaughter, Ellen Randolph Coolidge, picking up on a family story told by her brother Thomas Jefferson Randolph, attributed the paternity of Hemings's children to Jefferson's nephew Samuel Carr and accused him of being a "master of a black seraglio kept at other men's expense."[45] Although the *Nature* DNA study ruled out Carr and his brother Peter as possible fathers of Hemings's last son, the Jefferson family nonetheless might have selected them as scapegoats because they were known to participate in sex across the color line. Finally, and perhaps most telling, Jefferson was already known by 1802 to have facilitated the interracial sexual relationship of one of Betty Hemings's other daughters. In 1792, Jefferson had sold Sally Hemings's oldest sister, Mary, at Mary's request, to a white man named Thomas Bell. Bell subsequently freed Mary, and the couple lived together on Main Street in the nearby town of Charlottesville until Bell's death in 1800.[46] Many people who lived in Jefferson's neighborhood, then, believed the Hemings story because Virginia's slave owners and Jefferson himself had prepared them to believe it.

Yet even in Virginia, Callender's articles failed to have the impact he had hoped, for several reasons. For some Virginians, the Jefferson-Hemings story was as much as twelve years old by 1802, and Callender's claims were unlikely to change whatever opinions they already held. Other Virginians were unlikely to believe anything written by James Callender, given both his unhidden motives of revenge and his usual methods of operation. Those who strongly admired Jefferson also might have simply refused to accept that he might have sex with an enslaved black woman, who was by race and status as debased as Jefferson was revered. In addition, in July 1803, Callender, stumbling drunk through the streets of Richmond, fell into the James River and drowned. Other newspapers had picked up on the Jefferson-Hemings story, but their editors had neither the network of informants nor the desire for personal vengeance that animated Callender. When he died, a significant portion of the energy behind the story died with him.

Finally and most important, Callender misunderstood white attitudes toward interracial sex in Virginia, and thus failed to foresee that although his allegations might embarrass Jefferson and his white family, they were unlikely to provoke any larger consequences for his career or standing. To be sure, few white men (who constituted the entire voting population in the early nineteenth century) would publicly voice their approval of sex across the color line. Children of mixed race confused an ideally bifurcated racial order, and sex with black women was thought to degrade whites morally, a sentiment Jefferson himself expressed on numerous occasions throughout his life.[47] As Callender observed, "It is only doing justice to the character of Virginia to say that this negro connection has not a single defender, or apologist, in Richmond, as any man, that even looks through a spyglass at the hope of a decent character, would think himself irretrievably blasted, if he had lisped a syllable in defence of the president's mahogany coloured propagation."[48]

But the silence Callender witnessed among white male Richmonders did not necessarily mean that they were outraged or disgusted by the suggestion of interracial sex. Most white men, especially slave-owning white men, understood that the systematic sexual abuse of enslaved women helped bolster slavery by reminding all slaves that their masters held power over their bodies. Moreover, because slaves followed the condition of their mothers, all children produced by sex between white masters and slave women would still be slaves and hence far less potentially destabilizing to the social order than free people of color. Finally, and ultimately, what a man chose to do with his own slave property was for the most part his own business. With Virginians being of at least two minds about interracial sex, a story about a white man, no matter who he was, having sex with his own female slave could hardly be expected to elicit universal outrage.[49]

No great tumult was likely to occur when it came to Thomas Jefferson, not only because of who he was but also because of how he conducted himself in his relationship with Sally Hemings. In the slave South, ethical norms governed even activities not generally perceived to be intrinsically ethical, such as interracial sex. If a white man engaged in a sexual relationship of any duration with one of his own slaves, he could never prevent people in his community from gossiping. No one in his community, however, was likely to say anything to him directly provided that he kept his affairs discreet, which entailed never acknowledging any rumors about his sexual behavior and never demonstrating that he cared for his enslaved sex partner or that he treated any mixed-race offspring as legitimate blood relations.[50] From 1789 until the day he died, Jefferson never directly addressed the rumor of his relationship with Hemings, and he maintained appropriate racial boundaries between his black and white families. Whatever the nature of their sexual association, Jefferson acted with sufficient discretion that, according to his grandson, not "a motion, or a look, or a circumstance" would lead anyone "to suspect for an instant that there was a particle more of familiarity between Mr. Jefferson and Sally Henings [sic] than between him and the most repulsive servant in the establishment."[51] Jefferson also rarely showed affection toward his children with Hemings, and apparently never in front of others, including members of his white family. As Jefferson and Hemings's son Madison recalled, his father "was not in the habit of showing partiality or fatherly affection to us children."[52] If there ever was such a thing in white eyes as the ethical amalgamator, Thomas Jefferson was the prototype.

That Jefferson conducted his relationship with Hemings within the boundaries of what whites in his society considered propriety points to why Callender's intimation that Jefferson violated familial norms fell flat. Historian Jan Lewis has argued that Callender's publication of the story coincided with and helped contribute to a rethinking of familial affairs as sacrosanct rather than as acceptable weapons for public political warfare. Such an evolution of the public mind was still in its early stages even by the time Jefferson left office, but one means by which Jefferson's defenders tried to deny the Hemings accusation was to note his singular devotion to his white daughters and their upbringing. Such a defense carried with it two implications: that it was impossible to imagine a man so concerned with the well-being of his white family would jeopardize the feelings of that family by having an ongoing sexual relationship with a slave, and that it was unseemly for Callender even to make Jefferson's family life a matter of public discussion.[53]

In the pages of the Richmond *Examiner*, for example, Meriwether Jones maintained that Jefferson's reputation as a family man was beyond reproach. According to Jones, Jefferson had been a widower for twenty years, yet he "reared with parental attention, two unblemished, accomplished and amiable women, who are married to estimable citizens. In the education of his daughters, this same Thomas Jefferson, supplied the place of a *mother*—his tenderness and delicacy were proverbial." Jones maintained that "not a spot tarnished" Jefferson when it came to his family until Callender came along. Referring to Callender as a "brute," Jones suggested that he would get his just reward, asking him rhetorically if he was not afraid that "some avenging fire will consume your body as well as your soul."[54] Jones's claim that a slave owner could not see himself or appear to others as dedicated to his white family while also having a sexual relationship with one of his own slaves—indeed, even while raping his own slaves—was disingenuous. It masked not only the realities of Jefferson's relationship with Hemings but also the larger realities of life under slavery. Still, Jefferson never did accord Hemings or his children by her the kind of respectability and legitimacy that might have suggested he viewed them as family members. And in the end, that pretense put Jefferson's sexual behavior largely outside the bounds of public scrutiny, even to those who believed it very possible that Jefferson and Hemings had children together.

Just as he failed to appraise accurately how most Virginians were likely to respond to his revelations about Jefferson, Callender never understood that in Virginia and other parts of the South there were honorable and dishonorable ways of sharing information about the interracial sexual affairs of elite men. The integrity of a man's honor depended primarily on others accepting his self-presentation at face value. When it came to honor, appearance was reality, and Callender's very public figurative unmasking of Jefferson as less than he appeared to be was implicitly to call Jefferson a liar, the ultimate insult to a gentleman.[55] Virginians may have found Jefferson's sexual behavior wonderful material for gossip; some even fed Callender information knowing he would print it, but no one, not even Callender's informants, would ever say anything about it to Jefferson directly. Had Callender understood why this was so, he might have foreseen that even people who believed Jefferson's sexual behavior was less than admirable might also feel that his own behavior in publishing the story was at the very least distasteful. The Frederick-town *Herald* from nearby Maryland, for example, believed Callender's reports and thought the entire Hemings matter to be a subject of great hilarity. But its editors also called Callender a "sad fellow" and claimed they would not pursue the story. "Modesty," the paper argued, "orders us to drop the curtain. . . . We therefore assign it over to less scrupulous hands, confessing at the same time, that there is a merriment in the subject, which we should be graceless enough to pursue at the President's expence, were it less offensive to serious and decent contemplation."[56] By moving the rumor of Jefferson's interracial sexual affairs from private gossip to public discourse, Callender touched off whole new rounds of discussion about the president all over the country, but he also succeeded in cementing his own reputation as a scoundrel. As one hostile letter writer to the *Recorder* castigating Callender asserted, "He has no character, no honor, no sensibility."[57] Such a judgment has lasted for two hundred years.

Why There Was No Scandal: Massachusetts The fiercest enemies of Jefferson and his Republican Party, though, were primarily not in Virginia or even in the South, but further north, particularly in New England. Yet even in the hotbeds of Federalism, within a few months of the appearance of Callender's stories in the papers, opposition editors and politicians drew little attention to the matter of Sally Hemings. Although printed allusions and references to her and to Jefferson's relationship with her never completely stopped appearing during Jefferson's presidency, the revelations became just one of a litany of criticisms, and not even a particularly significant one, that political enemies incorporated into their larger critique of Jefferson as both a person and a president.

To understand why Jefferson's political rivals never took the Hemings affair much beyond what James Callender published in the Richmond *Recorder*, it is instructive to examine in some detail the only instance in which a legislative body did formally discuss Jefferson's character and whether it ought to take any official action that could be read as a condemnation of the president. On January 18, 1805, an unsigned article constituting a wide-ranging and sweeping attack on Jefferson's private morals and public actions appeared in the *New England Palladium*, a Boston newspaper. Entitled "The Monarchy of

Federalism," the piece recounted charges dating back to the 1780s, among them that Jefferson had acted in a cowardly fashion when he was governor of Virginia during the Revolutionary War, that he was a religious infidel, that he had defrauded one friend on a debt repayment and attempted to seduce another friend's wife, that he had undermined the strength of the navy, that he threatened the independence of the judiciary, and, of course, that he had "taken to his bosom a sable damsel."[58] The owners of the *Palladium* were also the official printers for the Commonwealth of Massachusetts, prompting a Jefferson supporter in the Massachusetts House of Representatives to introduce a resolution that the state's contract with the printers be terminated for their "indecent and libellous publication against the personal character of the President of the United States."[59]

The resolution seemed implicitly to ask the Massachusetts House to evaluate and judge the character of the president. If the resolution passed and the printers were fired, it could be interpreted as a vote of confidence in Jefferson and an indication that House members believed the *Palladium* charges were groundless. Conversely, if the printers were retained, it might mean that the House accepted the validity of the charges. The resolution was sent to a special committee, which was asked to make a recommendation to the full body. The committee reported that it believed the contract of the printers ought to be retained, but not because the charges leveled in the newspaper were necessarily true. Rather, the committee defended the printers by contending that people living in a republic had a right to know about the "*conduct, integrity*, and *talents* of those . . . who have been, or who may be called to offices of trust and honour," and that such knowledge depended on the rights of a free press. Whether the accusations were true and whether the printers were guilty of libeling the president were entirely irrelevant to the Massachusetts legislature, which was not a judicial body. Consequently, for the legislature to decide whether the president was of spotless or dubious character was just as irrelevant. Despite the fact that Federalists formed a majority of the Massachusetts House and might have relished the chance for a debate that they could use as an excuse to take their own public cracks at Jefferson, most of the legislators concurred with the committee. "Believing Mr. Jefferson's character was not a proper subject for legislation," the legislature concluded that in even considering whether to discuss the matter they were "foolishly squandering the time of their constituents."[60]

Notwithstanding the desire of most legislators to put the matter aside and move forward with pertinent business, some of Jefferson's supporters insisted that the president's reputation had to be unambiguously vindicated. A debate therefore ensued over whether the House ought even to discuss the truth or falsity of the charges against the president. This debate over whether to debate inevitably did bring a discussion of the charges to the floor, including that Jefferson had a sexual relationship with Hemings. Yet amid all the charges levied against Jefferson, even to his Federalist opponents the Hemings affair was of minimal importance. The only legislator to address the issue on the floor of the House was John Hulbert, the leader of the Federalist majority. Hulbert claimed to have examined the charges against Jefferson and indicated that he believed them all "substantially true and capable of undeniable proof." Moreover, it elated him to be able to say they were true, and that "he would be willing to have it written in the stars, that he might never look up without beholding it."[61] Hulbert then proceeded to detail evidence that he believed proved each charge. But when it came to discussing Jefferson's relationship with Hemings, the aggressiveness with which Hulbert had been pursuing his topic curiously failed him. He noted that the matter was well circulated and "rarely denied," but he would not even say publicly whether he thought it was true or false. As Hulbert put it, he felt "no disposition to scrutinize this charge. If it be true, it is to be presumed, that Mr. Jefferson considers it excusable. He was told that the custom of the country where Mr. Jefferson resides, warranted the practice, and, *de gustibus non est disputandum."*[62]

Hulbert's hesitation to say anything conclusively about Jefferson's relationship with Hemings might appear inexplicable, especially considering how "undeniable" he seemed to believe every other accusation made in the *Palladium* against Jefferson's character. Similar attitudes and ethics as those that structured the response of white Virginians, however, shaped how Hulbert chose to discuss or not discuss Sally Hemings and her relationship with the president. Racism, for example, certainly helped shape Hulbert's mind-set. Immediately before mentioning Jefferson's relationship with Hemings, Hulbert discussed, at some length, the accusation that in 1768, Jefferson had tried (and failed) to seduce Elizabeth Walker, the wife of his friend and neighbor John Walker. In Hulbert's words, Jefferson took advantage of his familiarity with the Walker family, and he "treacherously and basely attempted the honour of Mrs. Walker."[63] In 1805, the Walker affair was over forty years old in its origin, and John Walker himself had known about it for more than twenty years.[64] But the Walker affair involved the honor of a white woman, and to Hulbert, Jefferson's decades-old trespass on a white marriage mattered more than whether he was presently involved in an ongoing sexual relationship with a slave. To Hulbert, Sally Hemings, unlike Elizabeth Walker, had no honor to be defended. Hulbert's Latin observation, translated roughly as "There is no accounting for taste," was a snide indication that he was repulsed by the idea of having sexual relations with a black woman, but concluded that if Jefferson wanted to do so, then that was his business.

Hulbert's opinion of the Hemings matter, though, was that Jefferson's relationship with her was a matter not just of taste but of custom. To Hulbert, if it was acceptable practice in Virginia for white men to have sex with their slaves, then he would not criticize it. In later decades, Massachusetts would prove a hotbed of abolitionism, and abolitionists would use precisely the customary sexual exploitation of enslaved women that Hulbert implicitly condoned as a means of condemning the South and the institution of slavery. Some would turn specifically to Jefferson's relationship with Hemings as a propaganda tool, inventing the notion that he had not only had children with her, but had in fact sold one of his daughters by her on the open market.[65] But in 1805, there was essentially no organized abolitionist movement, and if other white men in Jefferson's own state would not criticize his personal behavior, neither would the majority of members of the Massachusetts legislature, no matter how much they might disagree with the president on matters of political principle. In the end, by a vote of 91 to 85, the Massachusetts House of Representatives accepted the report of its special committee. The printers' contract was retained, and the official position of the House was that the private character of Thomas Jefferson was simply beyond its purview.[66]

This brief exchange in the Massachusetts House illustrates how elected officials in the early republic viewed sexual gossip and its relationship to political discourse. Even Jefferson's political enemies believed that his own conscience, not a legislative body, ought to determine whether he had acted rightly or wrongly in his relationship with Hemings. Racism, property rights, and gentlemanly honor were all bound up in the customary right of slave owners to have sexual relations with their slaves. Morally reprehensible though it may have been, that customary right shielded certain aspects of Jefferson's private life from detailed scrutiny, as did perhaps an emerging notion that the inner workings of family were not matters for political discussion.

Jefferson's opponents certainly accepted that the private morality of the president could be a matter of public concern. The special committee created by the Massachusetts House did maintain, after all, that the printers were fully within their rights to expose Jefferson's perceived faults to U.S. citizens, in the belief that responsible voters had to know the character of the men they chose to represent them. The printers themselves, who offered a written defense of the *Palladium* article, similarly argued that Jefferson's private affairs were very much the public's business. By their logic, U.S. government "is elective, the superior advantage of which, is a choice of wise and good men. Every one, therefore, who becomes a candidate for office . . . necessarily puts so much of his character, as concerns his fitness for office, at issue before the people."[67]

Moreover, the printers who criticized Jefferson believed that his sexual behavior did in fact concern "his fitness for office" and that it should have consequences for his political career. The printers concurred with Hulbert's observation that in Virginia, the practice of masters having sexual relationships with their slaves was "not without some countenance from custom." But contrary to individuals who might argue that the Hemings matter "impeaches only the private character of Mr. Jefferson, and is no disqualification of a first magistrate," the printers held that Jefferson seemed to skirt the Virginia law that prohibited interracial marriage. Jefferson and Hemings, obviously, never could have been married, but the printers argued that cohabiting with a person one was forbidden to marry still made one "a breaker of the law, and an *example*, instead of a terror to 'evil doers.' " By this reasoning, the printers suggested that it might be argued that Jefferson's relationship with Hemings did actually provide grounds for excluding him from public office.[68]

Even if the case that Jefferson broke Virginia law held legal water, which it did not, it is crucial to realize that the printers felt those responsible for taking action against Jefferson were not legislators in Massachusetts or Virginia and were not members of Congress.[69] Rather, their justification for publishing a critique of Jefferson's sexual behavior in the newspaper was that American voters had to decide if Jefferson's supposed crimes in his relationship with Hemings mattered enough to damage his political career. The purpose of political gossip about sexual and familial matters in the early republic was not to make opponents subject to investigations, especially when there was no evidence that the ability of the subject of the rumors to execute his public duties had been compromised by his actions.[70] The Massachusetts printers argued that the Hemings affair pointed to Jefferson's corrupt character, and that his having perhaps broken the law made him ill-fitted to execute the nation's laws. But they never implied that Sally Hemings indicated any political corruption on Jefferson's part. Politicians of Jefferson's era gossiped about one another as a means of demonstrating their own stellar reputations and of sullying those of their opponents. And because the personal and the political were so deeply intertwined, a ruined reputation could potentially mean a ruined career.[71] If the voters cared. And in 1804, the voters decided that they did not care that Thomas Jefferson had a sexual relationship with Sally Hemings. Even in Federalist strongholds, the revelations seem to have had a negligible impact on Jefferson's reputation, and certainly had none whatsoever on his electoral fortunes. Jefferson had lost the popular vote in every New England state in 1800 and gained the presidency only after the election was thrown into the House of Representatives. In the 1804 election, however, he won every state in New England except Connecticut, and his victory overall was so overwhelming that it can hardly even be considered a contest.

Notes

1 See, for example, reportage in *New York Times*, 1 November 1998, 1, 24, and *Washington Post*, 1 November 1998, A1, A16. Also see Eugene A. Foster et al., "Jefferson Fathered Slave's Last Child," *Nature* 396.6706 (5 November 1998): 27–28.

2 Two of the first examples include Jan Ellen Lewis and Peter S. Onuf, eds., *Sally Hemings and Thomas Jefferson: History, Memory, and Civic Culture* (Charlottesville: University Press of Virginia, 1999), and "Forum: Thomas Jefferson and Sally Hemings Redux," *William and Mary Quarterly*, 3d Series, 57.1 (January 2000): 121–210 (essays by Jan Lewis, Joseph J. Ellis, Lucia Stanton, Peter S. Onuf, Annette Gordon-Reed, Andrew Burstein, and Fraser D. Neiman).

3 Eric S. Lander and Joseph J. Ellis, "Founding Father," *Nature* 396.6706 (5 November 1998): 13, 14.

4 William Safire, "Sallygate," *New York Times*, 2 November 1998, A27.

5 Even as the Federalist newspapers reprinted and snickered at Callender's 1802 reports, in fact, Jefferson's administration seemed to be gaining popular momentum. As Robert M. S. McDonald writes, "At the same time reports of 'dusky Sally' filled Federalist papers, John Quincy Adams decried the president's 'democratic popularity' and moaned that 'the strength of the present administration is continually increasing.' " McDonald insightfully discusses the national response to Callender's articles in "Race, Sex, and Reputation: Thomas Jefferson and the Sally

Hemings Story," *Southern Cultures* 4.2 (summer 1998): 46–63, quotation on 51.

6 For just one of the innumerable treatments of Jefferson's popular and political legacy, see Merrill D. Peterson, *The Jefferson Image in the American Mind* (New York: Oxford University Press, 1960), quotation of James Parton on 234. Also see Peter S. Onuf, ed., *Jeffersonian Legacies* (Charlottesville: University Press of Virginia, 1993).

7 Nearly every study of the politics of the early national period stresses their fragility and fractiousness. See, for example, Joanne B. Freeman, *Affairs of Honor: National Politics in the New Republic* (New Haven: Yale University Press, 2001). For recent studies of the Burr-Hamilton duel, see Joseph J. Ellis, *Founding Brothers: The Revolutionary Generation* (New York: Knopf, 2000), ch. 1; Arnold A. Rogow, *A Fatal Friendship: Alexander Hamilton and Aaron Burr* (New York: Hill and Wang, 1998); W. J. Rorabaugh, "The Political Duel in the Early Republic: Burr v. Hamilton," *Journal of the Early Republic* 15 (spring 1995): 1–23; and especially Joanne B. Freeman, "Dueling as Politics: Reinterpreting the Burr-Hamilton Duel," *William and Mary Quarterly*, 3d Series, 53.2 (April 1996): 289–318.

8 John Chester Miller, *The Wolf by the Ears: Thomas Jefferson and Slavery* (New York: Free Press, 1977), 154. For a thoroughly devastating critique of how most professional historians treated the Hemings matter prior to the 1998 DNA study, see Annette Gordon-Reed, *Thomas Jefferson and Sally Hemings: An American Controversy* (Charlottesville: University Press of Virginia, 1997). The only biography of James Callender (and one of the only judicious treatments of the man and his career) remains Michael Durey, *"With the Hammer of Truth": James Thomson Callender and America's Early National Heroes* (Charlottesville: University Press of Virginia, 1990).

9 On sex across the color line in Jefferson's Virginia, see Joshua Rothman, *Notorious in the Neighborhood: Sex and Families across the Color Line in Virginia, 1787–1861* (Chapel Hill: University of North Carolina Press, 2003).

10 On the centrality of gossip to the making of U.S. politics in the early national period, see Joanne B. Freeman, "Slander, Poison, Whispers, and Fame: Jefferson's 'Anas' and Political Gossip in the Early Republic," *Journal of the Early Republic* 15 (spring 1995): 25–57.

11 Durey, *"With the Hammer of Truth,"* chs. 1–5, quotation on 91.

12 On the Reynolds affair, see Jacob Katz Cogan, "The Reynolds Affair and the Politics of Character," *Journal of the Early Republic* 16 (fall 1996): 389–417. On Callender's role specifically, see Durey, *"With the Hammer of Truth,"* 97–102, and Charles A. Jellison, "That Scoundrel Callender," *Virginia Magazine of History and Biography* 67.3 (July 1959): 297–98. Durey suggests that Jefferson himself played a central

role in giving Callender information to use against Hamilton. Quotation from Callender's 28 September 1797 letter to Jefferson in Worthington Chauncey Ford, ed., *Thomas Jefferson and James Thomson Callender, 1798–1802* (Brooklyn, NY, 1897), 8 (hereafter cited as *TJ and JTC*).

13 Richmond *Recorder*, 3 November 1802; James A. Bear and Lucia C. Stanton, eds., *Jefferson's Memorandum Books: Accounts, with Legal Records and Miscellany, 1767–1826*, 2 vols. (Princeton: Princeton University Press, 1997), 2:963.

14 For additional payments from Jefferson to Callender, see Bear and Stanton, *Jefferson's Memorandum Books*, 2:971, 979, 980, 984, 986, 990, 1005, 1018, 1028, 1042.

15 Jefferson to Callender, 6 October 1799, *TJ and JTC*, 19.

16 As Callender wrote to Jefferson in September 1798, explaining his decision to leave Philadelphia, "I am entirely sick even of the Republicans, for some of them have used me so dishonestly . . . that I have the strongest inclination, as well as the best reason, for wishing to shift the scene" (Callender to Jefferson, 22 September 1798, *TJ and JTC*, 10).

17 Callender to Jefferson, 10 August, 26 September 1799, 14 March, 27 April 1800, *TJ and JTC*, 15–16, 17–18, 20–21, 21–22.

18 See Callender's letters to Jefferson from prison, *TJ and JTC*, 25–33.

19 Although Jefferson did send Callender $50 in jail, he never wrote to him, prompting Callender to implore Jefferson to write him "a few lines, at first or second hand." Ostensibly, Callender wanted acknowledgment that Jefferson was receiving political materials he had sent, but more important, he wanted some sign from Jefferson that he still remembered him and valued his support. Callender never got any signal. Michael Durey suggests that the Republican political strategy changed around Callender while he remained in jail, and that James Madison suggested to Jefferson that he assume a low profile during the election campaign, advice that Jefferson took (Bear and Stanton, *Jefferson's Memorandum Books*, 2:1028 n.53; Callender to Jefferson, 11 October 1800, *TJ and JTC*, 28–29 [quotation on 28]; Durey, *"With the Hammer of Truth,"* 139–40). On the delay in remitting Callender's fine, his overtures for a patronage position, and his subsequent fury toward Jefferson, see Durey, 143–48.

20 Callender to Jefferson, 12 April 1801, *TJ and JTC*, 33–34.

21 Callender to Madison, 27 April 1801, *TJ and JTC*, 35–37 (quotations on 35, 36).

22 Jefferson to Monroe, 26, 29 May 1801, *TJ and JTC*, 38–39. Jefferson clearly anticipated that Callender would carry out his threats. In his May 29 letter to Monroe, therefore, he also made a preemptive effort to shape the perception of his prior relationship with Callender by offering the disingenuous explanation that he had long wished Callender would end his activities as a political writer and that any money he had given

him was only as charity. Nearly a year later, Jefferson reiterated a similar and lengthier explanation of his association with Callender in another letter to Monroe (Jefferson to Monroe, 15 June 1802, *TJ and JTC*, 39–40). Jefferson's transparent strategy of trying to convince his political allies that he had never been a supporter of Callender was prescient. In the wake of the Hemings revelations, Jefferson's defenders claimed the president had never approved of Callender's work, prompting Callender at one point to print the letters Jefferson had sent him indicating otherwise.

23 Richmond *Recorder*, 1 September 1802; Fawn M. Brodie, *Thomas Jefferson: An Intimate History* (New York: Norton, 1974), 323.

24 One such poem appeared in July 1802 in the *Port Folio*, a Federalist newspaper in Philadelphia, and Callender reprinted the poem when he publicly revealed the Jefferson-Hemings story in the *Recorder* on 1 September 1802. The verse, written in dialect as if by one of Jefferson's slaves, included the following:

> "And why should one hab de white wife,
> And me hab only Quangeroo?
> Me no see reason for me life!
> No! Quashee hab de white wife too.
> Huzza, &c.
> "For make all like, let blackee nab
> De white womans . . . dat be de track!
> Den Quashee de white wife will hab,
> And massa *Jefferson shall hab de black.*"

25 Cited in Richmond *Recorder*, 22 September 1802.

26 Richmond *Recorder*, 1, 15, 22 September, 15 December 1802.

27 Richmond *Recorder*, 1 September 1802; Brodie, *Thomas Jefferson*, 323.

28 See, for example, Richmond *Examiner*, 9 June, 11 August 1802.

29 Richmond *Recorder*, 26 May 1802. Callender harped on this accusation even after revealing what he knew about Jefferson and Hemings, writing in the *Recorder* of 15 September 1802, for example, of Jones as "a fellow who converted his own house, and the bed of Mrs. Jones, into the receptacle of African prostitution."

30 *Aurora*, 25 August 1802; Richmond *Recorder*, 1 September 1802. Later, Callender explained that he had intended to wait until the election campaign of 1804 to reveal the Hemings story, hoping to cause maximum political damage for Jefferson. When the Republican papers brought his dead wife (she had died in 1798 shortly before Callender left Philadelphia, too poor at the time even to bring his four sons with him) into their personal conflict, though, he decided to run the report early. Writing to Duane at the end of October 1802 in the pages of the *Recorder*, Callender asserted, "If you had not violated the sanctuary of the grave,

SALLY, and her son TOM would still, perhaps, have slumbered in the tomb of oblivion. To charge a man as a *thief*, and an *adulterer*, is, of itself, bad enough. But when you charge him with an action that is much more execrable than *an ordinary murder* . . . is the party injured not to repel such baseness, with ten thousand fold vengeance upon the miscreant that invented it?" (Richmond *Recorder*, 22 September, 27 October 1802).

31 Richmond *Recorder*, 1, 15 September 1802. In his stories about Jefferson and Hemings, Callender never entirely dropped the subtheme that Jefferson had violated familial norms in his relationship with Hemings. On September 29, for example, Callender referred to Hemings as "Mrs. SARAH JEFFERSON" and suggested that Jefferson would call for Hemings "before the eyes of his two daughters" (*Recorder*, 29 September 1802).

32 Richmond *Recorder*, 1 September 1802.

33 Durey, *"With the Hammer of Truth,"* 142.

34 Richmond *Recorder*, 1 September 1802.

35 Sally Hemings gave birth to a son in 1790, a daughter named Harriet in 1795 (who died in 1797), a son named Beverley in 1798, an unnamed daughter who was born and died in 1799, and another daughter named Harriet in 1801. Hemings and Jefferson would have two more children after 1802: a son named Madison in 1805 and another named Eston in 1808. The "President Tom" of Callender's articles referred to the eldest child, who indeed would have been roughly twelve years old in 1802. Generations of oral history suggests that "President Tom" grew up to become a man named Thomas Woodson, but the same DNA study that linked Jefferson to Hemings also cast significant doubt on the genetic link between Jefferson and the Woodsons. It therefore seems most likely that the son Hemings gave birth to in 1790 died shortly after being born, as her son Madison later recollected his mother told him ("Life Among the Lowly, No. 1," Pike County [Ohio] *Republican*, 13 March 1873). Callender's insistence that a twelve-year-old son of Jefferson and Hemings lived at Monticello in 1802 was not his only error in his reports on the Jefferson-Hemings relationship. But it was by far and away the most significant and persistent one. For a supposition as to how and why Callender blundered in this regard, see Joshua D. Rothman, "James Callender and Social Knowledge of Interracial Sex in Antebellum Virginia," in Lewis and Onuf, 102–103.

36 Richmond *Recorder*, 8 December 1802. The original source of the information could easily have been the enslaved population of Albemarle County. Everywhere in the South, enslaved African Americans had kin and community networks that extended across vast distances. Slaves at Monticello knew of the association between Hemings and Jefferson and had greater access to details of their relationship than nearly

anyone else. Edmund Bacon, Jefferson's overseer between 1806 and 1823, described the entire Hemings family as "old family servants, and great favorites," and Jefferson's grandson, Thomas Jefferson Randolph, reported that other slaves envied the special treatment afforded the Hemingses and suspected ulterior motives, "account[ing] for it with other reasons than the true one," which he claimed lay in their trustworthiness and intelligence. Israel Jefferson, meanwhile, a Monticello slave who worked as a postilion, scullion, and waiter, confirmed late in his life and after gaining his freedom that Jefferson and Hemings were sexually involved, based on his "intimacy with both parties." Israel Jefferson also claimed in this interview that he had been Jefferson's personal attendant for fourteen years, which was not true. He probably overestimated his "intimacy" with both Jefferson and Hemings. Nonetheless he, like other Monticello slaves, believed they had a sexual relationship. Given Callender's disgust for African Americans, however, it is unlikely that he spoke directly to any Albemarle slaves. See Hamilton W. Pierson, *Jefferson at Monticello: The Private Life of Thomas Jefferson* (New York, 1862), 106–107; Randolph, quoted in Lucia Stanton, " 'Those Who Labor for My Happiness': Thomas Jefferson and His Slaves," in Onuf, 151–52; "Life Among the Lowly, No. 3," Pike County (Ohio) *Republican*, 25 December 1873. On the Hemings family, also see Stanton, " 'Those Who Labor,' " 147–80, and James A. Bear Jr., "The Hemings Family of Monticello," *Virginia Cavalcade* 29.2 (autumn 1979): 78–87.

37 Henry Randall to Hugh Grigsby, 15 February 1856, in *The Correspondence between Henry Stephens Randall and Hugh Blair Grigsby, 1856–1861*, ed. Frank I. Klingberg and Frank W. Klingberg (Berkeley: University of California Press, 1952), 29–30.

38 Brodie, *Thomas Jefferson*, 216–17.

39 Richmond *Recorder*, 20 October 1802. The Richmond *Examiner* had pointed out the error in the timing of Hemings's presence in France nearly a month before Callender printed his retraction. Callender, though, certainly trusted his own sources more than Jeffersonian editors, and though the *Examiner* notice may have prompted him to investigate the matter, he probably waited to confirm the error himself before taking any action in print (Richmond *Examiner*, 25 September 1802).

40 Richmond *Recorder*, 10 November 1802.

41 Ibid.; Lucia Stanton, *Free Some Day: The African-American Families of Monticello* (Charlottesville: Thomas Jefferson Foundation, 2000), 118–19; Rayford W. Logan, ed., *Memoirs of a Monticello Slave, as Dictated to Charles Campbell in the 1840s by Isaac, one of Thomas Jefferson's Slaves* (Charlottesville: University Press of Virginia, 1951), 13.

42 Richmond *Examiner*, 25 September 1802.

43 In 1796 alone, two different French visitors noted seeing such individu-
    als on Jefferson's resident plantation. The Duc de La Rochefoucauld-
    Liancourt mentioned "particularly at Mr. Jefferson's" slaves who had
    "neither in their color nor features a single trace of their origin, but they
    are sons of slave mothers and consequently slaves." The Comte de Vol-
    ney, meanwhile, similarly noted slaves at Monticello "as white as I am."
    Quotations in Stanton, " 'Those Who Labor,' " 152 (La Rochefoucauld-
    Liancourt) and 173 n.13 (Volney).

44 Historians have generally accepted that Wayles and Betty Hemings had
    as many as six children together. Madison Hemings claimed that his
    grandmother "was taken by the widower Wales as his concubine." Isaac
    Jefferson, formerly enslaved at Monticello, said of Betty Hemings's
    children that "folks said that these Hemings'es was old Mr. Wayles'
    children." Thomas Turner, a Virginian commenting on Jefferson's re-
    lationship with Hemings for a Boston paper in 1805, reported that Sally
    was "the natural daughter of Mr. Wales, who was the father of the actual
    Mrs. Jefferson." See "Life Among the Lowly, No. 1"; Logan, *Mem-
    oirs of a Monticello Slave*, 13; Turner, in Boston *Repertory*, 31 May
    1805.

45 Ellen Randolph Coolidge to Joseph Coolidge, 24 October 1858, re-
    printed in Gordon-Reed, *Thomas Jefferson and Sally Hemings*, 260.

46 Thomas Jefferson to Nicholas Lewis, 12 April 1792, in *Papers of
    Thomas Jefferson*, ed. Julian Boyd (vols. 1–20) and Charles T. Cullen
    (vols. 21–27) (Princeton: Princeton University Press, 1950–), 23: 408.
    On Mary Hemings, Thomas Bell, and their family, see Lucia Stanton,
    "Monticello to Main Street: The Hemings Family and Charlottesville,"
    Magazine of Albemarle County History 55 (1997): 95–126.

47 In a letter to an Albemarle neighbor in 1814, for example, Jefferson
    wrote that African Americans' "amalgamation with the other color pro-
    duces a degradation to which no lover of his country, no lover of ex-
    cellence in the human character can innocently consent" (Jefferson to
    Edward Coles, in *The Writings of Thomas Jefferson*, ed. Paul Leicester
    Ford, 12 vols. [New York, 1897], 9: 477–79).

48 Richmond *Recorder*, 29 September 1802.

49 On how interracial rape and sexual relations between masters and slaves
    generally helped bolster slavery, see, for example, Darlene Clark Hine,
    "Rape and the Inner Lives of Southern Black Women: Thoughts on the
    Culture of Dissemblance," in *Southern Women: Histories and Identi-
    ties*, ed. Virginia Bernhard, Betty Brandon, Elizabeth Fox-Genovese,
    and Theda Perdue (Columbia: University of Missouri Press, 1992), 177–
    89; Catherine Clinton, " 'Southern Dishonor': Flesh, Blood, Race, and
    Bondage," in *In Joy and in Sorrow: Women, Family, and Marriage in
    the Victorian South, 1830–1900*, ed. Carol Bleser (New York: Oxford
    University Press, 1991), 52–68; Catherine Clinton, "Caught in the Web

of the Big House: Women and Slavery," in *The Web of Southern Social Relations: Women, Family, and Education*, ed. Walter J. Fraser Jr., R. Frank Saunders Jr., and Jon L. Wakelyn (Athens: University of Georgia Press, 1985), 19–34; Thelma Jennings, " 'Us Colored Women Had to Go Through A Plenty': Sexual Exploitation of African-American Slave Women," *Journal of Women's History* 1.3 (winter 1990): 45–74; Karen A. Getman, "Sexual Control in the Slaveholding South: The Implementation and Maintenance of a Racial Caste System," *Harvard Women's Law Journal* 7 (1984): 115–52; Eugene Genovese, *Roll, Jordan, Roll: The World the Slaves Made* (New York: Vintage Books, 1974), 413–31.

50 On the ethics of sex across the color line among southern elites, see Bertram Wyatt-Brown, *Southern Honor: Ethics and Behavior in the Old South* (New York: Oxford University Press, 1982), ch. 12, especially 307–10. Wyatt-Brown, who doubted the Jefferson-Hemings story's truth, adds that ethical behavior also demanded that a man's enslaved partner was seen as sexually attractive to white men, which usually meant that she had light skin, and that a man's sexual practices were not part of a larger pattern of alcoholism or other dissoluteness. Jefferson's relationship with Hemings fit these patterns as well, with Thomas Jefferson Randolph describing her as "decidedly good looking" (Randall to Parton, 1 June 1868, reprinted in Gordon-Reed, *Thomas Jefferson and Sally Hemings*, 254).

51 Randolph, in Randall to Parton, 1 June 1868, reprinted in Gordon-Reed, *Thomas Jefferson and Sally Hemings*, 255.

52 "Life Among the Lowly, No. 1."

53 Jan Lewis, " 'The Blessings of Domestic Society': Thomas Jefferson's Family and the Transformation of American Politics," in Onuf, 123–32, especially 126–27.

54 Richmond *Examiner*, 25 September 1802. Decades later, Jefferson's granddaughter continued to maintain that his dedication to his white family made the very idea of his having sex with Hemings beyond comprehension. Writing to her husband in 1858, she asked, "Is it likely that so fond, so anxious a father, whose letters to his daughters are replete with tenderness and with good counsels for their conduct, should . . . have selected the female attendant of his own pure children to become his paramour? The thing will not bear telling. There are such things, after [all], as moral impossibilities" (Coolidge to Coolidge, 24 October 1858, reprinted in Gordon-Reed, *Thomas Jefferson and Sally Hemings*, 259).

55 On the centrality to honor of public acceptance of a man's appearance, see Kenneth S. Greenberg, *Honor and Slavery: Lies, Duels, Noses, Masks, Dressing as a Woman, Gifts, Strangers, Humanitarianism, Death, Slave Rebellions, the Proslavery Argument, Baseball, Hunt-*

ing, and *Gambling in the Old South* (Princeton: Princeton University Press, 1996), chs. 1–2.

56 The restraint shown by the editors of the *Herald* wore off within a few months. By December they were running stories on Jefferson and Hemings based on information received from their own informants, justifying their change of heart by claiming that "although the subject is indeed a delicate one, we cannot see why we are to affect any great squeamishness against speaking plainly of what we consider as an undoubted matter of fact interesting to the public" (Frederick-town *Herald*, quoted in Richmond *Recorder*, 29 September, 8 December 1802).

57 Richmond *Recorder*, 12 January 1803.

58 *New England Palladium*, 18 January 1805, quoted in *The Defence of Young and Minns, Printers to the State, Before the Committee of the House of Representatives; with an Appendix, containing the debate, &c.* (Boston, 1805), 14.

59 *Defence of Young and Minns*, 2.

60 Ibid., 3–4.

61 Ibid., 53.

62 Ibid., 55.

63 Ibid., 54.

64 John Walker heard about Jefferson's overtures toward his wife as early as 1784 and would claim that Jefferson kept making advances to his wife for more than a decade, even after Jefferson had already married. Jefferson's actions served as the foundation of a long-standing personal rift between him and Walker. The story became a matter of public discussion at the same time the Hemings story did, thanks to Callender, who wrote not only about Hemings but about the Walker affair in 1802 in the pages of the *Recorder*. In the wake of the debate in the Massachusetts legislature, Jefferson confessed to friends that he had indeed once pursued Mrs. Walker (although he would not concede Walker's version of events) and that he had been wrong in doing so. On the Walker affair, see Dumas Malone, *Jefferson and His Time*, Vol. 1: *Jefferson the Virginian* (Boston: Little, Brown, 1948), 447–51, and Jan Ellen Lewis, "The White Jeffersons," in Lewis and Onuf, 138–40.

65 William Wells Brown's 1853 novel, *Clotel; or The President's Daughter: A Narrative of Slave Life in the United States*, is loosely based on this story.

66 *Defence of Young and Minns*, 4.

67 Ibid., 5.

68 Ibid., 14–15.

69 It would have been practically impossible to make the argument that Thomas Jefferson broke the law in his relationship with Sally Hemings. Technically, it might have been maintained that they committed the crime of fornication, or having sexual relations outside of marriage. But

given that Hemings remained Jefferson's property, such a crime would almost certainly have been unrecognizable in any Virginia court, even presuming that a grand jury would bring an indictment, the chances of which were nil.

70 As Robert McDonald notes, "Revelations of unseemly personal deeds among men in prominent posts titillated newspaper readers, but many citizens—maybe most—cared more that their leaders faithfully executed public duties" (McDonald, "Race, Sex, and Reputation," 55).

71 Freeman, "Slander, Poison, Whispers, and Fame."

2

Class, Racc, and Gender in the Clinton Scandal

On "The Dalliances of the Commander in Chief"

Christian Right Scandal Narratives
in Post-Fordist America

The day after the 1998 elections, Christian Coalition Executive Director Randy Tate held a news conference to publicize the Coalition's spin on the election results. Somehow, the GOP had just managed to snatch defeat from the jaws of victory, losing five congressional seats in a midterm election to the party of a second-term president, something no party had accomplished since the 1830s. Tate declared that the Republicans had lost by failing to articulate a systematic agenda addressing the multitude of problems facing the nation. Instead, he lamented, the GOP had myopically concentrated on the president's conduct in the Monica Lewinsky affair, ensuring its own burial by wrapping itself in the shroud of a stained blue dress.[1]

Tate's indictment of his fellow partisans was more than a trifle disingenuous, however. Throughout the preceding seven years, the harshest criticisms of the president's personal behavior had been lodged by the Christian right. No force within the U.S. political spectrum had more seethingly and with such loathing condemned the private conduct of Bill Clinton and those close to him, or more vigorously sought to make it the basis of electoral judgment, than had evangelical conservatives. The Christian right besieged Clinton from the controversies over Gennifer Flowers and the young Clinton's trip to Moscow, which punctuated the 1992 campaign, through Vince Foster's suicide and the succession of presidential scandals involving Arkansas state troopers, real estate deals, and a familiar parade of women. The chorus of outrage reached a crescendo during the investigation of Clinton's relationship with Lewinsky.

Yet, as the 1998 elections demonstrated, the Christian right's assault on Clinton appeared to undermine the movement's prospects of continuing to accumulate electoral and party power. Why, then, did the movement pursue this seemingly self-defeating course of action? One reason is simply (or not so simply) the sex itself. Evangelical norms militate against extramarital sex, nonmissionary sex, and the idea that young and unmarried women might actually consent to sex rather than being seduced or bullied into it.[2] Clinton's sexual affair with Lewinsky, moreover, affronted not just "the family" as such, in Christian right eyes, but also the symbolic coherence of the first family as a signifier of the nation's unity. This problem was encapsulated in the opening lines of James Dobson's September 1998 letter to the constituents of Focus on the Family, a leading Christian right media organization. Denouncing "the dalliances of the commander in chief," Dobson bewailed that the president's conduct had "brought humiliation on himself, his family and our nation."[3] One might further attribute evangelical conservatives' wrath against Clinton to the fact that (to them) he came to stand for a panoply of evils which, according to conservative narratives, were loosed on the United States by "the sixties," as George Shulman argues in this volume. Deservedly or not, Clinton became a lightning rod for Christian right animosity toward the counterculture, feminism, out and proud queers, and "tax-and-spend liberalism," especially expansionary federal policy to improve political and economic conditions in black America. Insofar as the movement perceived these various forces as elements within a totalized structure of antipatriotic, anti-Christian evil, the president's infidelity incited ire as few other actions could, for it is the family that the movement elevates as the linchpin of the godly politicocultural order it desires.

Clinton's actions in the Lewinsky affair, however, not only grated against Christian right narratives of nation, race, and family—they also flouted a particular vision of political leadership that the Christian right holds dear, threatening to expose its internal contradictions. This narrative was developed and deployed on Dobson's nationally popular radio talk show *Focus on the Family*, among other Christian right media outlets, and was related in specific ways to the political economy of elections, policymaking, and the public sphere in the post-Fordist United States. Antidemocratic trends in campaign finance, along with other forces, have steadily weakened public officials' accountability to the public, especially lower-middle-class, working-class, and poor Americans. During the 1990s, however, national leaders of both parties sought to generate the sense that society was becoming more, not less, democratic by mobilizing hyperpopulist and personalistic rhetorics through newly available electronic channels. Christian right narrative reflects and reinforces this socio-historical contradiction. The broadcasts I examine present the self-contradictory figure of a political leader who is at once accountable to the people and beholden only to God for his public authority. By stressing the leader's personal similarity and accessibility to his followers, *Focus*'s narrative seals the breaches between these conflicting desires concerning political leadership. In doing so, it manages political-economic contradictions for Christian right constituents, making the simultaneous invocation of egalitarian aspirations and invasion of Congress and the electoral system by social privilege seem a harmonious state of affairs.

The Christian right's narration of political scandal is central to its narration of political leadership, for narrative intervention is most needed precisely at those points where the public feels itself betrayed, to recertify the leaders' authority. *Focus*'s stories of Watergate and the Iran-Contra affair and of the villains-turned-conservative-heroes implicated in these events thus furnish crucial genealogical reference points for the Christian right's reception of the Clinton scandals. *Focus on the Family* transforms these earlier scandals into occasions to legitimate a political-economic status quo fractured by an accountability crisis, by channeling egalitarian expectations toward personal identification with the morally upright leader so as to justify authoritarian leadership. To be sure, the reflection of sociopolitical contradictions in these narratives, and the resultant discord in the latter, preserve within Christian right narrative a residue of negativity toward society and thus a ground for criticizing the status quo. But inasmuch as Christian right narrative operates as socially legitimating ideology, events challenging this narrative's structural coherence are likely to evoke extreme consternation among the movement's adherents. Clinton's refusal to step down posed just such a challenge, by driving a wedge through the fusion of private and official virtue that anchors the forced reconciliation of authoritarian and egalitarian elements within Christian right narrative. In other words, Bill Clinton drew the unquenchable fury of the Christian right not only because a good many (though hardly all) of his policies, along with his peccadilloes, flew in the face of the movement's morals and political objectives — he was also vilified because he placed at risk a core mode of ideological adjustment to basic societal contradictions, not least by adapting key aspects of the Christian right narrative for his own ends. Thus, the most salacious and consequential Clinton sex scandal was not simply born of narrowly conceived partisan tactics for damaging a popular president. More profoundly, it manifested both the power and the limits of a broader hegemonic project—based on the political right but also penetrating mainstream discourse in significant ways—to secure public consent for a deeply self-contradictory political economy of democratic accountability in the post-Fordist United States.

Watergate in Christian Right Narrative Critics of the Christian right often characterize the movement's politics as "theocratic" and, hence, thoroughly authoritarian. They allege that the Christian right hides a yearning to reinstate established religion behind a cloak of veneration for the Constitution, an ambition presaged by the movement's efforts to censor educational materials, publicly funded arts presentations, and Internet content.[4] There is some truth to these claims; we should not underestimate the depth of philosophical disagreement between many evangelical conservatives and more consistent defenders of the classical liberal tradition in political thought and governance. Nevertheless, the common assumption that the Christian right's support for liberal egalitarianism is merely lip service, a façade behind which lurks the theocratic monster, relies on too simplistic a reading of Christian right discourse. An examination of the radio program *Focus on the Family* suggests that important dimensions of this discourse are more complicated and internally embattled than most critics of the movement suspect. More specifically, *Focus on the Family* encourages listeners to view a certain kind of egalitarianism as an integral rather than superficial feature of legitimate political leadership.

This aspect of egalitarianism comes through vividly in one of Dobson's discussions on the air with Charles Colson. A former Nixon aide who figured prominently in the Watergate scandal, Colson professed to have been "born again" after his indictment in the Ellsberg affair. He now heads Prison Fellowship Ministries, an evangelical outreach service for prisoners, hosts the radio talk show *BreakPoint*, and is a much beloved Christian right media personality. As a measure of Colson's stature in both the Christian right and the new right more generally, it is worth noting that then-Governor George W. Bush publicized his administration's cooperation with Prison Fellowship Ministries on the 2000 campaign trail, apparently to emphasize his ideological compatability with GOP Christian conservatives.[5]

On *Focus on the Family*, Colson offers testimony to his personal struggle to become an authentic political leader. The Nixon White House, in Colson's account, becomes the site of inauthentic leadership: activity that is merely a self-serving quest for power, betraying a foolish entrancement by the elitist trappings of high office. Forced out of this domain, Colson experiences a personal and spiritual rebirth that enables him to engage in "true" leadership. One mark of such leadership is that Colson shares crucial characteristics of the people he leads. Not only does he claim to have been "saved"; he stresses that he has "come to Christ" in the same way as have countless other evangelicals: by reading C. S. Lewis's popular book *Mere Christianity* at the urging of another believer. By invoking the potent signifier of Lewis's text, Colson makes it possible for Dobson's listeners to identify with him as someone who is just like them. He also does this by unashamedly remembering the tears he shed in "calling out to God" for the first time and reminding listeners that all persons are mortal beings.[6]

Personal humility is thus integral to Colson's vision of right leadership. At the same time, his narrative views humility—that is, sharing a common identity with ordinary individuals rather than being exceptional in terms of his access to state power or his fitness to use it— as enhancing rather than undercutting his capacities to shape world politics as a leader, and vice versa. It is only as a political "outsider," Colson insists, that he has been able to undertake those actions most decisive for the global fate of democracy. Specifically, he marvels that evangelical conversions of political leaders on several continents have (he says) brought down communist governments, doing what official cold war operations could never have done on their own:

Today I was just in Korea, for example, and we had our conference of Prison Fellowship international convocation [*sic*]—people congregated from all over the world. I met men from Russia and eastern Europe who had been converted reading my books, and a whole delegation got off a bus at the conference center in Korea—Russians—and they came rushing up to me. One of them was a city councilman in St. Petersburg, another one was a journalist from Moscow, another one was an Orthodox priest who'd been in prison—many of them came rushing up to me and started embracing me and kissing me on both cheeks. All I could think of was, I spent most of my life—a Marine Lieutenant during the Korean War—learning how to kill communists. I was in the Senate during the big arms buildup in the fifties, working on the defense budget. I was in the White House with four years of briefings on missile tonnage and megatonnage and throwweight, and how we're going to have a nuclear standoff, and listening to the intelligence summaries coming in every day from the Soviet Union. All my life fighting the Cold War, and now suddenly God has brought an *end* to that, and look at the marvelous and mysterious ways—what could never be done politically—these men are now standing on a street corner embracing me and kissing me on both cheeks, telling me how my book *Loving God* had transformed their lives, and you tell *me* which gives you the greatest thrill![7]

The clear message here is that the leader's Christian humility is perfectly compatible with his ability to exercise prodigious political influence, even though this influence may not operate through conventional political channels. Indeed, humility becomes the very source of the greatest political potency. In turn, exercising power through divinely ordained channels reconfirms the leader's sense that he has acted well by repudiating conventional ambitions and embracing a humbler way.

Colson's narrative of political leadership is distinctly evangelical. It is a narrative of personal salvation, which the individual gains both by adhering to the path of humility and by laboring to bring God's "good news" to the world. By virtue of the latter element, the narrative inextricably binds the redemption of society at large to Colson's personal redemption in a seemingly harmonious totality. The coherence of this totality is guaranteed by the humble leader's apparent reconciliation of his exceptional status as a defender of global democracy with his identity as an ordinary man of the people.

Nevertheless, within this beatific vision of right political leadership certain notable inconsistencies abide. Colson's constant references to the important people he has known and the exclusive places he has visited create no little friction with his attempts to cast himself as an evangelical everyman. More important, even if his persona as one of the people is allowed to stand, the manner in which he appears to have been authorized by them to lead on their behalf runs into sharp conflict with his professed commitment to democracy. Above all, the sanction of Colson's leadership by his "public" depends on the virtual collapse of the traditional public sphere (even as a nostalgic ideal of late capitalism) into a sphere of religious intimacy. The final image of his story of his trip to Korea perfectly encapsulates this process. On the one hand, the physical embrace of Colson by the public official, the journalist, and the priest vividly signifies the materialization of egalitarian hopes. On the other hand, it expunges any sense of critical distance among the realms of the state, civil society, and mediating institutions of the public sphere. And although the ratification of Colson's leadership seems to depend on anonymous encounters with his book through an evangelical Christian version of a public sphere, his remarks make it clear that *Loving God* has stimulated not rational-critical debate but experiences of inspiration and "conversion." Thus, the humble leadership narrativized by Colson lacks any solid sense that the leader is and must be held *accountable* to the followers he inspires.

The narrative seems aware of this problem, as it were, and tries to evade it by incorporating an explicit discussion of the need to hold evangelical leaders accountable for their actions in the name of the collective body of the faithful. Even here, however, an evidently egalitarian aspiration is disappointed by blatantly authoritarian counter-ideals and -practices. Colson insists that pastors are responsible to their parishioners, but he stresses far more strongly that "the Church is being assaulted" and that therefore "the lay people need to get behind their pastor. . . . Now, I think the pastor's got to have authority over that church, because *he* is the one ordained by God to speak to that congregation on God's behalf. He needs to be *accountable* to the church and *held* to account, but clearly that pastor needs authority."[8] Moreover, he explains to Dobson, pastors are to be "held to account" not by a general and public parish review but by the private supervision of the pastor by an elite circle of peers:

> One of the things that I talk about in the book (*The Body*, 1993) and feel very strongly about is the accountability that is necessary in the Christian life. I know you've done it, Jim, and I've done it—I've gone to certain members of my board and I tell them, "Doesn't matter what area of my life, it's open to you, you come in, you look at my books, you ask me questions. . . ." [Ideally, pastors and board members] sit around in a circle and they have seven questions and they ask one another these questions. They go down the list and it's all of the obvious temptations— "Have you lied?" and sexual immorality—and they finally get to the last one . . ."Have you just lied to me?" But they hold one another to account in that way.[9]

Not only is a very limited segment of the collective empowered to scrutinize the pastor's conduct, and not only is the pastor's probation clearly meant to occur behind closed doors; in addition, holding the pastor accountable blurs the distinction between the pastor's private morality and his faithful or unfaithful execution of church affairs. Indeed, the former ultimately appears to be the more pressing point of evaluation and the main criterion of the latter; this much is suggested when Colson and Dobson repeatedly refer to statistics showing the disturbing frequency with which pastors engage in "inappropriate sexual behavior with someone in their present church."[10] Colson's widely popular early 1990s book about rejuvenating the Church is entitled *The Body*, and it is quite literally the corporeal containment of the pastor that here guarantees the rectitude of the Church, not the critical mediation of a religious-public sphere or any other mechanism for ensuring the pastor's accountability to protecting the self-articulated interests of the larger body of believers. Even if this distribution of power and responsibility could be deemed an acceptable model of church organization (a contentious issue among Christians, to say the least), it suffers from obvious flaws as a vision of legitimate political leadership in a democracy. Yet Colson plainly presents it as such, because it is precisely the distinction between religious and political leadership that his story of his post-Watergate career actively blurs.

In sum, even though Colson's redemption narrative insistently evokes his fundamental equality with ordinary people, this egalitarian sensibility does not substantially qualify the "humble leader's" actual authority. This is the core contradiction within the narrative, which figures the people alternately as the ultimate seat of power to whom leaders must be held to account and as obedient "soldiers" (indeed, "Marines") in what Colson describes as a "cosmic struggle" against evil. The contradiction extends, inexorably, to Colson's narrativization of Watergate. Initially, he describes this scandal as catalyzing his personal transformation and forcing him to confront the spiritual waywardness of his "blind ambition" (to recall a phrase popularized by another self-berating Watergate conspirator, John Dean). Ultimately, however, Colson argues that he was justified in plotting "a conspiracy to defame [Daniel] Ellsberg," who had leaked documents to the media detailing secret U.S. actions in Southeast Asia. The reason? "National security," Colson intones, more specifically the need to prevent further leaks revealing "the names of CIA agents operating abroad at that moment [whose] lives would have been in instant jeopardy." Thus, in the Watergate scandal, "God's will" unfolds as an apparently harmonious "plan" weaving together the testing of Colson's personal virtue with the probation of national leaders' abilities to contain their powers (by stopping "leaks") and exercise authority without the meddling of the public or the press.[11] But this grand design remains far from coherent in the roles it assigns to ordinary citizens, whom it designates as the personal but not the political equals of their leaders.

Iran-Contra: The "Humble Leader" and National Redemption The Iran-Contra affair provided another opportunity for *Focus on the Family* to intervene at the site of scandal and disseminate its distinctive narrative of political leadership. Shortly after the dismissal of charges against Oliver North in 1991 for his alleged misconduct in the Iran-Contra affair, North and his wife, Betsy, joined Dobson in *Focus's* broadcast studio. In this series, Dobson frames the story of Iran-Contra in the same way he casts the account of Watergate: as the tale of a populist hero who successfully endures the trial by fire of his mettle as a leader, protecting the security of the nation, establishing himself as the people's authentic representative, and hastening the redemption of his own soul and the social body alike. Once again, however, this narrative figure seems Janus-faced, alternately displaying democratic and authoritarian features.

Just as *Focus on the Family* stresses Colson's identity as an ordinary private individual by extensively discussing his faith-life, so the program puts North on a level with Dobson's listeners by dwelling on his personal life. Cohost Mike Trout insists that "despite all of his responsibilities, all of his involvements in the government, he's a *family* man, he's a *father*," whose family members went through a protracted trauma and survived it because of their commitments to God and each other.[12] As "the husband of one and the father of four," "Ollie" (or "Larry," as Betsy affectionately calls him) comes across as someone who is just like Dobson's listeners by virtue of his commitment to the traditional family. Together, the Norths remember how the family struggled to keep up its daily routines once the congressional hearings had begun. "Ollie" jokes about having been "the most photographed commuter in America" and having "put in some long hours" at the office preparing to give testimony. Betsy recalls having to get up extra early to feed the ponies, take care of the children, and "fix [her] hair" before making the drive downtown.[13] By redefining Iran-Contra as a test of one family's ability to stick together and preserve its conventional lifestyle under circumstances of great stress, *Focus on the Family* invites the listener to identify with the Norths. North explains: "Everybody goes through something like this in their lives. Thankfully, for most of us, it's not that public, it doesn't become a front page issue. But every family faces some terrible ordeal of one kind or another, everybody is under fire at some point—whether it's a relationship between a husband and wife, or . . . family conflict . . . or whether it's a matter of how we approach the government."[14] The transformation of Iran-Contra from an extraordinary public event into a common personal affair, and the characterization of North as a humble average person, is completed when Dobson and North celebrate the fact that North's voting rights are no longer in jeopardy as a result of the dismissal of charges against him. Even politically, the former White House insider comes across as the equal of Dobson's constituents, for just like them he treasures the ballot that safeguards his individual rights and freedoms.

Precisely this personal equality with ordinary Americans fosters the sense that when North exercises exceptional powers as a public official, he does so in a way that is consistent with egalitarian norms. Like Colson, North paints himself as a defender of democracy in the global sphere. Prompted by Dobson, he justifies his deception of Congress in the same way that Colson rationalizes his execution of Nixon's dirty tricks: he claims that withholding information from Congress was necessary to protect the lives of those working for freedom in other countries, in this case including both U.S. undercover agents and friendly heads of foreign, anti-communist resistance movements.[15] North thus lays claim to rightful authority to determine the security interests of the nation and act in accordance with his independent judgment. But his power seems to express rather than contravene the will of ordinary Americans because North himself is a "regular guy": a "family man," a Christian, a voting citizen, a dependable comrade-in-arms who takes the Marines' motto (*Semper fidelis*) to heart and who will always be "faithful" to his fellow soldiers, just as he remains steadfastly faithful to his family.

In short, North turns his experience in Iran-Contra into a narrative of redemption that is at once personal and collective. The hero of this narrative gains salvation through his great humility, inasmuch as the North family's successful passage through the stormy waters of public scandal verifies the solidity of the traditional ways embraced by the humble soul. At the same time, this personal response to God motivates the humble leader's action for the good of others and society as a whole. His own salvation experience impels him to bring words of "encouragement" to others who endure their own family strains; in turn, this exhortation to keep "faith" in the family is one element in a more encompassing disposition of "faithfulness" that includes maintaining solidarity in the global fight for freedom and trust in the wisdom of national leaders.

Yet the way the people authorize the humble leader's political powers is no more substantively democratic in North's account than in Colson's. Adhering to the pattern in the Colson broadcasts, North invokes the reverent, passionate, but vague acclaim of a plebiscite rather than the rational-critical judgment of an informed public sphere as the basis for (his) legitimate political authority. He demonizes the media and Congress, the main institutions by which the people could hope to hold North accountable for abuses of public power, by positioning reporters and members of Congress as the rabid, faithless, self-seeking persecutors of the American family, symbolized by the Norths.[16] Instead of being formally mediated by these institutions of the public sphere and representative government, the people's "consent" to North's leadership is demonstrated when they deluge him with letters, prayers, and financial donations for his legal defense.[17] Indeed, for Dobson's listeners political consent as such becomes redefined as an act of faith in the leader, which the leader deserves to the degree that he sustains his own faith in God and God's fundamental gift, the family. Insofar as North admits that his conduct in the Iran-Contra affair was blameworthy, it is only because his improprieties violated God's will: "There's no doubt I made mistakes. I'm a mortal just like everybody else, I made some very serious mistakes, I admitted those mistakes that I made during the hearings, I admitted them again in my own trial. . . . I have always known where I was going, not because I was a good person or because of my work or because of my efforts or my energy—it's because He died to save me. And I know that He has forgiven me for the errors in judgment and the mistakes that I made."[18] The people themselves, however, clearly have no right to usurp God's authority to judge the leader's conduct and bestow or withhold forgiveness.

As in the Colson shows, then, in the North series the egalitarian strain in the narrative of the humble leader clashes mightily with a counterposing authoritarian current. When *Focus on the Family* confronts the Iran-Contra scandal, as when it confronts Watergate, it expresses desires regarding political leadership that are deeply contradictory. These desires are embodied in the figure of the humble leader whose countenance constantly shifts between that of the ordinary man of the people and that of the imperious theocrat.

Post-Fordism and the Accountability Deficit How are we to interpret the politics of *Focus*'s self-conflicting narratives of Watergate and Iran-Contra? In the most straightforward sense, Dobson's conversations with Colson and North circa 1990 promoted deference to the national security apparatus at a time when its legitimation needs had increased because of the end of the cold war. Moreover, these broadcasts function in obvious ways to recuperate the tarnished images of prior Republican administrations, enhancing their ability to serve as useful referents for nostalgic appeals by contemporary GOP politicians. In these respects, the internal contradictions of the narrative are strategically productive. By suturing the egalitarian spirit of evangelicalism to pointedly authoritarian notions of political leadership, the Christian right facilitates endeavors of far-right Republicans. It thus carries forward a long-standing pattern of movement support for an aggressively militarist foreign policy, earlier instances of which, for example, included active collaboration with the Reagan administration's anticommunist campaigns in Central America, the Philippines, and southern Africa.[19]

A different sense of this narrative's political and social significance arises, however, if we assign a less instrumentalist character to the specifically religious elements of *Focus*'s narratives. Whatever else it may be, *Focus*'s story of the humble leader remains an evangelical redemption narrative, recognizable to Dobson's listeners as this above all else. As such, it retains a certain religious-cultural coherence: it attempts to reformulate tradition with reference to contemporary society while preserving tradition's integrity. In the manner suggested by Theodor W. Adorno's theory of cultural dialectics, we might thus consider whether the structure of the narrative manifests something significant about the structure of contemporary U.S. society. Adorno argued that a cultural phenomenon's "passionate striving toward identity," toward an internal consistency and harmony, could be interpreted as an expression of historical processes aimed at securing the stability, cohesiveness, and legitimacy of the political economy. In turn, the *failures* of this phenomenon's exertions might furnish a window into political-economic antagonisms that stubbornly resist these processes' efforts to resolve, displace, or suppress them. What, then, is the "social physiognomy" of *Focus*'s narrative of the "humble leader"?[20]

The rise of the Christian right has coincided with and, in part, effectuated the onset of post-Fordist political-economic conditions in the United States. Certain political economists in the neo-Marxian tradition are in the process of formulating a theory of post-Fordism to describe and account for systematic developments in the political economy since the 1970s brought a halt to postwar expansion. Fordism was an earlier structure of capital accumulation and political regulation that ensured business profitability and social cohesion through a combination of these factors: a Taylorist labor process directed toward the mass production of standardized commodities; wages and benefits high enough to generate mass demand for these goods; an unprecedented level of government intervention in the economy to ensure the stability of markets and class relations; and well-established political cooperation among key business, labor, and party leaders.[21] Due to a variety of endemic crises in this regime, which became obvious with the declining profitability, ballooning public deficits, and social unrest of the late 1960s and 1970s, Fordism appears to have been supplanted by a new structure of accumulation and regulation. Post-Fordism's chief characteristics include capital's organizational and geographic restructuring ("downsizing" and the "export" of capital and jobs), followed by the current period of financial expansion; the intensification of global economic competition; the capitalization of previously undeveloped areas of the world; the declining availability of high-reward manufacturing jobs accompanied by the proliferation of both low-reward service industry jobs and high-skill occupations demanding "flexible specialization"; the decline and retrenchment of the welfare state; the distintegration of the alliances among labor, capital, and party leaders that had previously provided economic steering and ensured political legitimation; and the heightening of class antagonisms.[22]

In two major ways, the advance of post-Fordism has depended on concomitant changes in the electoral and public policy processes that offer the main institutional anchors for democratically holding leaders accountable. First, systemic alterations in the electoral environment have facilitated the defection of key sectors of business and the working class from the Fordist grand compromise among corporations, labor, and the state. This Fordist compact was initially threatened by the growth of the Sunbelt economy, the major industries of which (including natural resource exploitation, real estate speculation, certain branches of high technology, and service industries) have had little economic incentive to cooperate with organized labor or to accede to extensive government regulation. Conservative Sunbelt interests thus provided a powerful alternative financial base for Republicans who wanted to shed the burdens of the GOP eastern establishment's Fordist commitments. The Fordist compromise was further fractured by the growth of conservative single-issue campaigns (especially opposition to property taxes, racial integration, gun control, and abortion), the spread of the direct primary system (which undermined the power of the established major party coalitions), and the advent of new campaign technologies (such as direct mail and polling innovations).[23] Each of these innovations undermined the historical links between the major parties and their postwar social bases.

Second, the reconfiguration of electoral power dynamics and institutions has helped ensure that post-Fordist shifts in the morphology of advanced capitalism meet with only weak and sporadic political resistance. Single-issue campaigning, direct primaries, and technology-intensive electioneering have not only aided the electoral prospects of the new right; their more general effect has been to heighten the decisiveness of money in elections at the expense of the organizational loyalties at the heart of Fordism. The societal transition to post-Fordism has thus generated a mounting crisis of democratic accountability, making core institutions less able to serve as conduits for working-class and poor citizens' demands and expressions of discontent. Disturbing developments in the system of campaign finance, legislators' career aspirations, the legislative process in Congress, and the oversight of public officials' ethics provide telling measures of this accountability crisis.

The changing nature of campaign finance bears much of the blame for the diminution of political leaders' accountability to the public. The number of corporate political action committees (PACs) has grown exponentially since the early 1970s, and these PACs' "receipts, expenditures, and contributions to congressional candidates have increased significantly" over the same period.[24] Candidates' and office holders' intensifying pursuit and spending of PAC funds constrain citizens' options for holding officials accountable through voting by allowing incumbents to conduct early, preemptive campaigns and diminishing the prospects (and thus the likely candidacies) of challengers who do not seek or receive the support of PACs.[25] Indeed, members of Congress now need to raise money perpetually to compete effectively in the next election. In the late 1990s, the average successful candidate for a House seat had to raise $6,730 every week; this figure topped $10,000 for challengers, who do not enjoy the substantial electoral resources of congressional office.[26] A comparable dynamic holds in presidential politics, where the explosion of "soft money" contributions has rendered obsolete existing campaign finance regulations. Nearly half of all soft money contributions to the two major parties in 1995–1996 arrived in bundles of $100,000 or more, and soft money spending by corporations outdistanced similar expenditures by labor unions by a ratio of more than fifteen to one.[27] In a society with a high degree of economic inequality, such as the United States today, these conditions translate into atrophied accountability to wealthy individuals and private corporations and little accountability to the rest of the population.

Trends within the legislative apparatus suggest, moreover, that politicians victorious at the polls face additional insulation from broad public accountability once they settle into their posts. Since at least the mid-1960s, Congress has reshaped its institutional structure along lines established by the executive branch. Specifically, Congress has delegated much of its policy-determining authority to administrative agencies and professionalized the work of committee and member staffs.[28] These changes have distanced elected officials from responsibility for the actions of the federal government. Moreover, they have invited interest groups' "increased formal penetration . . . into the bureaucracy (advisory committees), the presidency (White House group representatives), and the Congress (caucuses of members)," compounding the accountability deficit further still.[29] The nesting of interest groups in intragovernmental policy processes was particularly accelerated by "congressional reforms that opened up the legislative process during the 1970s [and] provided a much larger number of access points for today's lobbyists."[30] The evolving aggregation of interest groups' discretion over federal legislation showed no signs of abating in the 1990s, as the intimate involvement of pharmaceutical firms, insurance companies, and physicians in mid-1990s health care reform initiatives illustrated.[31] And interest groups' broader sway over the substance of public policy carries with it biases toward social groups with greater financial, educational, technological, and organizational resources, further detracting from the degree of accountability on which most citizens (but particularly female, nonwhite, and poor or working-class Americans) can depend.[32]

The expansion in regulation and complexification of policy processes that has hastened Congress's abdication of its legislative responsibilities has in turn nurtured a transformation of the professional norms among legislators. The increasing quantity of federal regulations and the spread of procedural obstacles to passing legislation have multiplied opportunities for members who seek to maximize their services to interest groups. Accordingly, congressional service has become more attractive (because it is potentially more lucrative) to individuals who aim to work in legislative posts for limited periods, capitalizing thereafter on the relationships with "rent-seeking" interest groups cultivated while in Washington. By contrast, individuals who aspire to careers in public service constitute a declining proportion of the House and Senate memberships.[33] Pace the vitriol vented against "career politicians" by conservative term limits advocates, those who intend to make public service a career are likely to be more attuned to their responsibilities to the public than officials whose goals are much more self-consciously and thoroughly private and pecuniary.

The proliferation of rent-seeking behaviors, along with the rapidly rising costs of political campaigns, reinforces the trend toward what Dennis Thompson has defined as "institutional corruption" in Congress. In Congress, there have been increasing numbers of ethics scandals and multiplying attempts to regulate members' behavior according to ethical standards since the mid-1970s.[34] For the most part, this rash of scandals does not reflect the proliferation of "individual" offenses, such as bribe taking or other misuses of public office for purely private gain. Rather, it indicates the growth of a type of corruption that "encompasses conduct that under certain conditions is a necessary or even desirable part of institutional duties."[35] A particularly common kind of institutional corruption is the routine combination of fundraising and constituent service in congressional offices and the progressive integration of these functions into a unified and normalized process. Precisely this sort of conduct was at issue in the January 2000 controversy over Republican presidential candidate John McCain's interventions with numerous federal agencies on behalf of powerful campaign contributors. What McCain did was not illegal; rather, it was a form of action that had become such a regular feature of congressional operations that even a leading advocate of campaign finance reform could not avoid engaging in it. Nevertheless, a certain kind of corruption has doubtless developed when institutional convention sanctions an ever tighter synthesis of official intervention, the granting of access, and the pursuit of campaign donations, especially in a political environment where money has assumed such extraordinary influence over members' electoral prospects. And the collective, diffuse character of this corruption, the fact that it is "more systematic and more pervasive" than isolated cases of individual corruption, suggests that these tendencies are eroding the accountability of national political institutions in general.[36]

One would hardly suspect that accountability has been seriously eroded in the electoral, legislative, and public spheres, however, with all the recent enthusiasm in the United States about the supposedly imminent flowering of democratic participation promised by the "new media," especially highly interactive forms like the Internet and radio and TV talk shows, but also television news magazines and MTV.

Politicians and media leaders alike celebrate these new communications technologies and formats as yielding unprecedented opportunities for activism by citizens to determine the national policy agenda and to hold leaders directly accountable to the public. These electronic venues, however, define the processes of holding political leaders accountable and exerting agency as a citizen in very distinctive ways. They constitute these processes as rituals in which ordinary Americans and their leaders make specific uses of their increased (virtual) personal access to each other—the latter, to launch appeals directly to "the people" with mounting frequency and intensity; the former, to judge their leaders by the degree to which they are able to identify with them personally. In the present political culture, "democracy" is everywhere and incessant, demanding breathless participation, but in an ideologically personalistic and populist form.

Historically, evoking a sense of identity with ordinary Americans has been a vital aspect of political leaders' strategies to legitimate their authority in this country.[37] But the populist component of leaders' legitimation took on a new urgency and centrality as the twentieth century drew to a close. The presidential campaign of 1992 was a watershed event in this regard. With the air of leading a populist revolt against the entrenched and corrupted power of the traditional news media, Bill Clinton and Ross Perot charted new directions in political candidates' participation in "soft" media shows: Clinton played the saxophone on the *Arsenio Hall* show and chatted with young people on MTV's *Rock the Vote*, and Perot famously announced his candidacy on CNN's *Larry King Live*. These were only the most memorable and vivid of many instances in the campaign that collectively helped to generate a populist tone that was both more pronounced than and qualitatively different from its abundant precedents in earlier campaigns. In addition to exploiting television talk shows and news magazines, talk radio, and MTV, all the major presidential candidates widely distributed economic plans (following Paul Tsongas's lead in the Democratic primary), documents that far exceeded conventional issue papers in their detail and length. Perot's bar charts and long, content-heavy infomercials on the national budget projected a similar confidence in the capacity of ordinary individuals to sort through complex policy questions. Democratic candidate Jerry Brown financed his campaign by asking voters to call an 800-number to make donations. And Clinton conducted "electronic town meetings" in which he spontaneously answered questions from the audience, a practice that his administration continued after the election.[38] Meanwhile, the popularity of talk radio exploded on the political right as Rush Limbaugh and his local-market clones gained vast audiences, billing themselves as the facilitators of "democracy in action," as arenas for ordinary people to have authentic and honest political conversations with one another.[39]

There was a common message underlying these innovations, many of which had become stock features of presidential politics by the 2000 campaign, despite their disparate emphases in terms of public policy. Only that political leader was worthy of support who exposed himself to greatly intensified scrutiny by the "real" public (not just the elites who read the *New York Times*), actively sought personal and intimate conversations with average citizens, stressed in both word and deed his trust in the people's rational judgment, and energetically engaged in the interactivity distinguishing the new media from traditional media. Indeed, precisely this was the deeper current of ideology that encompassed the broad political spectrum from Limbaugh to Clinton, the underlying concordance among their evidently antagonistic discourses.

The actual democratizing effects and potential of the shift toward the new media have been much debated, and there are persuasive arguments and empirical evidence that electronic populism has so far produced little in the way of enduring and consequential participatory norms.[40] In particular, the new populism tends to substitute an empathic response by leaders to personalized policy issues for what Lisa Disch calls "power-sensitive" discussion of policy alternatives' differential outcomes on structurally unequal social groups. The new populist public sphere radiates the warm, personal intimacy and identification of leaders with ordinary citizens. In place of actual democratic deliberation, it offers this version of "democracy" along with choreographed and fetishized versions of rational-critical discussion, as in presidential debates, the Clinton administration's televised "town meetings" on health care and race, and, as Jodi Dean points out in her contribution to this collection, the media's self-evaluations regarding its reporting on the Clinton-Lewinsky affair.[41]

Recent political sex scandals furnish some particularly vivid examples of this ideology of personalistic populism. How did the Clinton camp respond when the story broke in early 1992 about their candidate's tawdry dealings with Gennifer Flowers? With two masterful strokes of political strategy, given the conditions of the present era: they convened an electronic town meeting with New Hampshire voters (highlighting Clinton's populist appeal) and they put Bill and Hillary on CBS's *60 Minutes* to discuss their commitment to struggling through marital difficulties (inviting the public, especially middle-aged swing voters, to identify personally with the Clintons). As a result, Clinton was not only able to stay in the race but ended up in a strong enough position to control the spin on the 1992 New Hampshire election results, which was not Tsongas's preordained victory but rather Clinton's "better than expected" finish. In a similar way, the *means* chosen by Clinton's enemies in Congress and the Independent Counsel's Office to carry out their assault on Clinton are vitally important. Of course, Clinton's antagonists aimed to discourage the public from identifying personally with him by including (porno)graphic content in their public transmissions, describing the prurient details of the sex acts he and Lewinsky performed. But at the same time, Starr, Hyde, and their associates attempted to endow their project with legitimacy in the eyes of the public by trying to show their own commitment to electronic populism and their facility with its machinery. They did this repeatedly: when they released the Starr report over the Internet, as well as when they supplied the media with Clinton's videotaped testimony before the grand jury and Linda Tripp's tapes of her conversations with Lewinsky and ensured that the impeachment hearings would be televised.

The main point here is that the ideology of personalistic populism has proven capable of legitimating power during the present era as democratic, when democratic accountability is actually declining in all the ways discussed earlier in this section: in the realm of campaign finance, in the career plans of elected officials, in the legislative operations of Congress, and in the monitoring of legislators' ethics. A political elite enamored of the channels of direct access to ordinary Americans opened up by the new media has, at this point, successfully preempted any sustained criticism of these antidemocratic trends — even in the debates in 2000–2001 over campaign finance reform, when the mainstream press allowed politicians' (laudable) enthusiasm for banning soft money to occlude recognition of the enormous political advantages for corporations and socially privileged individuals that would remain even with the enactment of the McCain-Feingold legislation. Needless to say, the prevalent, personalistic-populist ideology also helps prevent examination of the deep origins of these more immediately apparent patterns of governance in post-Fordist structures of labor, capital accumulation, and state action.

The Christian Right and Clinton's Humility Deficit   How are the Christian right's narratives of high political scandal related to these contradictory ideological and institutional dynamics of democracy in the post-Fordist United States? It is possible to discern within the many variants of Christian right discourse traces of concern about the accountability crisis, displaced onto anxiety or furor over the federal government's imputed departure from genuine American values. Some Christian right discourses, redeploying the rhetoric of Jerry Falwell's Moral Majority, itself a further permutation of Nixonian references to the Silent Majority, lament that government has lost all accountability to the supposed major portion of ordinary citizens who see homosexuality as perverse, abortion as murder, and school prayer as essential to the common culture. Other discursive currents identify and condemn the same tendencies in federal policy but have given up on the movement's triumphalist claim to represent an actual majority of Americans. They instead reinvoke the more world-despairing and even apocalyptic pessimism of Falwell's contemporary Francis Schaeffer, whose 1981 book *A Christian Manifesto* argued that only a *"minority* of the Silent Majority" in 1968 were truly principled people and viewed the Reagan coalition with similar skepticism.[42] One hears plenty from both perspectives—the notion that evangelical conservatives are decidedly outside the mainstream of U.S. culture, even at war with it, and the idea that evangelical conservatives *are* the American mainstream—on *Focus on the Family*, sometimes from the same individual. In both cases, the Christian right gestures obliquely toward the accountability crisis when it chastises national leaders either for being a cultural elite that does not represent the "moral majority" or for accurately representing the corrupted mainstream but not the smaller remnant of "true Americans."

The narrative continuities and discontinuities of *Focus on the Family*, however, also tell a more specific story about the embattled status of U.S. democracy under the contradictory conditions of post-Fordism. This story becomes audible when we listen to Dobson, North, and Colson in a way sensitized to the interpretive categories provided by Adorno's theory of the dialectics of culture, alert to the relation of reflection and reproduction sustained between the formal contradictions of the cultural object and the social contradictions rending the polity.[43] Precisely such a relation exists between the internal antagonisms of the narrative of the humble leader and the historical juxtaposition of the accountability crisis with the ideology of personalistic populism. On the one hand, the testimonies of Colson and North express the structural deterioration of democratic accountability in a variety of ways. They do this, above all, when their shared narrative logic portrays the humble leader as responsible to God rather than to the public, bids ordinary citizens to submit to "God's plan" for the nation and its plebiscitary leaders, and dismisses and demonizes the critical mediation of political relationships through the public sphere. On the other hand, *Focus on the Family* registers not only this historical tendency but also the ambivalent attempt to assimilate it to democratic expectations. As we have seen, vying for primacy with the humble leader's authoritarian visage is this figure's egalitarian aspect: the face (and voice) of "Chuck," who gets saved by joining the millions of other readers of *Mere Christianity* and embracing life as an "outsider" to power, the chummy banter of "Ollie" the family man. This is the countenance, in short, of a leader who is on an equal plane with his constituents, knows them well because he interacts with them constantly through a personalizing public sphere, and at once symbolizes and enables their active participation in self-government. In this respect, *Focus*'s narrative of the humble leader manifests the imprint of the new populist ideology that is currently redirecting public attention away from the accountability deficit. Thus, the sociopolitical contradiction between the ideology of personalistic populism and the actual decay of democratic accountability finds expression in the constitutive tensions of *Focus*'s narrativization of Watergate and Iran-Contra.

The Christian right narrative of the humble leader actively reinforces the accountability crisis even as the former reflects the latter in its compositional structure. Those who listen regularly to *Focus on the Family* and accept the program's forced reconciliation of the humble leader's warring aspects are so much more likely to assume that genuine popular democracy is consistent with the current rules of campaign finance, the decline of careerism in Congress, and the delegation of legislative discretion to interest groups. This is perhaps why so many evangelical conservatives find it possible to lambaste "Washington" as the lair of usurpers while energetically throwing themselves into conventional lobbying activities and electioneering for federal office candidates who oppose campaign finance reform, support industrial deregulation, and deride the public service norms traditionally attached to legislative office.

Yet the fissures in *Focus*'s narrative of the humble leader persist, along with the clash between ideology and institutional tendencies in the post-Fordist United States. Precisely this abiding instability in the narrative, rather than what is commonly assumed to be the rigid and thoroughgoing coherence of Christian right discourse, conditioned the Christian right's reception of the revelation of President Clinton's affair with Monica Lewinsky and the former's subsequent refusal to accept political punishment for his misdeeds. More specifically, one reason the Christian right so relentlessly pursued Clinton, despite all the signs that this course of action was strategically unwise, may well have been that Clinton *adapted* this evangelical-conservative narrative of leadership for his own purposes rather than simply ignoring or rejecting it. In doing so, he threatened to expose the narrative's internal contradictions, thus incapacitating the narrative as a mode of ideological adjustment to post-Fordism. Let us now examine how Clinton himself played with the terms of the narrative and the consequences with regard to political-economic consent by the Christian right and the general public alike.

In his September 1998 letter to *Focus*'s constituents, Dobson implored Clinton to "follow in the path of Watergate figure Charles Colson, a man who came clean with the truth, owned up to his misdeeds and found, at the height of his public humiliation, a new life and a new purpose."[44] Heedless of Dobson's advice, Clinton refused to act the role of the humble leader—or at least, he did not play the part to the hilt. Shortly before the broadcast of the videotaped grand jury testimony in which Clinton admitted to an "inappropriate" relationship with Lewinsky, the White House informed the media that Clinton had selected two evangelical pastors to provide him with spiritual counseling. To those uninitiated in the ways of the evangelical subculture, the *New York Times* explained, "Such informal groups of spiritual advisers, sometimes called 'accountability circles,' are not uncommon among Christian evangelicals, particularly among leaders of large churches and organizations. Men—and it is more often men—meet with a small group of peers to pray and provide support for those facing personal crises."[45] Clinton, startlingly, seemed much more hip to contemporary evangelical conservative practices of leadership than either his Christian right foes or his liberal-progressive friends would have assumed, and seemed not to care about their authoritarian overtones. He even linked his experiment with accountability circles to a set of appeals right along the lines of egalitarian, personalistic populism that we have seen in the testimonies of North and Colson: he publicly confessed that he had "sinned," announced his determination to "atone" for his betrayals, and admitted his need for pastoral counseling. All of this was meant to generate public empathy for the president as an ordinary human being, and an ordinary believer, with both iniquitous tendencies and a meek trust in God's grace. Here, too, the resonances with *Focus*'s narrative were palpable. Of course, Clinton could hardly have been hoping to win over adherents of the Christian right. Instead, his performance of these rituals was meant to resonate in a positive way with a broader public that, as I have argued, has grown distressingly comfortable with the notion that national leaders are more properly held accountable by unseen powers than by the people themselves.[46]

Yet, at a certain point, the president's story diverged decisively from the Christian right narrative by drawing a line between his personal conduct and his fitness to exercise public responsibilities. The presidential body (and its infamous leaks), Clinton insisted, were not the legitimate objects of supervision and regulation for the sake of the national interest. In making this claim, Clinton modulated the authoritarianism of the narrative by suggesting that the condition of equality on which legitimate authority is based could be political rather than merely personal, that is, the equality of citizens who *were* capable of holding their president accountable for the discharge of his *public* responsibilities (and of making an appropriate critical judgment distinguishing issues of public concern from private matters). At the same time, Clinton's defense of privacy directly assaulted the North-Colson narrative's egalitarian component, because it implicitly disputed the idea that political order depends on an identity of moral values, conduct, and lifestyle among the citizenry and a moral-sentimental *identification* of citizens with leaders.

Let us recall, now, that the narrative of the humble leader on *Focus on the Family* attempts virtually to resolve the institutional and ideological tensions of post-Fordism, as I argued above, and does so successfully, apparently, for Dobson's constituents. Perhaps it was precisely a concern to defend this discourse against the unraveling tendencies set in motion by Clinton's refunctioning of it that helped motivate the Christian right's hypervehement response to the Lewinsky affair and Clinton's defiance—beyond the movement's personal odium for Clinton, its opposition to particular policies associated with the progressives in the Clinton coalition, and its interest in deepening its influence in the Republican Party. The narrative of the humble leader furnishes one template for securing popular consent to conditions of labor, capital accumulation, and state action that predated, have outlasted, and will continue to persist beyond the factional fireworks of the late 1990s in which the Christian right was embroiled. These conditions include the systematic weakening of the labor movement through international free trade agreements, the advancing globalization of capital, and the ongoing retrenchment of the welfare state. These political-economic circumstances have inspired leaders of both major parties to ratchet up the intensity of their populist and personalist appeals. *Focus on the Family* registers and conjures away, through the device of narrative closure, the contradiction between the democratic pretensions of this populist ideology and actual institutional tendencies with an atypical acuteness, and in the specifically religious, culturally exclusive idiom favored by its listeners. With so much riding on this discourse, it is no wonder that the Christian right would rush to defend its integrity, even in the face of obvious short-term strategic disincentives.

Focus's tortured narrative of leadership is an extreme articulation of post-Fordist contradictions that encompass the American citizenry at large, a way of expressing these contradictions that allows them at once to crystallize and to seem to have been overcome. Clinton's adjustment of this narrative, of course, aimed at much more immediate political goals than the broad, structural project of legitimating post-Fordism, above all avoiding removal from office, preserving some vestige of policymaking authority for his administration's final months, and cutting the losses charged to his legacy by the scandal. Still, it is interesting to ponder how the peculiar narrative of leadership devised by Clinton during the months of the scandal's greatest intensity may have fit, or failed to fit, with the requirements of this macrosocial project of legitimation. Did Clinton's grafting of the North-Colson narrative onto a more classically liberal appeal to privacy, and to the law's capacity to enable citizens to hold public officials accountable for their public actions, accomplish the same act of ideological transfiguration that I have attributed to *Focus on the Family*, and for the benefit of an even broader popular constituency? Perhaps it did not do this quite as well as the North and Colson stories seem to do for Dobson's listeners. *Focus* posits a notion of equality that is made superficially consistent with authoritarian politics by the confinement of the former (mostly) to the sphere of private (faith, family, and work) life—superficially, because precisely this maneuver establishes the contradiction between the egalitarian and authoritarian principles as a contradiction between social spheres, generating an oddly inverted image of the structural contradiction in liberal democracy criticized by the early Marx (for whom the inequalities of civil society belied the imaginary nature of the equalities presumed to exist in the political realm). By contrast, the discourse deployed by Clinton mingled two contrary notions of politics, one authoritarian and the other liberal-democratic, with the emotional and privatistic egalitarianism of his populist appeal. This multiplication of ambivalences would seem, in comparison to *Focus*'s narrative, to invite criticism of current political institutions, if in no other way than by reminding the public that a choice exists among disparate political ideals and that some form of democratic politics might still be the object of aspiration. To the extent that even the mild requisites of liberal democracy, in terms of citizen participation and the social supports for political engagement, conflict with the imperatives of post-Fordism, then, the Lewinsky scandal may have forced Clinton into the position of partially and involuntarily disclosing the impossibility of reconciling post-Fordist institutional and ideological contradictions.

Indeed, it could even be argued that the contradictions in Christian right narrative themselves make a faint echo of this impossibility audible to critical listeners. Returning briefly to Adorno, we can see these contradictions as formal elements of negativity within the compositional structure of Christian right narrative, aspects that silently pronounce judgment against the post-Fordist antagonism between the democratic claims of the personalistic populist ideology and the antidemocratic trends in Congress, the electoral sphere, and society as a whole. In Adorno's terms, this mute protest would be the social "truth-content" of *Focus*'s narrative: its involuntary witness to the brokenness of historical conditions, even as it strives to represent them as harmonious. To be sure, the practical purchase of this negative element is minimal, although it would be a mistake to exaggerate the ideological uniformity of the evangelical conservative subculture and hence to presume the utter impossibility of any of *Focus*'s constituents hearing and being at least vaguely troubled by the narrative inconsistencies discussed above. Here there is at least a small kernel of opposition to the forced but hegemonic synthesis of personalistic populism and the accountability deficit, a negative moment that Clinton's adaptation of the narrative brings slightly closer to the surface.

Our time needs a strategy, however, that is more ambitious than either the silent expression of uncompromising negativity that so captivated Adorno or the overly accommodating soft-touch conservatism of Clinton, whose brand of politics tried timidly to forestall the consequences of measured capitulations to ever more authoritarian versions of personalistic populism through late-hour invocations of a traditional-liberal respect for the public/private distinction. In terms of public discourse, a narrative of leadership is conceivable and desirable that explicitly recognizes how the accountability crisis and the dramaturgy of personalistic populism alike preclude the realization of the universally autonomous and equal individuality toward which liberalism aims. Such an alternative narrative would furthermore emphasize that the political autonomy of the individual and the democratic character of political society require a political-economic reorientation in directions that critically develop the egalitarian possibilities of post-Fordism rather than tacitly accepting the current realignment of forces in the class struggle in capital's favor.[47] Clinton's limited defiance of his antagonists was enough to suggest that the rituals sanctioned by the ideology of personalistic populism need not be the sole repository of Americans' hopes for democratic leadership and citizenship. The difficult task remains, however, of formulating a more progressive narrative of leadership that thematizes economic justice as a condition of political democracy and liberty, and that validates the leader's declared commitments to equality insofar as that person challenges the exercise of class domination through elections and legislative processes and the patterns of post-Fordist development fueling these practices.

Notes

1 Randy Tate, executive director, Christian Coalition, televised news conference, Washington, DC, 4 November 1998.

2 Along similar lines, Thomas L. Dumm has argued that the specific nature of Clinton's acts with Lewinsky threatened to leave unfulfilled the "desire for a patriarchal figure to be the representative of the nation to itself." Dumm locates the root of this desire in the emergent norm of "infantile citizenship," which Lauren Berlant has theorized as the mode of political belonging characteristic of the United States in an era when "social membership" has become contingent on "personal acts and identities performed in the intimate domains of the quotidian." The citizen is rendered "infantile," for Berlant, because "no vision of sustained individual or collective criticism and agency accompanies the national system here." In turn, according to Dumm, the fact that Clinton's guilt or innocence on the charge of perjury hinged partly on whether or not he had sucked on Lewinsky's breast compromised the president's ability to signify effectively the parental authority figure that is the necessary complement to the infantilized citizen. In addition, Dumm contends, Clinton's "sexual practices characterize him as a deviant from the heterosexual norm," because "oral sexual acts and their representation in public undermine the compulsory heterosexuality that secures the nation." See Thomas L. Dumm, "Leaky Sovereignty: Clinton's Impeachment and the Crisis of Infantile Republican-

ism," *Theory and Event* 2.4 (1999). See also Lauren Berlant, *The Queen of America Goes to Washington City: Essays on Sex and Citizenship* (Durham, NC: Duke University Press, 1997), 4–5, 51.

3 Focus on the Family, *Family News from Dr. James Dobson* (Colorado Springs: Focus on the Family, September 1998).

4 See Sara Diamond, *Roads to Dominion: Right Wing Movements and Political Power in the United States* (New York: Guilford, 1995).

5 George W. Bush, "The Duty of Hope," speech, Indianapolis, 22 July 1999, accessed through the George W. Bush for President Web page 28 October 1999.

6 "Being Light in Darkness," *Focus on the Family*, 14 January 1993.

7 Ibid.

8 "Being Light in Darkness," *Focus on the Family*, 15 January 1993.

9 Ibid.

10 Ibid.

11 "Being Light in Darkness," 14 January 1993.

12 "A Visit with Lt. Col. and Mrs. Ollie North," *Focus on the Family*, 23 October 1991.

13 Ibid.

14 "A Visit with Lt. Col. and Mrs. Ollie North," *Focus on the Family*, 24 October 1991.

15 "A Visit with Lt. Col. and Mrs. Ollie North," *Focus on the Family*, 25 October 1991.

16 "A Visit," 24 October 1991.

17 "A Visit," 23–25 October 1991.

18 "A Visit," 25 October 1991.

19 Diamond, 237–41.

20 For Adorno, "social physiognomy," or "dialectical criticism," means "naming what the consistency and inconsistency of the work in itself expresses of the constitution of the existent. . . . Where it comes across inadequacy it . . . seeks to derive it from the irreconcilability of the object's moments. It pursues the logic of the object's aporias, the insolubility located in the task itself. In such antinomies it perceives those of society." Theodor W. Adorno, "Kulturkritik und Gesellschaft," in *Prismen: Kulturkritik und Gesellschaft* (Frankfurt am Main: Suhrkamp, 1963), 23. Writing in an earlier essay with Max Horkheimer, Adorno contends that this antinomial "logic" is the key to the object's transcendent capacity, that is, its ability to provoke the demand for revolutionary transformation: "The moment in the work of art which enables it to transcend reality . . . does not consist in the harmony achieved, of the dubious unity of form and content, the internal and the external, the individual and society, but rather in those features in which discrepancy appears, in the necessary failure of the passionate striving toward identity." Max Horkheimer and Theodor W. Adorno, *Dialektik der Aufklä-*

rung: Philosophische Fragmente (Frankfurt am Main: Fischer, 1988), 139. Both translations are my own.

21 See Michel Aglietta, *A Theory of Capitalist Regulation: The U.S. Experience*, trans. David Fernbach (London: New Left, 1979), 111–22, 151–61, 179–98; Giovanni Arrighi, *The Long Twentieth Century: Money, Power, and the Origins of Our Times* (New York: Verso, 1994), 4–13, 269–300; Mike Davis, *Prisoners of the American Dream: Politics and Economy in the History of the U.S. Working Class* (New York: Verso, 1986), 182–95; David Harvey, *The Condition of Postmodernity: An Enquiry into the Origins of Cultural Change* (Oxford: Basil Blackwell, 1989), 125–40; Michael J. Piore and Charles F. Sabel, *The Second Industrial Divide: Possibilities for Prosperity* (New York: Basic, 1984), 49–132.

22 See Aglietta, *A Theory of Capitalist Regulation*, 122–30, 161–69; Arrighi, *The Long Twentieth Century*, 300–324; Davis, *Prisoners of the American Dream*, 195–230; Harvey, *The Condition of Postmodernity*, 141–72; Piore and Sabel, *The Second Industrial Divide*, 194–280.

23 Davis, *Prisoners of the American Dream*, 158–62.

24 M. Margaret Conway and Joanne Connor Green, "Political Action Committees and the Political Process in the 1990's," in *Interest Group Politics*, 4th ed., ed. Allan J. Cigler and Burdett A. Loomis (Washington, DC: Congressional Quarterly, 1995), 158–61.

25 Ibid., 165–66.

26 Dan Clawson, Alan Neustadtl, and Mark Weller, *Dollars and Votes: How Business Campaign Contributions Subvert Democracy* (Philadelphia: Temple University Press, 1998), 2.

27 Ibid., 114–16. Also see Anthony Corrado, "Financing the 1996 Elections," in *The Elections of 1996*, ed. Gerald Pomper (Chatham, NJ: Chatham House, 1997), 135–71.

28 Theodore J. Lowi, "Toward a Legislature of the First Kind," in *Knowledge, Power, and the Congress*, ed. William H. Robinson and Clay H. Wellborn (Washington, DC: Congressional Quarterly, 1991), 9–36.

29 Burdett A. Loomis and Allan J. Cigler, "Introduction: The Changing Nature of Interest Group Politics," in *Interest Group Politics*, 5th ed., ed. Allan J. Cigler and Burdett A. Loomis (Washington, DC: Congressional Quarterly, 1998), 1.

30 Ibid., 26–27.

31 Burdett A. Loomis and Allan J. Cigler, "Introduction: The Changing Nature of Interest Group Politics," in *Interest Group Politics*, 4th ed., ed. Allan J. Cigler and Burdett A. Loomis (Washington, DC: Congressional Quarterly, 1995), 24–25. On the secular trend toward the delegation of policymaking power by legislators to interest groups, see Theodore J. Lowi, *The End of Liberalism: The Second Republic of the United States*, 2d ed. (New York: Norton, 1979).

32 Burdett A. Loomis and Eric Sexton provide evidence of the pro-corporate tilt of influence in Congress by analyzing the predominance of corporate advertising, especially advertising by defense contractors, in the major periodicals read by Capitol Hill staff and other elites in the policymaking processes: *National Journal* and *Congressional Quarterly Weekly Report*. See Burdett A. Loomis and Eric Sexton, "Choosing to Advertise: How Interests Decide," in Cigler and Loomis, 1995, 194–210.

33 Glenn Parker, *Congress and the Rent-Seeking Society* (Ann Arbor: University of Michigan Press, 1996), 86–90.

34 Dennis Thompson, *Ethics in Congress: From Individual to Institutional Corruption* (Washington, DC: Brookings Institution, 1995), 1.

35 Ibid., 7–8, 31–32.

36 Ibid., 31–32.

37 See Edwin Diamond and Robert A. Silverman, *White House to Your House: Media and Politics in Virtual America* (Cambridge, MA: MIT Press, 1997), 15–31.

38 See ibid., 2–11.

39 See ibid., 140–45.

40 See Richard Davis and Diana Owen, *New Media and American Politics* (New York: Oxford University Press, 1998), 23, 127–28, 151–52, 162–63; Diamond and Silverman, *White House to Your House*, 164; Marion R. Just, Ann N. Crigler, Dean E. Alger, Timothy E. Cook, Montague Kern, and Darrell M. West, *Crosstalk: Citizens, Candidates, and the Media in a Presidential Campaign* (Chicago: University of Chicago Press, 1996), 142–47.

41 See Lisa Disch, "Publicity-Stunt Participation and Sound Bite Polemics: The Health Care Debate 1993–94," *Journal of Health Politics, Policy and Law* 21.1 (spring 1996): 3–33.

42 Francis A. Schaeffer, *A Christian Manifesto* (Westchester, IL: Crossway, 1981), 73–79.

43 To be sure, here I am loosely rather than scrupulously adhering to Adorno, who would not have allowed that a "mass-cultural" form such as *Focus on the Family* could have the necessary compositional integrity to be capable, in the first place, of such a dialectical relation to social conditions. For a critique of Adorno's theory of the culture industry and a more extensive defense of the applicability of his theory of cultural dialectics to mass-cultural phenomena, see Paul Apostolidis, *Stations of the Cross: Adorno and Christian Right Radio* (Durham, NC: Duke University Press, 2000).

44 Focus on the Family, *Family News from Dr. James Dobson*.

45 Laurie Goodstein, "Clinton Selects Clerics to Give Him Guidance," *New York Times*, 15 September 1998, A22.

46 The fact that one of the pastors was the well-known, politically mod-

erate (indeed, "liberal" by reputation) evangelical author, professor, and minister Anthony Campolo, and that Clinton additionally turned to Jesse Jackson in a public way for spiritual advising, underscores that Clinton was not trying to appeal directly to the Christian right in forming an accountability circle. At the same time, it offers evidence of the penetration of authoritarian sensibilities into the mainstream political culture, and even the segment of the post–civil rights left represented by Jackson.

47 For explorations of aspects of democratization to which post-Fordism might potentially give rise, see Joshua Cohen and Joel Rogers, "Secondary Associations and Democratic Governance," in *Associations and Democracy*, ed. Erik Olin Wright (New York: Verso, 1995), 7–98; Alain Lipietz, "Post-Fordism and Democracy," in *Post-Fordism: A Reader*, ed. Ash Amin (Oxford: Blackwell, 1994), 338–57.

Narrating Clinton's Impeachment

Race, the Right, and Allegories
of the Sixties

This essay explores the racial and sexual subtexts, the nationalist rhetoric, and thus the political implications of the conflicting
narratives created by the right and the left about Clinton's presidency and impeachment. Surely, the right's attack on Clinton joined
race, sex, and "the sixties" in ways that expose the dominant meaning
of nationalist political rhetoric in U.S. political history. In response,
many on the left took up the meanings projected onto Clinton to defend a left project and the emancipatory legacy of the sixties. Indeed,
Toni Morrison famously claimed that Clinton is "our first black president," whose victimization signaled a constitutional crisis that she narrated in unabashed—and for her unprecedented—nationalist terms.
The irony and force in Morrison's intervention was that her writings
until then had exposed the dangers in, and seemed to refuse, a language
of American nationalism.

I use her intervention, therefore, to pursue several questions: How
are we to relate race, sex, and the sixties in our narrations of the Clinton presidency, impeachment, and its aftermath? Does an effective left
politics depend on reworking, not rejecting, a language of nationhood
or national belonging? How are we to judge Morrison's example of
such a reworking? To pursue these questions is to explore other issues
central to both political theory and left politics: the relationships between symbolism and policy, between constitutionalism and democracy, between narrative and politics.

Morrison's engagement with nationalist language, by way of the
Clinton impeachment episode, at first appeared in her now famous
New Yorker piece of October 1998. It follows the structure and themat-

ics of her recent nonfiction essays about Clarence Thomas and O. J. Simpson: she dismisses an "official story" to disclose the actual or real one:

African-American men seemed to understand it right away. Years ago, in the middle of the Whitewater investigation, one heard the first murmurs: white skin notwithstanding, this is our first black President. Blacker than any actual black person who could ever be elected in our children's lifetime. After all, Clinton displays almost every trope of blackness: single-parent household, born poor, working class, saxophone-playing, McDonald's-and-junk-food-loving boy from Arkansas. And when . . . the President's body, his privacy, his unpoliced sexuality became the focus of the persecution, when he was metaphorically seized and body-searched, who could gainsay these black men who knew whereof they spoke? The message was clear: "No matter how smart you are, hard you work . . . we will put you in your place or put you out of the place you have somehow, albeit with our permission, achieved . . . Unless you do as we say (i.e. assimilate at once) your expletives belong to us."[1]

She suggests that Clinton is coded "black" by the Christian right, and by inverse response, he is "blacked up" by her, too. Or rather, as if she is retelling a story pervasive among blacks but not known to others, she deploys racial meanings in three ways at once.[2]

In part, by reporting this story, Morrison exposes the unvoiced racial subtext of the right's hatred for and attack on Clinton; to show the racial meaning of Clinton's body to the right is to expose the racial meaning of, and so debunk, their claim to moral virtue. As racial projection accounts for conservative hatred, and thus also for African American sympathy, Morrison reports how Clinton is identified as one of "us." In part, then, she seems to buttress racial solidarity by reporting (and repeating) a story of racial victimization, which draws from and sustains a deep investment by African Americans in the notion that the white psyche is profoundly pathological. In this regard, she focuses not on his policies as president, but on who he appears to be or even is: he is "blacker than any actual black person who could ever be elected in our children's lifetime."

In this story, Clinton appears the victim of what Clarence Thomas called a "high-tech lynching." Morrison had attacked Thomas, who had fled his blackness, but she had defended O. J. Simpson and here Clinton to suggest the stakes that "we" have in saving "our" men. In other contexts, Morrison would have noted how this story discounts the predatory sexual behavior of these men and also how the victimized bodies of men, not of women, repeatedly are used to sustain the solidarity of a racial or national we. In other contexts, she was likely to note who was excluded and what was veiled precisely by such identificatory language. As always, though, she dramatizes the vicissitudes and stories of African Americans, who live in and as a second nation within an "American" nation governed by white supremacy.[3]

But in part, from this story of racial solidarity by identification with Clinton, Morrison also draws a narrative of an *American* nationhood. As Clinton stands in for blacks, his humiliation signifies a national crisis:

> Certain freedoms I once imagined as being in a vault somewhere, like ancient jewels kept safe from thieves. No single official or group could break in and remove them, certainly not in public. The image is juvenile of course, and I have not had recourse to it my whole adult life. Yet it is useful now to explain what I perceive as the real story. For each bootstep the office of the Independent Counsel has taken smashes one of those jewels—a ruby of grand jury secrecy here, a sapphire of due process there. Such concentrated power may be reminiscent of a solitary Torquenada on a holy mission of lethal inquisition. . . . But [this is] a sustained, bloody, arrogant coup d'etat. The Presidency is being stolen from us. And the people know it.[4]

The key word is "us," now denoting not only African Americans but an inclusive national community. Now, treasured national jewels—freedoms never before, in her writings at least, visibly possessed by blacks or protecting them—are a possession being stolen by thieves. Thus, the nation is neither an imagined community promising democracy nor an instrument of white supremacy, but a real democratic enterprise, however flawed, a republic whose continued existence is the basis of all other goods. And its fate rests on Clinton's victimization by a power whose pathology, clearly associated with whites and whiteness, threatens everyone. Here, a language of citizenship does not erase black particularity, but on the contrary, is rooted in it, because the (black) experience of lawless power now signifies a constitution in jeopardy; here, a language of national belonging, constituted by rights in a republic, asserts a we that must be given precedence over other differences, however significant.

Several months later, in December, I attended a rally at New York University Law School organized by Toni Morrison, among others. It went on for almost three hours; the speakers included Elie Wiesel,

Gloria Steinhem, E. L.Doctorow, Arthur Schlesinger, Sean Willentz, Alec Baldwin, Mary Gordon, and, as the last speaker, Morrison herself. From my notes, I can quote (not paraphrase) her words:

> We live in the greatest, the leading, democracy in the world, and justifiably proud of itself. But if we let this process go on, we will show how a great democratic power can reduce itself to an arrogant theocracy . . . to a nation controlled by a political cabal that allows no debate or dispute. . . . The majority of Americans now oppose this process but are completely disenfranchised. We have lost public spaces and no public body is obliged to pay us attention. . . . Whatever your race, age, sex, or class, this is not an entertainment. If you think so, you are deceived. . . . When this constitution . . . of this particular country is suspended, we *all* go down. So from our hearts, let us beg God to bless America.

And then, Odetta and Jessye Norman, standing next to Morrison, led the crowd in singing "God Bless America."

How should we assess this performance of American nationalism? Consider it first in terms of Morrison's own work: I was stunned at the time partly because Morrison, in her fiction and nonfiction, always had defended a black nation within a United States represented as an Egypt, not (yet) a Promised Land. She always had recognized the degree to which nationhood remains the organizing center of U.S. politics, and her work explores its persistent power to expose its danger. If the danger of national identity is its racialized practice as a form of white supremacy, its power is the fantasy of inclusion that effaces difference. Her work thus seemed to reject the redemptive rhetorics that premise national identity on racial domination, or on its final overcoming by realizing the promise of more perfect union.

Morrison, who never twinned the promise of democracy and the meaning of America, therefore had positioned herself as a racial outcast and voiced a counternational politics. But she refused the romance of a redemptive countercommunity lodged in outcasts; she relentlessly dramatized both the fault lines among them and the dangers in their longings for redemption. Those longings were not to be rejected outright, however, but, as *Beloved* demonstrates, to be worked through rather than merely repeated. Though I felt sure she would reject extending to U.S. nationhood her own parables about African American community, I still once asked: Does the left need to critically rework (not refuse) the language of nationhood and rhetorics of redemption?[5]

In the impeachment episode, then, Morrison seems to embrace precisely the language of nationalism from which she has distanced herself in the past. For here, an African American community is a counter-nation yet also aligned with a majority of Americans: her populist defense of an undifferentiated "people" speaks an unequivocal "we" and invokes a national interest and community transcending group differences. Her defense of democracy is thus not abstract or universalist, not about plurality or pluralism, but constitutional and national, defending the particular covenant binding a specific people. Invoking a proud heritage of rights and a common destiny, she seeks a providential blessing to embolden us to defend "our first black president" and, thus, our threatened jewels and jeopardized tradition. What crisis triggered this republican and national if not prophetic language?[6]

Any answer must begin with the meaning of Bill Clinton, of his two bodies, of the way the vicissitudes of his personal body come to signify both African American and national communities threatened by the Christian right. The logic appears simple: the right reads him as black; Morrison takes up their projection and then identifies (a blacked-up) Clinton with both a besieged black community and an endangered nation ("the people" opposing his victimization). At the rally, Doctorow displayed this logic: using the horrific example of James Byrd's death, he evoked an image of Clinton tied to the back of a pickup truck and "dragged/whipped" while a crowd drank beer and cheered. He ended his speech by saying, "Clinton is all of us." Who? We on the political and cultural left? We targets of racism and homophobia? We, the American people — minus beer-drinking bigoted crackers and punitive new right puritans?

By reference to the sixties, to cultural conflict since Wallace and Nixon in 1968, I think we can explain the intersecting fantasies that relate the right to Morrison and Doctorow, but we also can see how mistaken they are about Clinton and recent history. Let us begin with the meaning of Clinton to the new right, and then return to Morrison's claims about Clinton, constitutional jeopardy, and nationhood.

Surely, the right has connected sex and race in a jeremiad against the sixties, whose corrupting legacy they claim to oppose in Clinton and his "morals," his presidency, and the people who elected him. Pat Robertson, in his September speech to the annual Christian Coalition Convention, declared that the office once occupied by "Washington and Jefferson and Lincoln" had become "the playpen for the sexual freedom of the poster child of the 60's." Using images of drug use, draft dodging, and sexual appetite, Dan Quayle intoned, "The nation is finally coming to grips with the consequences of what we have tolerated," that is, "moral collapse." Those who promote or signify that corruption must recognize their sin and thus accept the necessity of punishment if they are to be redeemed. The *New York Times* article reporting the convention speeches was thus headlined: "To Christians, GOP Urges Punishment and Prayer."[7]

"What we have tolerated" bespeaks the relationship between possessive individualism and sexual puritanism in U.S. history. Simply put, self-reliance requires a self-controlling character if release from state control is to produce liberty rather than license. So economic liberalism has repeatedly demanded religious sanctions and patriarchal "family values" to secure a self-control cast as both moral and sexual. The connection between individualism and sexual politics appears here as hysteria about nonprocreative, nonmarital, and nonconventional sexual practices, which must be demonized and abjured. As "self-possession" is the condition of mobility in the market and economic success is the reward of "virtue," so moral and political corruption—corruption of both personal and political bodies—is the ruling fear in a propertied tradition of antistatist politics. Thus did Tocqueville identify Anglo-Americans as "a Puritan and trading nation."[8]

But as a resurgent right mobilizes against "big government" by using a trope of "welfare" to compare dependency and (sexual) profligacy to self-reliant virtue, so racial stigma accompanies the sexual Puritanism of self-making men in U.S. history. As this example attests, ambivalence about self-mastery and dependence, self-control and pleasure, violence and love have been projected onto black bodies since the advent of slavery. In part, those cast as racially other signify the impulses, desires, and longings that self-determining men must control and abjure. Sexual austerity and disciplined labor, not to mention an antistate politics, are sustained by images of slaves, fertile welfare queens, and libidinal, irresponsible men corrupted by welfare. By the logic of splitting and projection, of course, such racialized others are objects of (pornographic) longing, envy, and political nostalgia, not only of aversion. Thus, as Morrison argued about the meaning of Clarence Thomas, "the site of the exorcism of critical national issues [is] situated in the miasma of black life and inscribed on the bodies of black people."[9]

But mainstream press accounts of the new right's attack on Clinton and the sixties consistently elide the racial element in the sexual politics and moral meaning of possessive individualism. For instance, the day after the report on the Christian Coalition Convention, Peter Applebome in the *New York Times* contrasted Starr and Clinton as "Dueling Sons of the South" by associating one with tradition (and his hellfire preacher father) and the other with "modernization."[10] Both "sons" share an intense biblical religiosity, though Clinton links it to economic development and Elvis Presley. But Applebome ignores how conflict between traditionalists and modernizers has been shaped by struggle over segregation and race. Starr's father, a resolute segregationist, coded sin racially: in biblical discourse, sin is figured in sexual metaphors of impurity by mixing with people worshipping other gods. To the Starrs, father and son, Elvis thus means integration and miscegenation, so that white appropriation of African American cultural forms appears as sin rather than minstrelsy. Clinton, the child of this minstrelsy, is empowered but also rendered vulnerable by such appropriations, which represent his proximity to blackness and to actual black people.

The right, therefore, does not call Clinton a "black" president directly, but the language of sin and immorality, linked to sexual appetite, promiscuity, and loss of self-control, bespeak the racial meanings that Morrison named as such. As his genuine ease with African Americans is itself transgressive in the White House, a symbol of purity, so his sexual conduct marks the sinfulness that soils whiteness, that betrays both the marital bond and the public trust. Yet, despite repeated exposure, he escapes political punishment. That is because, so the argument goes, cultural changes initiated in the sixties have created the "toleration" that signifies moral corruption. To punish rather than tolerate Clinton, therefore, would signify redemption, the repudiation of a legacy joining sexual revolution and civil rights.

In response, as one *Times* article headlined, "Blacks Stand By a President Who 'Has Been There for Us.' "[11] The authors note that African Americans widely praise "the guiltless and unpatronizing egalitarianism in Clinton's relationship with blacks" and that in some polls he is more popular among blacks than Colin Powell or Jesse Jackson. As well, many African Americans believe that supporters of the Starr investigation seek to reverse gains made by blacks not only in the Clinton years but since the sixties. In this view, echoed by Morrison, a *racial* agenda Republicans could not enact electorally is being achieved by driving Clinton from office.

To be sure, the authors note, there is enormous anger at Clinton's compromises and failures, now because he has jeopardized any gains by African Americans. But as Christopher Edley, a black professor at Harvard Law School and consultant to Clinton on race, is quoted as saying, "Faith in redemption cuts the other way," that is, against the angry will to punish. "In the face of painful circumstances, you have to believe that faith will not only heal your [own] wounds but reform the master." Another respondent noted, "Forgiveness is part of [our] culture . . . we couldn't survive with all that pent-up hatred and fear, so we've had to forgive and move on."[12] Whereas the Christian right makes punishment the condition of redemption and so sanctions state power, these African Americans invoke the redemptive power of forgiveness on behalf of Clinton, but also toward "the masters," whose pathology (hate-full demonizing of others) is the unstated condition requiring redemption. To the Christian right, though, this very spirit of forgiveness is inseparable from "toleration" as "moral collapse."[13]

To many African Americans, according to both Morrison and the *Times*, Clinton therefore does indeed signify what the right says. Thus, the stakes in his struggle with the right also seem to be the standing of the civil rights movement, of civil rights more broadly, and of a culture valuing forgiveness rather than punishment. Views of Clinton on the right and left are thus mediated by mirrored allegories relating the fate of the nation to the sixties and the culture wars since then. But do these strangely intersecting versions of a blacked-up Clinton distort what is really going on? Consider an alternative narration.[14]

The sixties movements challenged acts of power in market and familial spaces deemed private, also segregation condoned as private choice, defending instead the rightful claims that a broader public could make on individual behavior. That time was "political" in part because what people did in private was brought to account; private behavior was made public precisely as a way of exposing hierarchy and power. Countercultural and feminist demands for freedom from patriarchal and market control were voiced in a language of private rights, but, as in the black struggle, demands for personal autonomy were linked to bonds of solidarity conceived as a way to transform personal and public life. Not only were (racist) acts once sanctioned in private made visible, but formerly proscribed (sexual) acts were made public, too, in terms of rights of expression that were both personal and collective. That time was "political," too, because the institutionalized power of the state and corporations was made visible and brought to account in public ways, through debate and what Arendt called "action in concert."

Beginning with Goldwater and then Wallace, new right discourse narrated this politics in jeremiadic terms as a fall into corruption associated with the demonic triangle of a state actively allied only with women and blacks. The problem was not a state allied with apartheid and imperial violence, but a state overtly hostile to working-class whites, to religious values, "law and order," and traditions of local control. Especially since Reagan's victory in 1980, the new right has realigned state power with a revalorized military, demonized taxes and welfare by renewing their racial coding, justified growing inequality, released corporations from public control in the name of economic growth, used the rhetoric of discrimination to protect privilege by race and gender, reauthorized punishment in criminal justice, demonized drugs, renewed a discourse of moral purity, and remade political discourse so that compulsory heterosexuality and "family values" govern the bestowing and policing of citizenship. By 1990, the right had succeeded in its project in regard to the economy, the military, and the relationship of racial reform and state policy, but failed to overturn the sexual revolution and feminism. What remains of sixties politics—a defense of sexual freedom and individual privacy against the state— has become the whole meaning of the sixties to the right, and its paramount target, even as it successfully cast national politics in terms of family values.[15]

In this context, how did Clinton win election? Mostly, he accepted rather than contested the elements of the Reagan revolution, but in ways that enabled him to hold together hard-to-reconcile constituencies. First, he attracted corporate elites by his loyalty to unfettered capitalism and global "free trade." Second, his ease with African Americans elicited their electoral support and thus held this key element in the base of the Democratic Party. But third, and crucially, he regained support from so-called Reagan Democrats, that is, non-college-educated men who identify themselves as white. For while his church-based cadences cemented black identification, he distanced himself from overt antiracist policies, punished black women in particular, spoke a moralized language of personal responsibility, embraced capital punishment, and promised to end welfare and the era of "big government." Clinton could embody "blackness" and embrace blacks culturally in ways that allowed him to sacrifice them politically; it was both his proximity and their sacrifice that made him attractive to Reagan Democrats.[16]

If one presumes the overwhelming power of new right discourse and the institutional constellation Clinton faced, and if one also presumes that the center could not have been shifted, then he appears to have fought, always, a defensive war to hold off superior force, to protect certain accomplishments arising from the sixties, and to make certain marginal advances. In this view, he encouraged a certain proximity to blackness, and to signifiers of the sixties, in his person; as well, his appointments were truly diverse, he symbolically affirmed the rights of women and gays, he defended affirmative action, and he initially sought to expand significantly state programs for health and education. In this view, associated with the Democratic Leadership Council, any majoritarian politics now must be premised on conceding and co-opting the right's discourse. For some further left, Clinton's importance thus rested on the symbolism of his person and (some) policies, which reflected left principles and had real impact under adverse conditions.

From the point of view I argue here, however, Clinton's political weakness followed precisely from not taking on the right's discourse directly, to shift the center rather than cede it. In this regard, Clinton never overtly defended any affirmative legacy of the sixties or challenged new right attacks on the cultural politics proceeding from that time. He did not defend the antiwar movement, sexual freedom, or the meaning of drugs in the counterculture. He allowed associations with these, but (as "slick Willy") he would not risk rejection by speaking on their behalf. Nor did he ever try to recast the place of "morality" in public life. Instead, he tried to resignify new right language and appropriate new right concerns about the family, crime, personal responsibility, welfare, and fiscal austerity. In my allegory of the sixties, then, he tried to ride the Reaganite tiger but in the end was eaten by it; even before impeachment he could create only a weak presidency relative to forces and discourses he did not contest head-on, and those forces remained committed to his destruction.

By using rather than contesting new right discourse, Clinton became its hostage, vulnerable to being demonized in terms of the very family values and moral responsibility he had legitimized. Though he had in fact ceded almost every element in the right's agenda, he still signified the last remaining cultural battle in its war to overcome the sixties. His symbolic proximity to blackness despite his policies on crime and welfare, his attachment to the women's movement, gay rights, and the environment, though repeatedly sacrificed, and his political facility sustained a hatred on the right that was intensified because public opinion tolerated (even enjoyed) his sexual desires while separating his "private life" from his "job performance" as a manager of the economy.

How does my narrative recast the responses to Clinton of Morrison and the nonacademic left? Three issues need to be considered: identification with Clinton and blackness, claims about a constitutional crisis, and appeals to national belonging to address it.

To begin with, Morrison did expose how racial projection onto Clinton's body fueled the hatred and symbolism of the impeachment campaign. Thus did she account for (and report) African American sympathy with him. The value of Morrison's *New Yorker* piece is precisely to suggest that the meaning of Clinton's policies and presidency must include his symbolic significance as itself a material political reality. (For in politics, as Machiavelli argued, appearances constitute reality, and who you appear to be is who you are.) And yet (just as Machiavelli also said that people can be deceived by appearances) she took up the right's projection as if he really were what the right said he was. Those who identified with him may have satisfied a blackface wish on his part, and their support may have helped save him, but the identification seems idealized or distorted because it was split off from Clinton's actual policies.

I have offered here a far more critical or disenchanted account than Morrison (or the other speakers at the rally) by arguing that Clinton ceded too much to the right, and not only in regard to racial issues. To say he defended a liberal legacy in adverse cultural and political circumstances is idealization unless one also credits how he contributed to those circumstances by both his silences and his own rhetoric. But it seemed very difficult during the impeachment episode to acknowledge Clinton's limitations and yet also defend him politically to thwart the right; it was as if recognizing his limitations compels us to repudiate him altogether, whereas defending him requires repressing (or idealizing) his politics.

Still, there is the issue of timing and context, that is, Morrison's claim in the *New Yorker* and then at the rally that impeachment signals a constitutional crisis requiring widespread action and protest. Here the issue seems less the meaning of Clinton himself and more the significance of the right's effort to impeach him.

The twinning of sex and race by the right and the intense battles that go under the sign of family values are at the core of white supremacy, patriarchal power, and homophobia, and are indeed profoundly threatening to democratic values in every way. In this sense, it seems true that the stakes in the impeachment struggle were far larger than Clinton's actual presidency and that the left had to defend Clinton in order to defend against the right. But Morrison did not really make this argument; she did not speak of democracy (or of a struggle for freedom) in a universalist sense. She depicted a specific nation whose constitution joins members despite our other differences; she claimed that a constitutional crisis put the democratic character of our nation in jeopardy. What are we to make of this claim?

If the right had succeeded in the Senate, that would have been something like a putsch to remove a democratically elected president. So efforts to sustain public opinion on Clinton's behalf were crucial to deterring that outcome. Moreover, Starr's investigation of Clinton did threaten to erode due process and privacy protections, which are important for all of us, and especially pertinent to gay rights and to the treatment of minorities by the criminal justice system. Indeed, the Starr investigation and the impeachment culminated years of work by the right to evacuate the meaning and scope of due process, and the right considered this struggle essential to its cultural politics more broadly. In ways that many at that rally did not recognize in their political radicalism thirty years ago, privacy rights and procedural safeguards are indeed essential to personal and political freedom.

But radical insights of thirty years ago remain pertinent. In part, procedural solicitude on the left indicates that paths for substantive action seem blocked, and then substitutes for struggling to shift the social forces and discourses that really govern legal and formally political process. In this regard, impeachment did not violate constitutional procedure, and its outcome hinged on the mobilization of public opinion and the election of 1998, not on procedural rectitude. Constitutional piety and a language of privacy rights remain suspect for other reasons as well, as theorists on the left (from Marx to MacKinnon) have rightly argued. Not only is the language of rights and safeguards repeatedly used to defend privilege, as the right itself has shown. More important, constitutionalism is not a resource to foster a *public* freedom because this language links freedom only to procedure, privacy, and separation from others. For these reasons, democratic politics is in tension with and not simply dependent on constitutionalism.

Morrison does gesture toward this other, call it republican or Arendtian, conception of freedom when she speaks of a majority of Americans who are "disenfranchised" because they have "lost public spaces and no public body is obliged to pay us attention." As crucial—and prescient—is her claim that a democratically elected president is being removed under pretense of law by a "political cabal that allows no debate or dispute." A left cannot be built on privacy claims, and appeals to constitutionalism all too often ignore the machinery of domination that constitutions make legitimate. But demands for public spaces, political voice, and accountable power can infuse a democratic, say political, dimension into the constitutional sentimentality that all too often reduces freedom to civil rights. How we read this tension in Morrison's speech, therefore, affects whether we credit her association of constitutional jeopardy and democratic crisis.[17]

Still, there remains her claim that impeachment affects the destiny of a *national* community anchored in the Constitution, a "we" on which the fate of *every* "I" depends. Nothing in her writings, at least by my reading, prepares one to hear her defend an undifferentiated "we" of national belonging. Is this a sign of desperation? Of a residual patriotism released by grave danger? Of the realization that, however much we on the left decry the failure of the republic, its survival is a condition of democratic possibility? Against the legacy of disappointed rage that drives the antinational politics of the academic left, does Morrison's intervention suggest that certain moments require—and dignify—a narration of nationhood?

Morrison evokes a national membership that she anchors in constitutional loyalty rather than blood and soil, in the universality of procedural safeguards as a condition for all other goods, and in democratic norms of representation; the national identification she invokes thus repeats ideal elements of liberal nationalism, promising to transcend or include all other loyalties and identifications. Morrison speaks here not as the literary artist and critic who addresses the experiences constituting a distinctive black nation within the "American" nation. She speaks not in the left tradition that joins Marx's "On the Jewish Question" and Malcolm X's "The Ballot or the Bullet"; she speaks not to show the constitutive inequality that mocks the inclusionary poetry of liberal nationalism, nor to stand with the excluded in a counternational community.

Rather, she has made a series of associations from blacks to Clinton to constitutional and national crisis: as Clinton stands in for blacks, his victimization signifies a national crisis, caused by the right's attack on constitutionally protected rights, and not only rights to due process and privacy but also to democratic elections (and assembly). Rights historically denied to blacks (and, not coincidentally, again in Florida in the 2000 election) are now "jewels" whose possession by all is endangered.

In effect, Morrison inverts the typical left critique of nationhood and nationalism: she makes particularity the bearer of universality. Like Frederick Douglass, Martin Luther King, and James Baldwin, she always worked against the language of nationalism by showing how the apparently inclusive "we" of American nationhood is the exclusionary voice of white supremacy. But now she also echoes their other claim, that African Americans bear a commitment to freedom defaulted on by a white majority, so that blacks can redeem whites (and thus an American nation) imprisoned by racism and the fears that drive it. Like her exemplars, Morrison here makes black experience the barometer and bearer of "American" freedom, but by using Clinton to mediate (or stand in) for blacks and their national significance.

She too readily collapses the difference between Clinton and the right's image of him, and thus the difference between black experience and Clinton's difficulties, but thereby explicitly takes on a side of politics she always seemed to devalue. Rather than show how the claim of a whole obscures the reality and suffering of a part, she shows how particular experiences and grievances can bear—and should be given— broader, resonant, significance. Moving from blacks to Clinton to the nation, she overtly claims that the language of a national "we" need not erase particularity, but can be a reminder of connections that are the condition of all other goods, the ground against which other differences are figures, the frame through which conflicts about erasure and inclusion can themselves be enacted. .

Strangely, then, Morrison sounds like Rorty, advancing a left nationalism, though Rorty speaks in terms of civic religion and the myth of American exceptionalism, whereas Morrison imagines democratic nationhood more through an expansive reading of the Constitution as a condition of any further democratic possibility. By rooting nationhood in the Constitution, she voices something like what Habermas calls a constitutional patriotism, as if to avoid the dangers of what Lauren Berlant calls "national sentimentality," to which Rorty is subject and which often sanctions or effaces white supremacy. But Morrison's own claims idealize, or sentimentalize, the relationship between the Constitution and democracy. Just as she too readily collapses the difference between blacks and Clinton, so also between constitutionalism and democracy. Her speech thus shows, contra theorists of a merely "civic" nationalism, how powerful the romance of America remains.

On the one hand, then, I affirm her effort to articulate a national we. Morrison's interventions indicate that the nation remains the organizing center of American life and that we must refuse not only the fantasy of inclusion by that identification, but also the fantasy of escaping it. As well, her intervention suggests that, whereas political critique depends on voicing erased particularity, efforts to achieve or exercise political power depend on generalizing from the experiences of a part to claims about the fate of the whole. That projection of meaning is dangerous but necessary if one interpretation—of history since the sixties,

of feminism, civil rights movements and democracy, of nationhood —
is to be advanced against others.

On the other hand, though, Morrison seems to repeat the language
of nationhood as a romance. The problem is not that she created associations among blacks, the Constitution, and the nation by way of
Clinton's two bodies, but that she did not also and openly resist full
identification between Clinton and the sixties, black experience, and
constitutional jeopardy, between the Constitution and democracy, and
between democracy and the nation. Granted, it was *Morrison* speaking; her appeal to a nation in crisis had authority precisely because of
her history of counternational testimony, which could remain unstated
to a largely left-liberal audience. Perhaps considerations of timing —
of crisis — also seemed to warrant an idealizing rhetoric, which leaves
to another moment a critical story showing how nationalism has been
practiced. Still, by collapsing these associations, Morrison suppressed
not only the political meaning of Clinton's real limitations, but also
the actual political legacy of both the sixties and the social movements
since then.

A more powerful challenge to the right, I think, would have to speak
out loud what Morrison left unstated, to analyze but resist, and not
only use, the meanings projected onto Clinton, to mobilize people not
by identification with Clinton, but on behalf of the legacies he partly
represented but mostly conceded and betrayed. And speaking on behalf of those legacies necessarily means telling a more complex story
about American nationhood and democracy. That story would, of necessity, voice the critical testimony whose negativity Morrison suspended at the rally, but it would also follow her example by recasting
the democratic aspirations that alone can redeem a national identity.

This assessment of Morrison's intervention is confirmed by key
events since then. Several warrant emphasis. First, public opinion
never accepted the right's case against Clinton, and indeed turned
against Starr. Second, the Christian and congressional right took this
famous "disconnect" as evidence of the very moral corruption they
lamented, and thus sustained a political crusade profoundly estranged
from popular culture. But third, Democrats offered no competing narrative to explain, let alone politically exploit, this disconnect. Indeed,
the right's story of moral failure, sanctioned and repeated by media
elites, was never challenged and governed the 2000 national election.
Every decision Gore made, from whether Clinton would campaign to
the selection of a vice-presidential candidate, was premised on Clinton's guilt. Thus, impeachment was never addressed by the Democrats;

the episode that controlled the election was never discussed. Fourth, even when a "cabal" of judges on the Supreme Court gave the election to Bush by disenfranchising (especially black but also Jewish) voters in Florida, Democrats rushed to confirm the "legitimacy" of government.

These highlights suggest how elements in Morrison's account of constitutional jeopardy and national crisis became more pertinent and literal in the 2000 election than anyone might have imagined a year earlier. Partly, disenfranchisement and constitutional usurpation reiterated how black experiences continue to signify the jeopardy or failure of democracy, showing why threats to the citizenship of some matters to all. Partly, the refusal to expose the motives disguised by the moral claims of the right continues to allow a "cabal" to govern both discourse and policy in ways unsanctioned by public opinion. In both regards, recent events suggest the necessity of creating a counternarrative to contest the hegemony of the right's discourse. Clinton's scandals and impeachment can be ignored, apparently forgotten, but require narration if the power of the right is ever to be overcome.

With the admitted advantage of hindsight, then, it also seems clear that taking on the right means addressing the meaning of the sixties, whose reverberations continue to echo and haunt our politics. A compelling narrative would have to retell the practice of nationhood in ways that make credible the social movements arising in the sixties and yet also acknowledge the profound confusion, rancor, and fear that remain their most palpable outcome. A compelling narrative also would have to depict as complex the social realities recurrently simplified in terms of sin, and yet also credit the longings that attach people to rhetorics of family and morality that they know are estranged from the actuality of their lives. By addressing the appeal of a rhetoric of moral failure and the power of a story of sin and redemption, a counternarrative might dramatize the meaning of the new right, reauthorize both public debate and political conflict, and so break the stalemate in American politics.

Notes

The first version of this essay was delivered as a talk at the American Political Science Association Convention, September 1999. It appeared online in *Theory & Event* February 2000, with two responses: Mark Reinhardt,"Constitutional Sentimentality" and Ebony E. A. Chatman, "Clinton's Black 'I': A Note on Public Property." This version, considerably revised, is much indebted to Reinhardt's defense of Morrison's interventions and to conversations with Peter Euben and Victoria Hattam.

1 "Talk of the Town," *New Yorker*, 5 October 1998, 31–32.

2 The *dual* nature of Morrison's use of Clinton was brought home to me by Stuart Clarke's commentary on the talk that became this paper. For at first, I emphasized only how she used the story of (black) victimization to narrate nationhood, but not also how this story bespeaks and sustains racial solidarity.

3 Lawrie Balfour, in private correspondence, made the observation about the way that Morrison here participates in rather than rejects the figuring of community through victimized men, not the women they victimize.

4 "Talk of the Town," 31–32.

5 Beloved, especially, I have argued, retold the redemptive narrative of deliverance from servitude crucial to any version of American nationalism, but also to black nationalism; that text dramatized, to work through rather than repeat, the redemptive language that always has entwined white supremacy and resistance to it, the exclusionary violence of special nationhood and opposition to it. See George Shulman, "American Political Culture, Prophetic Narration, and Toni Morrison's *Beloved*," *Political Theory* 24.2 (May 1996): 295–314.

6 She seems to use prophetic tropes to invoke a nation with a particular covenant tradition, whose god's blessings are conditional on its people incarnating justice. But perhaps her language is more republican: danger and desperation reveal (the Machiavellian insight) that continuation of the republic is essential to all other goods, the condition of all other possibilities, however much we have spent our lives lamenting and trying to overcome its failures. Indeed, unlike a Hebrew prophet, she does not say the republic deserves to perish, or that god is teaching us a lesson essential to our later redemption.

7 Laurie Goldstein, *New York Times*, September 19, 1998, 1.

8 Morrison read the fascination with Clinton's body and sexuality in racial terms, but did not explore how homophobic hysteria fueled attacks on Clinton's extramarital, nonprocreative, and nongenital sexuality. Pornographic fascination with that sexuality bespoke a disowned homoeroticism, even as the exposure and policing of Clinton were part of a larger struggle to prohibit gay sexual expression.

9 Toni Morrison, "Friday on the Potomac," in *Race-ing Justice, En-gendering Power* (New York: Pantheon, 1992), x. For arguments relating self-control in the market, sexual austerity, rhetorics of virtue, and white supremacy, see Winthrop Jordan, *White over Black* (New York: Norton, 1968); Richard Slotkin, *Regeneration through Violence* (Middleton, CT: Wesleyan University Press, 1972); and Michael Rogin,

Ronald Reagan: The Movie (Berkeley: University of California Press), 1984.

10 Peter Applebome, "Dueling Sons of the South," *New York Times*, September 19, 1998, The Week in Review, 1.

11 "Blacks Stand By a President Who 'Has Been There for Us,'" *New York Times*, September 19, 1998, 1.

12 Ibid.

13 Clinton repeatedly turned to black churches to show repentance and receive forgiveness; by going to African Americans for love, and receiving it, of course, another aspect of the racial imaginary is replayed.

14 I am indebted to Nikhil Singh for the term "allegory" to suggest how the sixties figures in contending political positions now. See Nikhil Sing, "The Black Panthers and the 'Undeveloped Country' of the Left," in, *The Black Panther Party*, ed. Charles E. Jones (Baltimore: Black Classic Press, 1998).

15 I am indebted to Michael Rogin for conceiving the various domains in which the right has sought to remake U.S. politics and life, and for placing Clinton in that context. See Christine Schofer, "Fatal Obsession" (an interview with Michael Rogin on the new right and Clinton), *Express*, 13 November 1998. The phrase "demonic love triangle" is my own, from a paper several friends and I wrote as graduate students in 1979. On how the right has reconfigured public and private, see Lauren Berlant, *The Queen of America Goes to Washington City* (Durham, NC: Duke University Press, 1997).

16 Clinton specifically punished black women—Sister Souljah, Lani Guinier, Jocelyn Elders—as though a cultural identification through masculinity enabled the politics signified in his relationship to actual and symbolic black women.

17 I would emphasize a studied ambivalence about privacy and legal protections. On one side are the arguments of Marx and MacKinnon, classic left diagnoses of the ways that "privacy" grants protection to power and legitimacy to domination. On the other side are the lessons of both the women's and gay rights movements: freedom does entail protection from state intrusion in certain regards, as well as protection to express sexuality publicly. Likewise, I would emphasize a studied ambivalence about constitutionalism. One side is represented by the arguments of Sheldon Wolin, for instance, for whom constitutionalism, by legitimating bureaucratic corporate regimes, threatens democratic politics. On the other side are the lessons of the past twenty years, which show that constitutional safeguards can retard the power of the right and provide some protection to vulnerable minorities.

ANNA MARIE SMITH

Sexual Risk
Management in the
Clinton White House

When Clinton left office, his aides mentioned time and time again that he was concerned about his historical legacy. Feminist historians will look back at the Clinton administration and give it a mixed review. On the one hand, Clinton will be remembered for a few key initiatives on late-term abortion, family leave, and the earned-income tax credit. His partnership with Hillary Rodham Clinton will be compared to that between the Roosevelts. Women and minorities also won a substantial number of the appointments to the Clinton administration. On the other hand, however, Clinton abandoned many of his best nominees, presided over a dramatic increase in the gap between the rich and the poor, and supported a draconian welfare plan that virtually eliminated the statutory entitlement to poverty assistance.

Above all, feminists will remember the Clinton-Lewinsky affair as a moment in which sexual harassment policy was turned inside out. Many of us have struggled for years to pass policies in our workplaces and to enact laws in our legislatures that reflect a feminist position on sexual harassment. We have had to confront some of our most recalcitrant male colleagues in meeting after meeting to make our point clear. No, we are not against sex, sexual expression, or freedom of speech. We insist that a person's right to equal opportunity in the workplace is violated wherever she or he is faced with unwanted sexual conduct. If a woman has been subjected to unwanted sexual behavior that is so severe that she cannot do her job or cannot pursue her studies properly, or if she has been effectively coerced into accepting sexual conduct as part of a quid pro quo exchange, then she has been denied one of her basic rights.[1] From a feminist perspective, the key question is this: Is the adult worker consenting to the sexual conduct in question, and is that consent freely given, or is consent produced by the coercive dimensions of the individual's workplace status?[2] The feminist perspective is absolutely agnostic on the moralistic questions that may arise. We do not care—and we should not care—whether the adults involved are male, female, transsexual, married, single, divorced, straight, or gay; whether the worker complainant holds a "decent" job or works on the street; whether the complainant and/or the accused have sexual histories that include moments of perversity, fetishism, nonmonogamy, sex with strangers, and so on; whether the sexual behavior in question is "tasteful" and "normal" or "tacky" and "perverse"; or whether the alleged sexual contact took place in an "appropriate" private venue or in a "pristine" public place.

In the Clinton-Lewinsky affair, as in the Thomas-Hill hearings, feminists lost control of the public discourse on sexual harassment. To take but one example, the taboo on adultery looms large in the Clinton-Lewinsky records. Starr and the Republicans seem to have assumed that the public would be outraged by their allegation that the president had abused his power specifically to conceal an adulterous sexual liaison. The fact that every sexual moment between Clinton and Lewinsky was fully consensual for both parties was hardly given any emphasis at all.

In the end, the pro-impeachment camp was bewildered by the fact that the American people were not really fazed by something as banal as extramarital sex. The ghosts of Chappaquidick and Gary Hart's *Monkey Business* cruise did not rise again. For all the apparent failures of Starr and the Republicans to mobilize popular opinion against Clinton in defense of "moral decency," however, feminists will look back at the Clinton years as a turning point in official discourse on marriage and the family. In his trademark "triangulation" style, Clinton picked a theme right out of the Republicans' repertoire—family values—and made it his own. At the same time, however, the neoconservative policies that he approved made it more difficult than ever for working-class and poor families to stay together.

Clinton's legacy includes the ironic logic of two juxtapositions. First, Clinton constructed himself as a pro-family and pro-marriage leader, even as his policies had severe antifamily effects and even as he continued to pursue his sexual fetishistic interest, namely, extramarital casual sex. Second, the Clinton-Lewinsky affair began at a particularly intense political moment for the White House, at the time of the government shutdown of 1995, and continued in an administration that had just shifted toward a much more restricted policy vis-à-vis access to the Oval Office. In the midst of what his own aides regarded as a dramatic intensification of time and space management, Clinton carved out the space for a secret sexual liaison that took place just out of sight and just beyond the earshot of the White House staff. Although some may regard the actual setting of the affair as an irrelevant detail, the fact that one of the most infamous extramarital affairs of the century was conducted in a workplace should be central to feminist discourse on the case.

The Clintons: Images, Policies, and Policy Image   The Clinton-Lewinsky affair can be located within a complex and contradictory tradition, namely, the regulation of sexuality through the deployment of marriage as a form of social control. By using the terms "regulation" and "social control," I do not mean to indicate that this tradition has taken the form of a totalistic conspiracy-like system that has been successfully and uniformly imposed on subordinate groups by a dominant class or an omnipotent state. There is a long tradition in early modern and modern Western societies of promoting popular heterosexual marriage to bring an otherwise unruly bachelor population into a disciplined condition and to prevent the social problems associated with a large wanton bastard population. As many researchers in the field of the politics of sexuality acknowledge, however, the promotion of heterosexual marriage and the nuclear family on the part of governments, religious institutions, social movements, and experts in the medical, psychological, and psychiatric professions has sometimes had a significant effect on the bourgeoisie as well as the working class, has often resulted in incoherent ad hoc policies or even failure rather than perfect social control, and has always been enormously differentiated across various classes, races, immigrant peoples, and colonial subjects.[3]

The Clinton administration's position with respect to gender, family values, and marriage was quite complicated. Clinton clearly owed his electoral achievements in part to gendered policies and images. When he succeeded in his 1996 reelection bid, the voting data demonstrated that although male voters were almost evenly divided between Clinton and Bob Dole, at 43 to 44 percent, women supported the incumbent by a 59 to 35 percent margin. Several analysts hailed the emergence of a new key voter, the white, middle-class, suburban "soccer mom," and contended that Clinton's vigorous defense of women's rights was a winning factor. Leading feminists such as Gloria Steinem did in fact ask women to cast their vote for Clinton on the grounds that there were significant differences between his positions and those of Dole and the Republicans, and that where Clinton had wavered, he had done so only because he did not have a strong enough progressive support base.

For all the media's emphasis on the gender gap, it should be remembered that other feminist analysts differed sharply with Steinem. This is not to say that there was no basis whatsoever for the feminist pro-Clinton argument. Clinton had in fact vetoed the ban on late-term abortions and had ensured that the unpaid family leave law, the Violence against Women Act, and the ban on assault weapons were passed. He had expanded the earned-income tax credit by increasing the subsidy for the 15 million low-wage full-time working recipients and by extending the eligibility requirements to include an additional 4.5 million workers. He had also appointed an impressive number of women and minorities to offices in his administration.

Katha Pollitt calls Clinton's record of positive achievements for women a "short [and] narrowly tailored list."[4] Clinton actually abandoned many of his women appointees, such as Zoë Baird, Lani Guinier, and Jocelyn Elders, when their views, or even the right's distorted constructions of their views, threatened to contradict his moderate image. He had constructed himself as a firmly pro-choice leader, but he had done nothing to improve access to abortion. Eighty-four percent of U.S. counties lack abortion facilities and states are free to impose mandatory counseling and waiting periods for all women and parental approval for women under the age of eighteen. The states are also allowed to exclude coverage for abortions by Medicaid, the health care plan for the poor. Clinton had promised to support gay rights, but he capitulated on the issue of gays in the military, gave no power to his AIDS "czar," distanced himself from his gay supporters, enthusiastically embraced the myth that children should be raised only by married heterosexual couples, and signed the 1996 Defense of Marriage Act, a bill that allows states to ban gay marriages. Given the overrepresentation of women and minorities among the poor in the United States, it is reasonable to suggest that the elimination of welfare entitlements will have an especially large impact on women, blacks, and Latinos.

Clinton had the good fortune to occupy the White House during an economic recovery, and it should be recognized that some of the fruits of the late 1990s upswing in employment and wages did in fact benefit everyone, even the poorest, to some extent. The gap between the rich and the poor nevertheless remains larger in the United States than in any other Western country. The economic recovery that Clinton presided over did not transform the fundamentally antiegalitarian nature of American society, and, insofar as it depended on market speculation and an increase in household debt and was not being used to fuel massive investment in public education, Clinton's recovery did not lay the foundation for more equality in subsequent economic cycles. If poor people are locked into low-paid jobs with no union protection and little opportunity for advancement, then it is simply common sense that they will encounter serious difficulties holding their families together as decent housing, adequate food, and basic health care remain beyond their reach.

Clinton also vigorously worked with the Republican-led Congress to secure the passage of the North American Free Trade Agreement (NAFTA), which is having a devastating effect on workers and unions. Progressive critics are divided on Clinton's decision to prioritize balancing the budget, but they all contend that he maintained an excessively generous level of military expenditures. Many of Clinton's otherwise promising policies remained empty rhetoric: his pledges for support for the inner cities were meaningless without a substantial jobs creation program and his increase in the minimum wage still left a family of four under the poverty line. Although he sponsored legislation that established uniform achievement standards for children from wealthy and poor school districts alike, the Republicans reduced his already insufficient education spending initiatives, thereby ensuring the further deterioration of the public elementary and secondary school system. Finally, he failed to act positively in key issue areas such as the environment and campaign finance reform and abandoned his own moderate proposals to reform the capitalist health care system.

Feminist critics also point out that Clinton's leadership style had a restrictive effect on the feminist movement itself. Wherever he was confronted by a credible source of opposition, Clinton's response was to appropriate his antagonists' arguments and to neutralize them. Fighting the Newt Gingrich–led resurgence of Republican popularity, Clinton adopted their balanced budget, pro–free trade, anti-immigrant, antiwelfare, and pro–law and order policies. With respect to feminist leaders, Clinton offered them government appointments and an unprecedented degree of access to the White House, yet feminists and progressive leaders who criticized him for supporting welfare reform were marginalized and censored at the 1996 Democratic Convention by his campaign staff. Reverend Jesse Jackson, for example, joined Patricia Ireland, the president of the National Organization for Women, to protest against the passage of the 1996 Personal Responsibility Act. It was only when Clinton faced impeachment hearings during the fall of 1998 and wanted to shore up his support among blacks that Jackson was brought into the White House for extensive consultation.

Frances Fox Piven contends that Clinton's neutralization strategy did in fact have an enormous impact on women's organizations and social welfare advocacy groups. In her view, progressive activists placed too much emphasis during the Clinton administration on what she calls the "insider strategy," and virtually abandoned their political independence insofar as they muted their criticism of Clinton's policies in exchange for political access.[5] Pollitt further argues that this pattern of incorporation and neutralization seriously weakened the feminist movement as activists' energies were directed away from grassroots mobilization to lobbying and fundraising for Clinton and moderate Democrats, many of whom ultimately supported welfare reform and other antiegalitarian policies. Although she admits that Republican administrations certainly would have pursued a more reactionary agenda, Pollitt concludes that they would not have occupied the sort of imaginary "middle ground" that Clinton staked out, and therefore would not have been able to neutralize the progressive opposition within and outside Congress to such an enormous degree.[6]

Given the fact that Clinton's policies were not remarkably pro-women in any sense, the gender gap cannot be explained in terms of his actual political agenda and concrete achievements. Zillah Eisenstein contends that Clinton was particularly adept at borrowing feminist and feminizing symbols during his 1996 electoral campaign. He presented himself to the voters as a "caring and sharing" leader: he claimed that he "felt the pain" of the voters and offered initiatives on popular symbolic issues such as teen smoking, school uniforms, violence on television, gun control, and crime. These initiatives, however, were conceived in the sort of low-cost manner that suited the downsized government tone of 1990s American public discourse.[7] Clinton also gained from the Republicans' failure to anticipate the importance of women voters. The 1995 government shutdown, the blatant extremism of Gingrich, Pat Buchanan, and the Christian Coalition, and Dole's own Washington masculine style made it relatively easy for the president to construct himself as the Republicans' feminine "other." Elizabeth Dole, Susan Molinari, and Colin Powell were pressed into service at the 1996 Republican Convention to give Dole's candidacy a more women- and minority-friendly feel, but their gestures never effectively compensated for the Republicans' antiwoman reputation.

Above all, Eisenstein argues, Clinton's marriage allowed him to emerge as a credible pro-woman leader. By staking out the pro-choice position and by constructing himself as the supportive spouse of an empowered and articulate woman and the loving father of an intelligent and independent daughter, Clinton cloaked himself in feminized images and thereby gained the political cover he needed to pursue the antiwelfare and antiegalitarian aspects of his agenda. When his health care initiative seemed destined for failure, it was Hillary Rodham Clinton who took the largest share of the blame. Throughout the health care debate, it was Hillary who became the masculine and aggressive "policy wonk," while Bill remained the master of the compassionate personal narrative. When rumors about his adultery began to circulate during the 1992 campaign and the most sordid details of his sexual encounters with Lewinsky became public in 1998, Hillary proved to be his most valuable asset as she came to his defense and "saved" their marriage.[8]

Sexual Management beyond the "First Marriage": The Role of Clinton's Staff While the "first marriage" operated as the president's most important symbolic counterweight to the sex scandals, the official record reveals that it was his staff who attempted to come between Clinton and ruinous sexual "excess" on the mundane, behind-the-scenes level. The Starr report includes a full transcript of Lewinsky's testimony before the grand jury on August 6 and 20, 1998. Lewinsky also gave a deposition before the independent counsel on August 26, 1998. From these documents, we can get a glimpse of not only Lewinsky's version of her affair with Clinton, but her remarkably consistent account of the activities of the White House staff as well.

In July 1995, Lewinsky began an internship in the correspondence division of Chief of Staff Leon Panetta's office in the Old Executive Office Building in the White House complex. She saw Clinton at various public functions and began to flirt with him. On November 15, 1995, they had their first private meeting and sexual encounter. It is significant that their affair began exactly at that time. The first day of the fiscal year in the U.S. budget is October 1. Under the 1985 Gramm-Rudman-Hollings Act and other laws passed in 1987 and 1990, the budget process begins with a meeting of the president and his director of the Office of Management and Budget (OMB) and the congressional leaders. Together, they establish agreements about spending and taxation that become more or less binding with respect to the rest of the budget process. Although the OMB now largely imposes broadly defined goals for the various appropriations, it is still entirely possible that intense contestation will take place between the president and Congress over budgetary matters. This is especially likely where a divided government exists, that is, where the president and the congressional majorities represent different parties.

In the standard budgetary process, the congressional leaders, having met with the OMB and the president and having received the president's budget, guide their budget resolutions through the appropriate authorizing and budget committees. The different budget resolutions from the Senate and the House are merged into a single budget reconciliation bill. Generally, the latter is passed by both bodies by midsummer. At this point, the president can use his veto power to reject the congressional budget and its accompanying appropriations bills. A two-thirds vote in both bodies is required to override the veto. On October 1, either the fiscal year begins and the budget is implemented, or, if a final agreement has not yet been reached, the beginning of the fiscal year is postponed. In the second situation, government funding is usually sustained through the passage of continuing resolutions until the president and Congress can reach a final budget agreement.

Newt Gingrich, the Republican speaker of the House, was at the height of his popularity in 1995. His neoconservative "Contract with America" seemed unassailable. By contrast, Clinton had failed to move his promised health care reform program even to a preliminary legislation phase. Congressional Republicans won majorities in both chambers of Congress in 1994 and continued to dominate national politics. Clinton's approval ratings sagged and he had to insist on the continuing relevance of his office.

Situated in this particular political environment, the 1996 budget was subject to tremendous antagonism and delay. There was a great deal of hostility between the Republican congressional leaders and the White House, such that the OMB could not wield its normal consensus-building powers. Clinton decided that he could not accept the congressional budget and therefore vetoed the appropriations bills. (The line-item veto became available to the president only in 1996.) Because the Republicans could not muster a two-thirds vote in both bodies, a stalemate ensued. The failure of the appropriations bills meant that the entire government machinery ground to a halt. Offices were closed and civil service employees were placed on "furlough," sent home without pay for an indefinite period. The federal government was literally shut down between November 14 and 20, 1995.

Essential employees were the only staff members who were allowed to continue working during the furlough. The White House staff of 430 people was reduced to ninety for the duration.[9] A special atmosphere must have prevailed in the White House in these conditions. Clinton had embarked on an enormously risky path: he would win the stalemate only if public opinion turned against the Republicans for having shut down the government. If that happened, he would emerge as the senior statesman who had rescued the country from Gingrich's brinkmanship. For historical reasons, Clinton's gamble was a long shot at best. In our current post–September 11, 2001 conditions, public opinion about the government—including popular support for the police and firefighters, but also voters' approval for large-scale bailouts of the airline industry—is shifting in a positive direction. During the fall of 1995, however, the government was overwhelmingly constructed in public discourse as a sprawling and self-serving monstrosity that fed corruption and wasted the taxpayers' money.

Clinton's gamble ultimately did pay off, and the showdown with the Republicans helped him to triumph over Dole the following year. In mid-November 1995, however, no one could have predicted this outcome with confidence; things easily could have gone the other way. Although Clinton himself may have actually preferred the excitement of this moment to the days when he had been forced to watch Gingrich's dizzying ascent from the sidelines, it was a dangerous time. Clinton's aides and cabinet members closed ranks and stood by their leader in the midst of great uncertainty. Meanwhile, the egalitarian effects of the disaster-time culture that prevailed in the White House were quite substantial. Unpaid interns were not only instantly promoted as they were asked to perform the tasks of the absent salaried administrative assistants; they also found themselves working shoulder-to-shoulder with heretofore remote senior officials.

Lewinsky, who normally worked during her internship in the Old Executive Office Building, reported in her testimony that during the furlough, she was assigned to answer phones in Panetta's West Wing office in the White House [730–31] (25–26).[10] Given her subsequent actions, it is highly ironic that Lewinsky was in Panetta's White House office at the time. Clinton's first chief of staff, Thomas "Mack" McLarty, ran what presidential experts regard as a fairly loose operation. After several errors, coordination failures, and scandals involving the firing of the Travel Office staff and the use of FBI files, Clinton replaced McLarty with Panetta in July 1994. One of the hallmarks of Panetta's leadership was a much more restrictive space and time management style where access to the Oval Office was concerned. The list of aides and advisors who could easily meet with the president was shortened; fewer meetings with the president were scheduled and small groups of people attended each meeting. Increased focus was brought to the president's daily considerations; an issue had to be studied and analyzed before it could be raised with him. Investigative journalist and presidential specialist Elizabeth Drew noted the effects of Panetta's controlled environment: "Walk-in privileges to the Oval Office were drastically reduced; not even his national security advisor, his legal counsel or his confidant [George] Stephanopoulos [senior advisor for policy and strategy] could get to the president except through Panetta. No decision papers went directly to the president; even those from the National Security Council went first through Panetta's review. No longer were policy decisions made by seminar. And perhaps most significantly, hierarchy and clear lines of authority and responsibility were established."[11]

For all of Panetta's efforts, the furlough disrupted everything. Lewinsky found herself placed in a highly favorable position to pursue the president. In her testimony, she stated that her relationship with him changed from flirtation in public settings to sexual interaction in a secluded workplace environment on November 15, 1995. Associate Independent Counsel Karin Immergut questioned Lewinsky about the transition:

Q. I wanted you to explain sort of how it came about.
A. It was during the furlough. I was up in Mr. Panetta's West Wing office answering phones. The President came down several times during the day. There was continued flirtation and around 8:00 in the evening or so I was in the hallway going to the restroom, passing Mr. Stephanopoulos' office, and he [Clinton] was in the hall and invited me into Mr. Stephanopoulos' office and then from there invited me back into his study. [730–31] (25–26)

It is at this point that Clinton and Lewinsky had their first private meeting. Although their actual interaction is rather brief, they acknowledged their mutual attraction and kissed for the first time. Later that evening, around 10, Clinton went into Panetta's office and invited Lewinsky to meet him five minutes later in Stephanopoulos's office. From there, they went into Clinton's back study, where they could be alone. They kissed, and Lewinsky performed oral sex on Clinton.

The furlough conditions also provided the opportunity for their next encounter.

Q. When was the next time?

A. On the 17th of November.

Q. And could you explain how that contact occurred?

A. We were again working late because it was during the furlough and Jennifer Palmeri [special assistant to the chief of staff] and I, who was Mr. Panetta's assistant [*sic*], had ordered pizza along with Ms. Currie [personal secretary to the president] and Ms. Hernreich [deputy assistant to the president and director of Oval Office Operations].

And when the pizza came, I went down to let them know that the pizza was there and it [was] at that point when I walked into Ms. Currie's office that the President was standing there with some other people discussing something. And they all came back down to the office and Mr.—I think it was Mr. Toiv [deputy White House press secretary], somebody accidentally knocked pizza on my jacket, so I went down to use the restroom to wash it off and as I was coming out of the restroom, the President was standing in Ms. Currie's doorway and said, "You can come out this way." So we went into his back study area, actually, I think, in the bathroom or in the hallway right near the bathroom, and we were intimate.

At that point they kissed.

Q. And how did that encounter end?

A. I said I needed to [go] back and he said, "Well, why don't you bring me some pizza?" So I asked him if he wanted vegetable or meat.

Lewinsky brought some pizza to the Oval Office area.

Q. Could you describe what happened when you returned?

A. Yes. I went back to Ms. Currie's office and told her the President had asked me to bring him some pizza.

She opened the door and said, "Sir, the girl's here with the pizza." He told me to come in. Ms. Currie went back into her office and then we went into the back study area again. [734–36] (29–31)

The pretext worked. Clinton and Lewinsky gained private time together and were able to have another sexual encounter. Again, Lewinsky's remarkable access to the president arises directly out of the government crisis situation. A complete unknown at the bottom of the White House hierarchy, Lewinsky suddenly found herself answering phones for the president's chief of staff and ordering a pizza with his assistant, the president's personal secretary, and a presidential assistant. Then Lewinsky had a legitimate reason to approach the Oval Office: she needed to tell Currie and Hernreich that the pizza had arrived. Up until the furlough, Lewinsky had to admire the president from afar as she stood with the rest of the interns in rope lines and reception crowds. In November 1995, however, she found herself sharing "study break" snacks with the president's closest personnel and moving with full authorization through the hallways and outer offices next to the Oval Office.

Lewinsky had previously applied for a paid staff position in the White House. She accepted a job offer for a position in the correspondence division of the Legislative Affairs Office at the White House on November 13, 1995. She continued to work as an intern for two weeks and then took up her staff appointment on November 26. On several subsequent occasions, she followed strategies for meeting with Clinton that they had clearly worked out together. Sometimes she would create a pretext for meeting with him in the Oval Office by carrying folders that she described to others as papers for him. At other times, they would either set up meetings by telephone or Clinton would invite her into the Oval Office after meeting her "accidentally" in another White House office or hallway.

At several points in her testimony, Lewinsky indicates that when she visited Clinton at the White House, he always escorted her out of the Oval Office—a room with large, uncovered windows—to the back study, the adjoining bathroom, and the rear hallway for their sexual encounters. Immergut questioned Lewinsky on Clinton's choice of locations for their sex acts:

Q. Why did you choose the hallway?
A. Because I believe it was—it was really more the President choosing the hallway, I think, and it was—there weren't any windows there. It was the most secluded of all the places in the back office. Well, that's not true. The bathroom is the most secluded, I guess, because you can close the door.
Q. And did you sometimes have sexual encounters in the bathroom?
A. Mm-hmm. . . .
Q. Okay. Did you notice whether doors were closed when you were physically intimate with him in the back study or hallway?
A. No, he always—well, I'm not sure about the door going in the dining room but I know that the door leading from the back hallway to the—into the Oval Office was always kept ajar so that he could hear if someone was coming. [754–56] (49–51)

Lewinsky also related that she would often enter Clinton's study or the Oval Office through one door and exit through another so that the Secret Service guards would not be able to tell how long she had been there.

As a member of the Legislative Affairs staff, Lewinsky was given a "blue pass," which allowed her to enter the hallways surrounding the Oval Office. The added mobility that came with the position was crucial to their affair. In one of her responses, Lewinsky not only details the White House rules that restrict the movements of interns, but indicates that Evelyn Lieberman, deputy chief of staff, had first become suspicious about Lewinsky's behavior while she had been an intern — that is to say, quite early on in her flirtation with Clinton.

A Juror: So that interaction that you had with Evelyn Lieberman was when she was telling you what?
The Witness: She stopped me in the hall and she asked me where I worked, in which office I worked, and I told her Legislative Affairs in the East Wing.
And she said, "You're always trafficking up this area." You know, you're not supposed to be here. Interns aren't allowed to go past the Oval Office. . . .
I went back to Evelyn Lieberman, to Ms. Lieberman, and I—I said, "You know, I just wanted to clarify with you that I work here, I'm not an intern. So, you know, I am allowed to go past the Oval Office." I don't think I said that, but I had a blue pass. And she looked at me and said, "They hired you?" And I was startled and then she said, "Oh well, I think I mistook you for someone else or some other girl with dark hair who keeps trafficking up the area." [1066–67] (265–66)

Lieberman's suspicions clearly became the basis for further steps that were taken to protect Clinton from scandal. Lewinsky was stopped only once by Clinton's Secret Service agents. This occurred on April 7, 1996, during an important turning point in their affair.

A Juror: Ms. Lewinsky, I wondered if you ever had any trouble with the Secret Service in trying to be near the President.
The Witness: No. The only time that I remember was when I went to see him on the last time in '96, I guess it was April 7th, Easter. And when John Muskett [Secret Service uniformed officer] was outside and he said he was going to check with Evelyn [Lieberman] if I could go in and then I don't remember exactly how it happened, but I sort of—I don't remember the exact discussion, but it ended up he ended up not talking to Evelyn and I went in. [1098] (297)

Lewinsky had in fact been fired from her staff position on April 5, 1996 and had been transferred to a position in the Pentagon. The Starr report evidence includes an October 16, 1996 memo written by a staff member in the White House named John that was addressed to Lieberman. (John could be John Hilley, an assistant to the president, director of legislative affairs, and Lewinsky's supervisor.) John had had a meeting with Lieberman the previous day in which she had made several suggestions for improving the management of his office. In the memo, he details changes that he had already made during the earlier months of 1996 with respect to White House personnel. John states, "I've also enclosed a brief memo on our correspondence operation. It was in bad shape when I came in. We got rid of Monica and Jossie not only because of 'extracurricular activities' but because they couldn't do the job" [2828] (710).

In her testimony before the grand jury, Lewinsky described an April 7, 1996 telephone call with Clinton in which she informed him that she had lost her position in the White House. According to Lewinsky, Clinton was not only upset that she had been transferred, but saw her transfer as a deliberate attempt on the part of his aides to protect him from scandal. In Lewinsky's account, Clinton acts as if he had not been consulted about her transfer to the Pentagon: "I told him that my last day was Monday. And he was—he seemed really upset and sort of asked me to tell him what had happened" [782] (77).

Lewinsky arranged to meet with Clinton at the White House, using the pass that she possessed as a member of the Legislative Affairs staff to gain entry to the Oval Office. Associate Independent Counsel Michael Emmick's line of questioning appears to have been designed to bring to light any special favors with respect to employment that Lewinsky subsequently received from Clinton. Lewinsky's answers, however, portray not a manipulative schemer, but the actions of a man trapped between his interest in pursuing a sexual relationship and the interest of his politically savvy staff. The romantic gloss that Lewinsky's account expresses—Clinton emerges as a heroic David promising to battle against the Goliath of his staff to make room for their relationship—may of course be a product of Lewinsky's fantasy that was not shared by Clinton himself. Indeed, because he never responded directly to detailed questions about their encounters, we will probably never know exactly how he felt about the whole situation. But on the question of mutual consent, the evidence is simply overwhelming.

Q. What I am going to ask you about . . . was your discussions with the President about the termination and about what the future would hold for you.
A. He told me that he thought that my being transferred had something

to do with him and that he was upset. He said, "Why do they have to take you away from me? I trust you." And then he told me—he looked at me and he said, "I promise you if I win in November [1996] I'll bring you back like that." [783] (78)

Lewinsky then had a telephone conversation with Clinton on the following Friday, April 12, 1996.

Q. Tell us about what the two of you talked about.
A. He told me that he had asked Nancy [Hernreich] and Marsha Scott [deputy director of personnel] to find out why I had been transferred, and that he had learned that Evelyn Lieberman had sort of spearheaded the transfer, and that she thought he was paying too much attention to me and I was paying too much attention to him and that she didn't necessarily care what happened after the election but everyone needed to be careful before the election. [784–85] (79–80)

Lewinsky signed an immunity agreement with the Office of the Independent Counsel on July 28, 1998. According to her handwritten notes for her oral proffer agreement, she states that when she informed Clinton about her transfer, he indicated to her that

Evelyn Lieberman spearheaded the transfer because she felt that the President paid to much attention to me and vice versa. Ms Lieberman told the Pres. that she didn't care who worked there *after* the election, but they needed to be careful until then [emphasis in the original].
     After the election, Ms. Lewinsky asked the Pres. to bring her back to the WH. In the following months, Mr. Clinton told Ms. Lewinsky that Bob Nash [assistant to the president and director of presidential personnel] was handling it and then Marsha Scott became the contact person. Ms. L. met with Ms. Scott twice. In the second meeting, Ms. Scott told Ms. L. she would detail her from the Pentagon to her (Ms. Scott's) office, so people could see Ms. L.'s good work and stop referring to her as "The Stalker." Ms. Scott told Ms. L. they had to be careful and protect the Pres. Ms. Scott later rescinded her offer to detail Ms. Lewinsky to her office. [709–10] (6–7)

Lewinsky returned to these details in her testimony, stating that in early 1997, Nash and Scott were assigned the task of considering Lewinsky for a position in the White House but ultimately did not follow through.

Beginning in April 1996, there was a break in the interactions between Clinton and Lewinsky. Either Clinton followed the wishes of his staff and chose not to pursue Lewinsky, or the politically sensitive efforts of his staff prevailed. In any event, Lewinsky did not see

Clinton again until late February 1997, well after his 1996 reelection. She clearly made an attempt to see him at this time. The Starr evidence includes a February 24, 1997 memo from Currie to Clinton entitled "Items of Interest." It includes only two sentences: "Monica Lewinsky stopped by. Do you want me to call her?" [3162] (711).

Lewinsky testified before the grand jury that she was called to the White House by Currie to attend Clinton's weekly radio address and to collect her Christmas presents from him on February 28, 1997. As is already well-known, Currie was the intermediary between Lewinsky and Clinton when their affair resumed, for Lewinsky had been transferred to the Pentagon and Clinton's aides had clearly developed concerns about their interaction. In Lewinsky's terms, "Betty always needed to be the one to clear me in so that, you know, I could always say that I was coming to see Betty" [775] (70). Having a meeting with Currie as a cover story was especially crucial because, according to Lewinsky's testimony, a member of Clinton's staff kept a list of his visitors and circulated it to the rest of his staff [1061] (260). Currie not only ferried messages back and forth between them; she also told Lewinsky when Clinton's aides would be absent from their posts in the White House. According to Lewinsky, for example, Currie let her know that Hernreich had yoga classes on Tuesday nights [778] (73).

Lewinsky indicated in her testimony that the concerns of Clinton's aides had not dissipated as a result of his reelection. Stephen Goodin, an aide to the president, saw Lewinsky waiting in Currie's office after the radio address on February 28, 1997. He immediately convened an unscheduled meeting in the Oval Office with Currie and Clinton. According to Lewinsky, she later learned from other White House staff that Goodin had told Currie and Clinton that they could not allow Lewinsky to be alone with the president at any time. After Goodin left the Oval Office, Currie did accompany Lewinsky and the three of them entered the president's back office. However, either sympathizing with Lewinsky or refusing to accept chaperon duties as part of her employment contract, Currie only partly implemented the Goodin plan, and Clinton and Lewinsky were able to begin what ultimately became the last phase of their sexual interactions. Immergut questioned Lewinsky on this point.

Q. Okay. And why did Betty come in the back office with you?
A. I later found out that—I believe it was Stephen Goodin who said to Ms. Currie and the President that the President couldn't be alone with me, so Ms. Currie came back into the back office with me.

Q. And then what?
A. And then left. [750–51] (45–46)

Questioned later by Emmick, Lewinsky reaffirmed that just prior to her meeting with the president that day, she had seen Goodin, Clinton, and Currie go into the Oval Office together. A few weeks later, she learned that Goodin had stated to Currie and Clinton at that time that "she [Lewinsky] can't be alone with him [Clinton]" [766–67] (61–62).

Emmick also pursued a line of questioning about Lewinsky's ability to evade Clinton's aides.

Q. Where are the aides at the time you are having your encounters, if we can call them that, with the President?
A. Most of the time they weren't—they weren't there. They weren't at the White House.
Q. And how was that arranged?
A. When I was working in Legislative Affairs [in the White House], I don't think—I don't know if it was ever verbally spoken but it was understood between the President and myself that most of the—most people weren't in on the weekends so there was—it would be safer to do that then. And then after I left the White House, that was sort of always a concern that Betty and I had just because she knew and I knew that a lot of people there didn't like me. [767] (62).

Emmick brought Lewinsky back to the same theme at a later point.

Q. Any discussion with the President about trying to make sure that there are fewer people around when you were to visit?
A. When I worked in Legislative Affairs, I think that was sort of the understanding that the weekend was the—there weren't a lot of people around. And there were times when I think that the President might have said, oh, there are too many people here because there was some big issue or some big event happening maybe. [778] (73)

Clinton as a Sexual Subject: Maiden in the Tower or Shame-ridden Fetishist? It goes without saying that every president of the United States enjoys the protection of one of the most tightly controlled security systems in the world. We need only refer to the measures that were taken by the Secret Service to protect President George W. Bush and Vice President Dick Cheney on September 11, 2001 to establish this point. Space and time management for the Clinton administration had in fact been intensified before the Clinton-Lewinsky affair began. The errors incurred under the McLarty regime had been extremely costly. Though it is true that the Clinton-Lewinsky affair occurred on Panetta's watch, it is possible that his enhanced management style saved Clinton from even worse disasters.

It should also be noted that during his first term, Clinton had to deal with much more than the issues of the day. He also had to prepare to fight what became, at that time, the most expensive electoral campaign in U.S. history. Before the 1990s, politicians typically shifted between distinct campaign and legislative phases in more or less regular political cycles. Given the fact that a presidential contender in the 1990s had to raise hundred of millions of dollars every year for his own campaign funds and his party's "soft money" funds, political campaigns became permanent and almost all-encompassing phenomena. Virtually every minute and every public gesture by the candidate counts. Election experts estimate that a record amount of $1.6 billion was raised and spent on the 1996 election; $800 million was spent on the presidential election alone, a figure that is three times greater than the 1992 spending level.[12] It makes sense, then, that Clinton is constructed in the official record as a prized race horse whose movements had to be scripted down to the smallest detail by his handlers.

There is also little evidence that Clinton shared Lewinsky's romantic view of their interactions. Lewinsky clearly saw herself during the affair as a heroine who was rescuing her lover from imprisonment — that is, Clinton's containment within the spatial and temporal rules imposed by his office — by using her erotic energy. She may have regarded Clinton as if he were a David locked in a battle with a Goliath-like staff for his personal freedom, but she constructed a different narrative where her relationship with him was concerned. In her discourse, he takes on the role of the powerless maiden locked in the tower and she becomes the heroic knight valiantly sacrificing personal gain in an all-encompassing struggle to liberate the trapped lover.

It appears that the idea that Clinton would eventually leave his wife and form a lasting partnership with Lewinsky was entirely the product of her own imagination. It is nevertheless plausible that Clinton did in fact see himself as torn between his sexual desire and his political ambitions. He may indeed have regarded his staff as denying him gratification when they fired Lewinsky; he may have even complained to her in a plaintive voice, "Why do they have to take you away from me?" But we also have to consider the possibility that Lewinsky's testimony suppresses the logic of desire that was at work in this scenario. In her account, the furtive nature of their encounters was a faute de mieux, a secretive arrangement that would always be second-best because it meant that their interactions had to remain brief sexual encounters in the Oval Office. True, the political costs were enormous for a Democratic president having any sort of extramarital affair in the era of the "Contract with America" family values. We should note, however, that other presidents have had little difficulty accommodating their extramarital affairs.

Three factors made Clinton's pursuit of sexual gratification especially dangerous. First, his particular fetish was not extramarital heterosexual intercourse with a long-term partner or sex with a trustworthy sex trade worker in a non-work-related private place; it was casual sex with women who were workplace subordinates in a workplace environment. Second, the evidence suggests that Clinton was not at peace with himself about his fetishistic interests. As we already well know from campaigns to promote safer sex where transmission of the HIV virus is concerned, shame can be deadly, for the only individuals who take precautions are the ones who can affirm their sexual interests in advance. The closeted married man stopping for sex with a male stranger in a public bathroom at the mall or in a rest area off the interstate highway is probably less likely to be carrying a condom than the "out" gay man cruising the bars. Similarly, Clinton's own sense of shame must have made it more difficult than it need have been for him to create a viable opportunity for the pursuit of his sexual interests. Third, it is perhaps the case that Clinton actually enjoyed taking the risk that he would be caught in the act. We know that he finds political risk taking peculiarly exhilarating and that he certainly did not experience any difficulties achieving an aroused state during his interactions with Lewinsky—some of which occurred just out of the sight and beyond the earshot of his aides.

Taking these factors together, it makes sense that Clinton did not do what he could have done to save himself from unnecessary scandal. He could have affirmed his fetishistic desires to his wife and closest aides. Then he could have made arrangements to see trustworthy and security-approved sex trade workers on a regular basis in private locations. He could have even asked them to stage casual sex scenes with simulated risk taking. Given his wealth and authority, he certainly would have had access to some of the best prostitutes in the business. And, as long as their contracts were fair and fully honored by their client, there would have been no contradiction between such an arrangement and Clinton's ostensible support for feminist demands.

If Clinton did have an interest in casual sex where the risk of discovery was part of the sexual scene, then Lewinsky's account inverts the situation entirely. She believed that Clinton really loved her and that if his official duties, political ambition, interfering staff, and overbearing wife had not been in the way, the two of them would have gone off together into the sunset. Her romantic discourse is structured by what Foucault calls the "repressive hypothesis," namely, the assumption that prohibition represses genuine desire and that the dismantling of a prohibitionary structure therefore allows for the authentic expression of the self.[13] If Clinton had pursued Lewinsky from the perspective of a risk-taking casual sex fetishist, however, it was precisely the pressure of the office, the possibility of interruption, and even the nearby movements of White House personnel and his spouse that made their sex scenes work for him. The space and time management techniques deployed by his staff become not a policing mechanism that threatened to extinguish romantic love but an erotic backdrop, a virtual sex toy.

The Antifeminist Impact of the Scandal This is one of the elements of the ubiquitous phenomenon of sex in the workplace that rarely receives any attention. Prohibition and taboo do not necessarily threaten the erotic; in some cases, they are the condition of possibility of the erotic. Sex in the workplace—that is, sexual relationships between coworkers and actual flirting and erotic behavior in physical work environments—is therefore inevitable. In the case of the Clinton-Lewinsky relationship, we have substantial evidence that the meeting of the sex partners in the workplace was not accidental or secondary to their connection. Further, it is also possible that even if they had had ample opportunity to leave the workplace and stage their sexual encounters in a private place such as a hotel room, they might not have done so. The kinkiness of Clinton and Lewinsky may not be unique; it is entirely plausible that many people find workplace sex especially gratifying.

What difference does any of this make for feminists? The one virtue of Kenneth Starr's own perverse and fetishistic pursuit of the most minute details about the Clinton-Lewinsky affair is the fact that his report absolutely lays to rest any lingering doubts about their consent. Will the consenting adults dimension of their relationship be remembered as its defining feature? In a sex-negative milieu like the contemporary United States, where erotic practices that fall outside the heterosexual and marital reproduction model are given titillating media coverage and subjected to moral condemnation at the same time, I would say no. This otherwise historical irrelevance will be framed instead by its taboo-breaking dimensions: the publicization of the president's erotic behavior, down to the most minute and sordid details of erections, pizza slices, and stained dresses; the juxtaposition of special symbolic sites connoting great imperial power with mundane orgasms; the cross-generational sex; and the adultery.

Feminists should pay close attention to one symbolic construction of the affair. The Clinton-Lewinsky relationship was never technically constructed as a sexual harassment case. But the affair came to public notice in the context of legal proceedings relating to Paula Jones's sexual harassment lawsuit against Clinton, namely, the written deposition in which Clinton claimed he had not had sexual relations with anyone employed by the federal government since the mid-1980s. And there were other allegations of further sexual misconduct in the workplace that were lodged against Clinton throughout the scandal. The dominant narrative for the Clinton-Lewinsky affair is therefore colored by the more general representation of Clinton as a sexual harasser. He may or may not deserve that particular reputation. For my purposes, the question is: To what extent does the symbolic force of that representation migrate outward from the specific Clinton-Lewinsky relationship such that it begins to define the much more general field of sexual wrongdoing? It is entirely possible that thanks to Clinton's reputation and the workplace character of the Clinton-Lewinsky interaction, this incident of consensual adult sex will begin to operate, in an unacknowledged and yet authoritative manner, as an exemplary sexual harassment case.

The point here is that there is a huge difference between workplace sex and sexual harassment. From a feminist perspective, sexual harassment entails coercion and exploitation. Consensual workplace sex is not necessarily a feminist concern, and feminists should not be co-opted by a conservative attempt to desexualize the workplace. We should take it as a given that our adult coworkers will engage in consensual sex; some of it will be casual, some of it will be romantic. They might slink off to a motel room; they might find new purposes for the broom closet down the hall. We might find this disgusting, embarrassing, annoying, or titillating. But should we feminists remain silent and stand on the sidelines as private corporations, government agencies, and educational institutions rush to adopt policies prohibiting consensual sexual relationships between supervisors and their subordinates and between horizontally situated colleagues? Shouldn't we simply insist that our existing laws prohibiting nonconsensual sex are fully enforced? Shouldn't we just allow consenting adults to muddle through?

Should we allow antidiscrimination law designed to address serious cases of coercion and exploitation to be twisted to serve fundamentally puritanical purposes? What if employers who anticipate sexual trouble on the job end up minimizing their risks by refusing to hire women and gay men?

This is not to say that I take it as given that feminists should embrace an "anything involving consenting adults goes" libertarian attitude. My argument is that I have not seen enough weight given to pro-sex feminist arguments in these policymaking processes. It may very well be the case that in a capitalist society, the workplace deserves to be recognized as a very special social site. Governed as it is by the capitalist wage labor contract, the workplace is, by definition and to its core, a fundamentally hierarchical environment. In a sense, coercive and exploitative relations are always present at work; the concept of free choice when it comes to getting hired or fired, earning wages, seeking a mentor, getting a letter of recommendation, and advancing one's career is already problematic. If keeping my job means that my family will be able to eat nutritious food next month, then can I really step back from a sexual invitation from my supervisor, position myself squarely in an ideal decision-making space in which I can exercise my free will, and make a decision that reflects my best interests? Do I really have access to a genuine exit option that the consent doctrine assumes is present in all consensual erotic encounters between adults? But, on the other hand, is a one-size-fits-all prohibition of sex in the workplace or the university, backed only by the threat of civil suits, the best solution? What about enhancing the collective bargaining rights of workers and students, such that we lessen the degree of their subordination and thereby give them more power to resist all forms of workplace wrongdoing? What if the existing policies require complainants to seek redress in an inherently isolating basis—namely, through the employee complaint and/or civil suit processes, in which the complainant faces the accused as a lone individual, rather than as a member of a union—and therefore leave the fundamental workplace hierarchies intact? And what if we start out with genuine concerns about women's rights in the workplace, but we lose control of the policy, such that we end up giving ammunition to the antisex conservatives as they launch yet another sexual witch-hunt? It seems to me that we have not even begun to address this issue from a feminist perspective.

The problem for feminists is that Clinton has been depicted not only as a proven liar, but as our quintessential Sexual Harasser, and that the repulsive nature of our Sexual Harasser in Chief has been amplified by antisex value judgments about "tackiness," "kinkiness," marital infidelity, and "immoral" behavior. Since when did we feminists agree to defend the institution of marriage against adultery? Since when did we sign up for hall monitorships? We never liked etiquette codes, we never promised to be "good girls" and "polite ladies," and we certainly should not give these new workplace rules on sexual conduct the benefit of the doubt. But who would want to stand up for a Clinton-like colleague or, for that matter, a Lewinsky-like subordinate, now that we have all consumed the Starr report's "disgusting" details? Attitudes toward sex in the workplace are shaped not only by specific legal findings and individual experiences; they are also constructed with reference to background sexual values emerging out of a wide range of sex-negative sociocultural phenomena: the AIDS crisis, the increasing failure of the traditional patriarchal heterosexual family, the rise of the religious right, and so on. The danger, then, lies at the symbolic level in which policy issues are often framed. It is entirely possible that the Clinton-Lewinsky scandal has helped conservative forces to close down the space for feminist debate on sexual harassment and sexual politics. Unless we maintain our distinct position, feminist opposition to sexual harassment will be interpreted by the moralistic right as simply one more contribution to the patriarchal campaign to protect traditional heterosexual marriage and to restrict legitimate sexual practice to the monogamous, heterosexual, reproductive, private, and marital bedroom.

Consistency was never one of Clinton's virtues, especially where ethical questions are concerned. We need not embrace the reactionary idea that marital fidelity is a prerequisite for public office to acknowledge that one of Clinton's most serious failures to conduct himself in a consistent and honest manner does in fact revolve around marriage. Monogamous patriarchal heterosexual marriage is currently being widely promoted in the United States by policy experts, politicians, religious leaders, and right- and left-wing communitarians alike as a solution to poverty and to antisocial behavior among the "underclass." Clinton, the very same leader who signed the key piece of pro-marriage welfare law, the Personal Responsibility Act (1996),[14] decried the "national epidemic" of teen pregnancy on numerous occasions, and approved the Republican Congress's antilesbian and -gay Defense of Marriage Act (1996), was not only a notorious philanderer, but was himself in a situation in which his marriage was being used as a strategy to keep him in line and out of trouble. And when we consider the actual policies of the Clinton administration, it is also highly ironic that this president claimed that his right to privacy was violated by the independent counsel's investigation,[15] for his welfare and antiterrorism policies have received very poor marks from human rights experts.[16] Of course, consistency is no virtue when it produces a right-wing result. During the 2000 presidential campaign, the leading contenders tried to outdo each other by trumpeting their "personal character," showcasing their support for "faith-based" institutions, proclaiming their "family values" credentials, and reducing women to the role of adoring and submissive wives. It is clear that the Clinton-Lewinsky scandal will cast an antifeminist shadow on U.S. political discourse for years to come.

Notes

I want to acknowledge the importance of the work of Zillah Eisenstein and Katha Pollitt with respect to the development of this essay. Many of my arguments were presented in a paper that I delivered at the "Democracy-Sexuality-Citizenship" Conference in Berlin on 9 October 1998; my thanks to Sabine Hark and the Heinrich Böll Foundation for their support. Thanks also to Gwen Wilkinson for her suggestions for the later revisions.

1 This is not to say that I unequivocally endorse the "hostile environment" doctrine, especially as it is being interpreted in same-sex sexual harassment cases and cases in which students complain that they were "harassed" by their feminist or queer instructors when the latter exposed them to sexually explicit material in the classroom. Feminists certainly need to hold extensive debates about these matters. I agree, for example, with many of the concerns expressed by Janet Halley with respect to *Oncale v. Sundowner* (83 F. 3d 118, 119–120 5th Cir. 1996; Janet Halley, lecture, Cornell University, 18 October 2001). In the end, the best feminist course might be to endorse a very narrowly designed policy that prohibits quid pro quo demands for sexual favors, while ensuring at the same time that existing criminal law prohibiting unwanted sexual behavior is aggressively applied to the workplace and educational institutions. The hostile environment doctrine is so vague and formal that it may constitute a serious threat to feminist speech as a result of conservatives' appropriations. Further, feminists should also work to safeguard the due process rights of the accused. This is true not only because a policy that fails to do so would be unjust, but also because when the accused is not treated fairly, she or he can become a cause célèbre for the antifeminist right, such that the entire concept of prohibiting discriminatory behavior in the workplace is brought into

disrepute. In my view, we more or less succeeded at Cornell University in meeting the specifically feminist challenge of ensuring due process in our sexual harassment policy. We did, however, leave the hostile environment language intact. Even though administrative concerns about employer/educator liability would have trumped our arguments about these matters, I do think we missed an opportunity for debate. See http://www.univco.cornell.edu/policy/SH.html.

2 As child labor has been banned in the United States and sexual harassment laws apply exclusively to the workplace, the relevant legislation and court decisions on sexual harassment anticipate an exclusively adult class of complainants.

3 See, for example, Jeffrey Weeks, *Sex, Politics and Society: The Regulation of Sexuality Since 1800* (New York: Longman, 1981).

4 Katha Pollitt, "We Were Wrong: Why I'm Not Voting for Clinton," *The Nation*, 7 October 1996, 9.

5 Barbara Ehrenreich, "Frances Fox Piven," *The Progressive* (November 1996): 34.

6 Pollitt, "We Were Wrong," 9.

7 Zillah Eisenstein, *Global Obscenities: Patriarchy, Capitalism and the Lure of Cyberfantasy* (New York: New York University Press, 1998), 63–65.

8 Ibid., 58.

9 Office of the Independent Counsel, *The Starr Report: The Independent Counsel's Complete Report to Congress on the Investigation of President Clinton* (New York: Simon and Schuster, 1998), 70–71.

10 *The Starr Evidence: The Complete Text of the Grand Jury Testimony of President Clinton and Monica Lewinsky* (New York: Public Affairs, 1998). Pagination from the original copy of the testimony and supporting documents as submitted by the Office of the Independent Council, 9 September 1998, and released by the U.S. Congress, 21 September 1998, is given in square brackets; pagination from the unabridged Public Affairs edition of the testimony is given in parentheses.

11 Elizabeth Drew, quoted in Theodore Lowi and Benjamin Ginsberg, *American Government: Freedom and Power* (New York: Norton, 1998), 247.

12 "Money Votes," editorial, *The Nation*, 11 November 1996, 2.

13 Michel Foucault, *The History of Sexuality*, vol. 1 (New York: Vintage, 1980).

14 On the relationship between welfare "reform" and the reduction of poor women's right to privacy, see Gwendolyn Mink, *Welfare's End* (Ithaca: Cornell University Press, 1998) and Anna Marie Smith, "The Sexual Regulation Dimension of Contemporary Welfare Reform: A Fifty State Overview," *Michigan Journal of Gender and Law* 8.2 (2002): 121–218.

15 See the following passages of Clinton's testimony before the grand jury on 17 August 1998: [477] (467), [529–30] (519–20), [545] (535), [553–54] (543–44), [559] (549), [599] (589).
16 Human rights activists have criticized Clinton for signing the 1996 anti-terrorism law that bans any person resident in the United States, citizens and aliens alike, from supporting the activities of a "foreign terrorist organization." The law also grants the secretary of state the power to determine which organizations fit this category based on a vague definition involving the use of violence. The concept of "supporting" such organizations is defined quite broadly; otherwise, lawful advocacy and fundraising activities on behalf of a named organization are now classed as a felony offense punishable by up to ten years in prison. Pro–African National Congress antiapartheid activism could have been criminalized under this law, and yet it leaves the most serious terrorist threats to American social order, such as domestic antiabortion violence and the right-wing militias, completely untouched.

3

Privacy and Publicity, and the Conditions of Democratic Citizenship

Privacy in the (Too Much) Information Age

T he American attitude toward privacy has undergone a dramatic shift in the wake of the Clinton-Lewinsky-Starr scandal. Gone are the days when come-hither thongs winked coyly above waistlines; we've tightened our belts in this chastened nation, as the age of "bring it on" has given way to the era of "too much information." In the early years of the new millennium, the nation finds itself in the throes of a privacy panic, with the American public spooked not by now quaint-seeming tales of ghost sightings or alien landings, but by unrelenting reports of a menacing and ubiquitous "unwanted gaze" looming above every street corner, peering at every credit card transaction, lingering over every mouse click.[1] Recent furors over issues ranging from business monitoring of online browsing to mandatory national ID cards to the protection of personal medical data attest to widespread public skittishness about imperiled privacy rights.

Those who welcome the privacy revival owe a special debt to Judge Kenneth Starr, who perhaps has done more than any other figure in recent history to galvanize Americans in support of privacy—not just as a legal right but as a cultural ethic. Starr's sprawling investigation of former President Clinton's role in the Whitewater land deal, which eventually led to an intensive inquiry into the president's intimate relations with White House intern Monica Lewinsky, sounded a blaring wake-up call to a public mesmerized by the pleasures of publicity culture. In its aftermath, the Starr probe unleashed a torrent of anxiety about dwindling privacy protections: If Starr could do what he did to the president of the United States, who would be next? The vagaries of the Starr probe revealed how little bite the legal right to privacy has in actual practice, a fact made apparent as Starr and his lackeys bulldozed

through Lewinsky's personal life and then stood idly by, first as tantalizing tidbits were leaked to the public and then as Congress took the
highly unusual move of voting to mount Starr's report on the Library
of Congress Web page for all the world to see. Beyond highlighting
the impotence of legal protections for privacy, the Clinton-Lewinsky-
Starr scandal reawakened the public to the importance of privacy as a
social norm. In the midst of the scandal, many found themselves extol-
ling the virtues of neglected notions like discretion and restraint as the
deluge of lurid details about a consensual presidential dalliance sent a
drowning public gasping for relief. It is difficult to say whether popular pleas for the restoration of privacy emanated more in embarrassment for those who were exposed or in horror at ourselves for lapping
up every salacious morsel, but at some point it became clear that the
public was not merely sated, but fed up. Privacy had proven itself no
idle ideal, but a nonnegotiable civic virtue, now widely recognized as
essential for the maintenance of a civilized public sphere.

Privacy Panic Though privacy may be staging a cultural comeback,
there are good reasons to suspect that the privacy revival soon will
prove a passing fad, for today's paeans to privacy mask the persistence
of more deeply rooted societal ambivalences. One need only contem-
plate the stunning success of reality TV programming in recent years,
or the willingness to trade privacy for security after 9/11, to doubt that
faith in privacy as a panacea for all of society's ills will last long. Indeed, what privacy enthusiasts have yet to reckon with is the fact that
the Starr probe did not just elicit anxiety about the loss of privacy; it
also disclosed underlying uncertainty about the meaning, value, and
relevance of privacy in contemporary society. For a time, the Clinton-
Lewinsky-Starr scandal focused public attention on a set of seemingly
trivial questions that proved deceptive in terms of both their significance and complexity: Does talk of the presidential penis belong on
the front page?[2] Should lying about sex be considered a crime like any
other? What difference does character make when it comes to leadership? Is marriage a public or a private institution? In inviting public
confrontation with questions like these, the scandal laid bare the over-
grown thicket of confusion shrouding the long-standing assumption,
deeply rooted in the liberal political culture of the United States, that
the domains of public and private can, and must, be clearly circumscribed.

   Jodi Dean's recent call for "interfacial" analysis at the juncture between political theory and cultural studies suggests the need to explore the dense network of associations and ideologies—the "constellations" of meaning—surrounding the idea of privacy in the political culture of the United States.[3] Privacy has long been a prominent notion in the United States, but little attention has been paid to privacy's myriad and shifting cultural meanings, an inquiry preempted, perhaps, by the assumption that the American fascination with privacy is simply another form of "rights talk."[4] Liberal ideology mitigates against the cultural study of rights, insisting that the function of guaranteed rights is to establish an anchor of stability against the unpredictable forces of both politics and culture. But privacy, like freedom of speech and voting rights, has revealed itself to be one of those fundamental rights that generally is presumed to be absolute and eternal despite a long history that has proven it to be ambiguous and precarious in law and in society.

This is not to deny certain continuities in the cultural connotation of privacy over time. Indeed, one of the most significant though underappreciated points of stability in privacy discourse has been the projection of privacy onto the home, a practice that long predates cultural politics in the United States, extending at least as far back as Aristotle. In this regard, it seems especially appropriate that the White House became the mise-en-scène for a spectacular fin de siècle privacy crisis. Situated at the hazy intersection between the imagined domains of public and private, the White House was the ideal staging ground for acting out privacy's indeterminacy at a moment when home, as well as kindred constructs like domesticity and family, is being reworked to meet the needs, demands, and tastes of today's mediated, technologically enabled citizen-subjects.

Precisely because the cultural status of the home in the United States has changed over time, so too has the meaning of privacy. Simply put, the way the home is figured and configured in the cultural imaginary reveals a great deal about the role and function of privacy in society. In the United States, the home has stood at various times as a symbol of individual liberty, social propriety, and family values, to name just three moments. These notions of home have influenced the legal development of privacy doctrine. Likewise, feminist critiques of the ideology of domesticity have contributed to an understanding of the meaning—and limits—of privacy doctrine. Finally, recent shifts in cultural conceptions of the home create an imperative to move beyond the public/private divide as the governing metaphor for social space. The foregoing analysis suggests that privacy doctrine is less effective and more costly than has generally been acknowledged. In the end, privacy doctrine needs to be not so much reconceived from within as supplemented from without by alternative accounts of the social world.

Privacy's Hidden Meaning One approach to understanding the cultural meaning of privacy is to consider the evolution of privacy doctrine in the law. In the United States, privacy doctrine has never strayed far from the pre-Revolutionary declaration by a Massachusetts jurist that "a man's house is his castle." As a legal matter, the abstract notion of privacy has always taken the home as its primary site of projection. This pattern attests to more than the historically strong association between privacy rights and (private) property rights. As Justice Harlan explained in his 1961 dissent in *Poe v. Ullman*, "Certainly the safeguarding of the home does not follow merely from the sanctity of property rights. The home derives its pre-eminence as the seat of family life."[5] A review of the development of privacy doctrine in the United States suggests that as the social significance of the home and family life has changed, so too have the ends and objectives promoted by privacy.

The U.S. Constitution makes no explicit mention of a right to privacy, but it does identify the home as a place in which citizens are to be accorded special protections against government intrusion. The Third Amendment holds that "No Soldier shall, in time of peace be quartered in any house, without the consent of the owner" and the Fourth Amendment states that "The right of the people to be secure in their persons, houses, papers, and effects, against unreasonable searches and seizures, shall not be violated." These Amendments attest to the way the home, physically and symbolically, was politicized in the pre-Revolutionary era through a pattern of seizure and appropriation by the British. Stephen Holmes explains, "In the seventeenth and eighteenth centuries, to affirm private property was to attack the politics of confiscation."[6] In asserting the inviolability of the home, then, the founding generation declared an opposition to tyranny. The home stood as a threshold, literal and figurative, beyond which government could not pass.

One hundred years after the Constitution was ratified, the home had become a very different sort of battleground, this time a staging ground in a simmering class war. In the high Victorian era, privacy was regarded as a hallmark of refinement, a marker of class status. Noting the "distinctly class-based character" of concerns with privacy at the end of the nineteenth century, legal scholar Randall Bezanson roots the emergence of the modern privacy doctrine in a concern with "the 'problem' of access by the lower classes of society to information about the upper classes."[7] In a society in which status was equated with privacy, gossip posed a fundamental threat to the social order, breaking down the very barriers that defined the distinctions among classes. Against this background, one can understand the crisis precipitated by the marriage of the camera and the printing press, a development that for the first time allowed the mass circulation of revealing images of the shrouded world of upper-class privilege. It was to put an end to these virtual invasions that Samuel Warren and Louis Brandeis penned their famous *Harvard Law Review* piece "The Right to Privacy." First published in 1890, this article is today widely considered not only "the most influential law review article ever written" but the definitive articulation of privacy doctrine in U.S. law. Because Warren and Brandeis's case for judicial recognition of a privacy tort arose from an interest in containing a budding press, it was not surprising to hear throughout the Clinton-Lewinsky-Starr affair frequent references to their landmark treatise, with the implication being that the country had strayed far from the principles they had so ably defended.[8] What is surprising, however, is the fact that Warren and Brandeis's defense of privacy has little to do with an interest in protecting individual rights. In fact, Warren and Brandeis were far more concerned with the maintenance of social order and social hierarchy, goals that depended on the rigorous enforcement of a strict code of public morality. In their article, they denounce the press for crossing "the obvious bounds of propriety and decency," worrying that this development will "destroy at once robustness of thought and delicacy of feeling." They continue, "No enthusiasm can flourish, no generous impulse can survive under its blighting influence." Warning that "each crop of unseemly gossip, thus harvested, becomes the seed of more, and in direct proportion to its circulation, results in the lowering of social standards and of morality," Warren and Brandeis implore the courts to take a stand against the scourge of publicity. Their case for limiting intimate exposures rests not so much on a principled commitment to autonomy or a concern with personal dignity as a desire to limit the kind of gossip-mongering that threatened not just to corrupt public sensibilities but to destroy a social order that relied on privacy to maintain class distinctions.

Things are not so different today. Privacy remains a powerful sym-

The (Too Much) Information Age 217

bol of privilege precisely because the maintenance of privacy requires not just will, but means. Consider the flack during the Clinton presidency when it was discovered that the first family had cultivated an elite cadre of "first hosts," wealthy friends of the president willing to loan out their vacation homes for first family getaways. A front-page story in the *Los Angeles Times* reported in sober terms about the challenges posed for the Secret Service by "the first president in recent memory who has no place of his own to retreat to when he wants a break from official Washington."[9] But the real story came down to this: "Clinton has no real estate at all, not even a *pied-à-terre* in Arkansas. As a consequence, he and his family have turned first guests into a rent free term-of-art." Obliquely recalling the Lincoln Bedroom controversy—a brouhaha eventually eclipsed by the Starr probe—the article stood as a coy reminder that the Lewinsky matter was not the first time President Clinton had been accused of "sleeping around." And in a country notoriously squeamish about talk of social class, it was far easier for Clinton's foes to indict him for philandering than to mock his lowly origins directly. The not-so-subtle tone of disrespect underlying the report played on the easy slippage between disdain for those who sleep around for pleasure and disapproval of those who do so for lack of an alternative. In short, the suggestion was that Clinton prostituted himself to wealthy friends to compensate for his lack of personal resources. Worse still, without a ranch, estate, or family compound of his own to escape to, the president decided to convert the Oval Office into his makeshift love nest. Lacking real estate of his own, then, privacy was a privilege Clinton simply couldn't afford.

It might seem strange to suggest that privacy doctrine serves to further a social agenda, as today the right to privacy is popularly understood to do quite the opposite, that is, to prevent the legislation of morality. In fact, this civil libertarian conception of privacy doctrine is a relatively recent development, taking hold in the 1960s, when the right to privacy was enlarged by the courts to afford protection for certain sorts of controversial activities in the home. The Supreme Court first gave explicit recognition to a constitutional right to privacy in its 1965 ruling *Griswold v. Connecticut*. This case arose from charges filed against the executive director and medical director of a local chapter of Planned Parenthood.[10] Both were charged as accessories to a crime for providing information and dispensing contraceptives to a married couple, actions violating a Connecticut statute outlawing contraceptive use by any individual.[11] The Court held the Connecticut law unconstitutional on the grounds of a recognition of a constitutional right to marital privacy. Declaring that "specific guarantees in the Bill of Rights have penumbras, formed by emanations from those guarantees that help give them life and substance," the Court went on to explain that this shadow extends to the marriage relationship: "We deal with a right to privacy older than the Bill of Rights—older than our political parties, older than our school system. Marriage is a coming together for better or for worse, hopefully enduring, and intimate to the degree of being sacred. It is an association that promotes a way of life, not causes; a harmony in living, not political faiths; a bilateral loyalty, not commercial or social projects. Yet it is an association for as noble a purpose as any involved in our prior decisions." Under any circumstances, such a declaration by high officials of a pluralistic nation would be alarming, but there is a special irony in the Court's delivering such a statement in the course of a decision purporting to be a vindication of privacy rights. The *Griswold* decision exposes the way privacy rights have been gerrymandered by the courts, contoured to protect certain citizens while exposing to public scrutiny others who challenge the moral mainstream. In 1986, the limits of *Griswold*'s conception of privacy were vividly exposed in the case of *Bowers v. Hardwick*. Here, the majority declared that the right to privacy does not imply that "homosexuals" have the right "to engage in acts of sodomy." Returning to the *Griswold* precedent, the Court held that because there is "no connection" between homosexual sodomy and "family marriage or procreation," there is no privacy claim at issue in this case. The *Bowers* decision suggests that the judicial recognition of privacy rights rests on a moral evaluation of the behavior privacy is supposed to shield.[12]

A review of the evolution of privacy doctrine in U.S. law discloses, then, a pernicious tautology at its core: the law exempts from public scrutiny only those acts that have already been scrutinized—and deemed acceptable. It is the same logic Slavoj Žižek describes when he suggests of liberal democracies generally that "our 'freedoms' themselves serve to mask and sustain our deeper unfreedom."[13] The right to privacy is simply the right to do whatever the law says you can do. That is why the right to privacy does not extend to individuals who, for example, wish to consume child pornography in their home or use controlled substances. In recent years, the ranks of the unprotected are growing as privacy rights are being denied not just to those who engage in prohibited activities, but to those deemed members of suspect classes, such as immigrants and high school students.[14] Paradoxically, in U.S. law privacy doctrine has become an instrument used by government to promote socially desirable ways of life, rather than a source of protection for those seeking relief from official coercion.

The Personal *Is* Political Instead of taking the current privacy crisis to signal a need to think critically about both the possibilities and limits of privacy rights, privacy advocates mostly have been on the defensive. In the popular press, a cottage industry of blame now hums along, churning out accusations left and right. On the one hand, Christian fundamentalists have been held culpable for promoting revelation politics, charged with coercing confessions from sinners seeking public office. Others accused of aiding privacy's demise include communitarians of various persuasions whose assault on the culture of individualism has been held responsible for the public's sense of entitlement not just to choose, but to truly know, our leaders. Then there are the media, whose high-brow contingent have been accused of selling out their professional standards, while the mercenary muckrakers of the low-brow wing are derided for peddling private lives for profit. After the Starr probe, however, it is "the feminists" who have emerged as prime suspects in the death of privacy, charged with unleashing the ethic of "the personal as political" on a hapless society. As the Clinton-Lewinsky-Starr scandal wore on, commentators from across the political spectrum increasingly portrayed the affair as an object lesson in the degrading and degenerative consequences of pursuing the The personal is political to its logical extreme. Writing in the *New Republic* during the waning days of the scandal, Peter Beinart opined that The personal is political "has left American politics in shambles," and he implored feminists to begin taking steps down "the difficult road toward a movement that does not degrade politics by turning it into a synonym for life."[15] Succinctly encapsulating the mood of the day, another commentator deemed The personal is political nothing less than a "powerful destroyer of private life."[16] Of course, the Clinton-Lewinsky-Starr scandal was not the first time feminist champions of The personal is political were charged with killing civility in the United States. In an essay appearing some time before the scandal broke, Jean Bethke Elshtain suggested that, with the popularization of The personal is political, "what got asserted was an identity, a collapse of the one into the other. Nothing 'personal' was exempt from political definition, direction, and manipulation—neither sexual intimacy, nor love, nor parenting. A total collapse of public and private as central categories of explanation and evaluation followed. The private sphere fell under a thoroughgoing politicized definition. Everything was grist for a voracious public mill, nothing was exempt, there was nowhere to hide."[17] Throughout the Clinton-Lewinsky-Starr affair, feminism seemed to make an easy mark for a public confronting a destructive scandal that turned on what many felt was fundamentally a family matter, best left at home. But blaming feminists for the Starr fiasco depended on a highly distorted perception of the feminist movement generally, and the meaning of the phrase The personal is political in particular. In popular discourse, feminism has been portrayed as a movement of ball busters (think Hillary Clinton), backstabbers (think Anita Hill), and, of course, home wreckers. Pitting women's liberation against the survival of society itself, antifeminists long have portrayed the struggle to free women from economic dependence, violence, and other forms of oppression in the home as an attack on the American family. This kind of oversimplification obfuscates vast domains of feminist theorizing, among them the voluminous feminist literature centered on the core concept of care, a literature whose very existence it is impossible to reconcile with the popular image of feminism as antifamily.[18] The same is true of the assumption that feminists are uniformly antiprivacy. Recent writings by scholars such as Anita Allen, Jean Cohen, and Patricia Boling defending a revisioned privacy right affirm the existence of lively debate within the movement about the meaning and merits of privacy doctrine today.[19]

The fact that some feminists endorse the principle of privacy might surprise those accustomed to the view that The personal is political is a war cry against privacy. The mistaken assumption of an antithesis between privacy and politicization rests on pervasive misunderstandings about the meaning and implications of The personal is political. Often traced back to a 1969 tract by activist Carol Hanish, the phrase immediately struck a chord with a budding generation of second-wave feminists activated by the recognition of their embeddedness in a dense network of patriarchal power. The slogan redefined reality for a generation of women who began to see themselves as effects of power, rather than passive outsiders to it. Carole Pateman describes the message behind the motto this way: " 'The personal is political' has drawn women's attention to the way in which we are encouraged to see social life in personal terms, as a matter of individual ability or luck in finding a decent man to marry or an appropriate place to live. Feminists have emphasized how personal circumstances are structured by public factors, by laws about rape and abortion, by the status of 'wife,'

The (Too Much) Information Age 221

by policies on child-care and the allocation of welfare benefits and the sexual division of labour in the home and workplace. 'Personal' problems can thus be solved only through political means and political action."[20]

In the years since the phrase was popularized, its underlying meaning has been lost. Instead, the slogan has been subject to opportunistic errors of interpretation that serve more to invalidate feminist perspectives than to promote understanding of the causes and consequences of the oppression of women. In this regard, perhaps the most significant confusion has been wrought by the assumption that The personal is political is prescriptive, when, in fact, the statement is merely descriptive. That is, The personal is political is a call for recognition of the ways the private sphere is ordered by patriarchal and other forms of political power. In this crucial respect, The personal is political departs from the more familiar modality of exhortative sloganeering ("Make love, not war"; "Think globally, act locally"; "Choose life"). The point is not that the personal *should be* political, but that the personal always and already *is* political—whether we like it or not. The critics who assail feminists for "politicizing" the personal and for "making a political issue" of matters properly kept private imply that absent feminist intervention, matters deemed private are not implicated in power. But if the personal is always already political, the only choice one has is whether or not to acknowledge this fact. Politicizing the personal entails merely a recognition, then, not a transformation—although, of course, this recognition may also be an important initial step toward change.

Misconstruing the meaning of The personal is political, many have suggested that sex scandals somehow exemplify an ineluctable telos inherent in the sentiment. In fact, sex scandals, at least of the sort we have been treated to in recent years in the United States, serve virtually the opposite tendency, promoting a radical depoliticization of the public sphere. Sex scandals rivet public attention on the minute details of a tiny cluster of individuals, creating a centrifugal force of obsessive fact finding. This force was evident throughout the Clinton scandal, during which time the public learned a stunning amount about the president's sexual predilections but virtually nothing about the complexities of sexual harassment law, the status of women in the contemporary workplace, or a host of other related issues of political relevance and social import. For early participants in consciousness-raising groups, The personal is political encouraged a shift in focus from complaints about individuals (husbands, bosses) to consideration of social structures and systems (patriarchy, sexism). Perversely, today the notion that The personal is political is most often deployed to achieve the opposite effect, that is, to justify a myopic focus on individual character. In form and content, sex scandals resemble soap operas, avoiding confrontation with big questions like the social status of marriage or the role of ethics in political affairs. But this is what it means to politicize the personal: to use the occasion of revelations about individual transgressions as an entry point for a critical examination of larger social forces at play. Sex scandals as we now know them, then, stand as a rebuke to the very notion of The personal is political, resisting politicization rather than promoting it.[21]

Regrettably, to date, the Clinton-Lewinsky-Starr affair represents as a missed opportunity to move beyond the familiar mode of scandal discourse. In this regard, Clinton himself was pivotal; had he taken The personal is political to heart, the scandal might have unfolded very differently. In considering Clinton's decision to lie when he was first approached by Paula Jones's lawyers, it is not difficult to understand his temptation to be evasive, but even those who believe the legal systems affords inadequate protections to the accused must view Clinton's decision to lie as short-sighted and selfish. His resorting to lying suggests that his sole objective throughout the crisis was to wiggle out of trouble, not to alter a system he believed to be unfair. But what if Clinton instead had sought a solution not only to his own dilemma but also for those who might find themselves in a similar predicament in the future? Had Clinton, for example, told the truth to the investigators but spoken out against a law that affords inadequate protections to the accused, he might have found a footing on the moral high ground. Instead of challenging the law, Clinton pretended to respect it, a pretense that proved impossible to sustain. Still, he hoped that the American people would share his view that, under the circumstances, lying was his best option, as honesty would have been tantamount to political suicide. In retrospect, however, it is clear how self-serving a construction of the situation this interpretation was, for throughout the scandal the public demonstrated a capacity and willingness to forgive that belied Clinton's insistence that telling the truth was not a viable option. Had he taken the tack of making a political issue of a personal affair, he might have turned a personal failure into an opportunity to make a difference for others. Instead, he cheapened the idea of privacy by using it as a cloak for disingenuousness.

Although the productive potential of The personal is political was radically underexploited throughout the Clinton/Lewinsky/Starr affair, its destructive power was vastly overestimated. The personal is political became an ideological scapegoat, distracting attention from the root causes of the excesses of publicity culture. Indeed, when commentators complain about the damage wrought by The personal is political, they usually are more concerned with the ways the personal has become *public*. Too often, a crucial difference between politicization and publicization has been overlooked: whereas the former entails an analysis of power relations, the latter discourages it, trading politics for the numbing comfort of gossip and psychodrama. The conflation of politicization and publicization enables critics to blame feminists for unwelcome cultural shifts, but those seeking to understand the fate of privacy would do well to look elsewhere to understand the forces behind the production of publicity culture. One obvious starting place would be with a consideration of the reigning corporate-cultural complex which has fed the public appetite for publicity with exceptional dedication. For an array of corporate interests, privacy stands in the way of the last frontier for profit seeking: the home. Today, many U.S. homes are subject to a daily seige of circulars, automated telephone pitches, and Web-based solicitations, and it is a remarkable accomplishment that in both law and society these interruptions are more likely to register as nuisance than as trespass. What we see in contemporary society are the effects of corporate-sponsored cultural engineering, whereby it is no longer cool to retreat behind dark shades and forbidding leather: today's hipsters soak up the sun and bask in the glow of the gaze, a shift epitomized by the legions of "real people" who today vie for the privilege of being locked in staged homes or stranded on desert islands while all the world watches their every move.

You Can't Go Home Again Much more lies behind privacy's shifting fortunes in U.S. political culture than a feminist campaign to unsettle normative domesticity. As a social ethic, privacy thrived during the neoconservative 1980s, when mainstream American life seemed for a time to revolve around the pursuit of nest eggs and feathered nests. By the early 1990s, however, privacy seemed poised on the brink of cultural obsolescence: gated communities were out, gateways were in. Suddenly, suburbia hummed with nanny-cams, caller-ID boxes, and high-speed Internet connections, as giddy infatuation with Internet-age values like access and connection sent Americans racing to reconfigure their homes for surfing, shopping, and surveillance. But with the dot-com boom having landed in the dot-compost heap, technologies we once thought of as enabling now just seem invasive. Nonetheless, any effort to return privacy to its exalted status in the cultural imaginary faces unprecedented challenges in the present moment, for it is not at all clear that the idea of privacy is still relevant—or even legible—in an age in which the home has become an outpost of the public sphere while the public sphere increasingly functions as a kind of home away from home. What is the meaning of public and private at a time when one can be both in and out, sitting in front of the home computer while chatting, buying, or just window-shopping? By the same token, with the proliferation of portable devices like cell phones and pagers, it has become possible to be out but also in. In retrospect, *Star Trek's* tantalizingly futuristic vision of instant transport—"Beam me up, Scottie"—didn't go far enough, for who needs travel when we have simultaneity, the technologically enabled capacity to be (at least) two places at once. What is the use, then, of the rhetoric of separate spheres, or more broadly, of social ontology based on metaphors of realms, domains, and divides, now that it is possible to be all over the place without ever leaving the comfort of one's own home?

In the face of these shifts, scholarly attention has been trained on the task of distinguishing the boundary between public and private, a project premised on the uncritical assumption that the public/private divide remains the major axis along which social life should be graphed. Reading the triumph of the private in the ascendance of VCRs over movie theaters, chatrooms over coffee shops, and SUVs over subways, one side in this debate claims that Americans live a radically privatized existence. In another corner are observers who insist that the late twentieth-century middle-American home has been annexed by the outside, reconfigured as just another portal to the 24/7 global marketplace.[22] However, more important than the shifting balance between public and private, I suggest, is the increasing incoherence of the public/private distinction itself. This is not to deny that many experientially and politically meaningful differences exist between, say, a public sphere that is virtual versus one that is physical, nor to dispute the fact that an evening spent in an anonymous chatroom is not the same as an intimate dinner with friends. To be sure, there is still much of value to be gained from further inquiry into the nature and character of private life and public space. Nonetheless, there are powerful indications today of a need to shift maps and to define new coordinates of social space as we seek to understand human experience in the contemporary setting.

In this regard, there has been a general failure to acknowledge, let alone to engage the fact that the current privacy crisis is due not simply to privacy being *taken* away, but to the fact that Americans in ever-increasing numbers are *giving* their privacy away. To some extent, the cultural renunciation of privacy rests on a recognition of a fundamental change in the nature of social life, a shift from a condition of familiarity to one of anonymity. The shift is exemplified by the lightning speed with which the background chatter of people on cell phones has billowed into a white noise tapestry blanketing the public sphere. It is interesting to note that the proliferation of cell phones signals the demise not just of the pay phone, but the phone booth; indeed, I suggest that the obsolescence of the phone booth is a cause, not an effect, of the popularization of cell phones. The purpose of the phone booth, it now appears, was never to shield society from the annoying strains of senseless chatter, for it is abundantly clear today that this is not a high social priority. No, the purpose of the phone booth is to protect the caller's privacy, and this shield is no longer deemed necessary by anonymous subjects, for who cares if you know *my secrets* if you don't know *me*? Though today little remains hidden from public view, we remain largely opaque to those around us. The example of cell phones suggests that the very idea of privacy is premised on the possibility of being known. By a similar logic, perhaps it is only in a confederacy of strangers that the kind of tell-all culture now thriving in the United States can be sustained. Shifts in the social terrain have rendered the idea of a private sphere unnecessary, as anonymity has displaced privacy as the contemporary subject's social shield.

In this anonymous public sphere, there are signs that the public finds privacy not only unnecessary, but undesirable. This is hardly surprising, for how could privacy maintain its appeal in a culture that regards social worth as a function of exposure?

The Social Revolt against Privacy Launched in April 1998, Voyeur-Dorm has become a highly successful X-rated Web site, indistinguishable in many respects from myriad other online pay-per-view porn destinations.[23] The VoyeurDorm site features not so much a dormitory as a mansion, one of those ubiquitous, postmodern communes first popularized on MTV's *The Real World* and now a staple of mainstream television programming. Home to a passel of twelve comely "coeds," VoyeurDorm is equipped with fifty-five strategically placed Web-cams feeding live to the Internet. At first glance, the principle behind VoyeurDorm's profitability seems obvious: it offers thrills to viewers who get off, quite literally, on the violation of privacy. And what better way to induce the titillation of transgression than to stage a virtual peep show inside the sacred space of a "real" home? But the site's free virtual tour makes it clear that there is more to Voyeur-Dorm than first meets the eye. The tour includes a page featuring a photograph of each VoyeurDorm resident, the snapshots accompanied by personal statements. In these statements, the residents share provocative tidbits about their sexual preferences and invite potential customers to have a closer look. But for a site based on the principle of voyeurism, these solicitations seem strangely out of place, undermining the voyeuristic pretense on which the whole site is premised. What happened to the guilty pleasure of stolen glances? Why isn't VoyeurDorm's fantasy space structured around a violation of privacy rather than the performance of consent? One might be tempted to dismiss this breach of pretense as a necessary concession to the reality of selling sex in an inflated sexual economy, one in which being sexy means shedding not just one's clothes but one's inhibitions as well. And though there is certainly something to the idea that sex today has been constructed as just another extreme sport, I suggest that the site's contradictory setup caters to a public whose pleasure depends not just on transgressing privacy, but overcoming it.

Consider first that today's spectator no longer seems in pursuit of a glimpse of the kind of unself-conscious disclosure that once lured the voyeur to the peephole. In the classical sense, voyeurs are seers who seek a way around the problem of what physicists call observation effects: the fact that the act of observing a phenomenon can alter its nature or trajectory. When watched, human beings perform, but what the voyeur craves is a glimpse of the real, a flash of authenticity. However, many of today's voyeurs may understand, at least intuitively, that wherever else the gaze may be, it is at the very least internalized. Thus, sex, like gender and other aspects of identity, is always a performance, even when no one is watching. Why go to the trouble of stealing glances when a good look is offered up for all who care to see?

Beyond the thrill of watching, customers who visit VoyeurDorm also pay to be desired. In a society in which subjectivity increasingly is defined by spectatoring, wanting my gaze is tantamount to wanting me. In soliciting the customer's gaze, VoyeurDorm's denizens act out the possibility of a *wanted* gaze, countering mounting social anxieties about the pervasiveness of the unwanted gaze. In this sense, the women of VoyeurDorm are (role) models, the ideal subjects of a surveillance society: they love to be watched. In the same way, in soliciting the gaze, the residents bring a degree of respectability to voyeurism, shifting the peep from the realm of the surreptitious to the level of any other commercial transaction. In a society that venerates privacy, the spectator is figured as a pervert or a criminal, a positioning subtly reversed by VoyeurDorm and other sites of its ilk. As subjectivity increasingly is defined by the act of watching, one can expect to see more efforts to dignify spectatoring subjectivity.

Not only do VoyeurDorm customers want to be wanted, they also seem to seek assurances that the objects of their gaze are objectively desirable. If there was a time when Peeping Toms took delight in glimpsing the forbidden body, today the hidden body is more likely to raise suspicions—if no one's looking, maybe it's because there's nothing to see. It's the same logical inversion that U.S. youth culture has witnessed around the issue of virginity: where once chastity was seen as a sign of personal restraint, now it is as likely to be read as evidence of undesirability. For what is privacy today but the consolation prize for those whom no one cares to watch? Far from cheapening its product, then, VoyeurDorm's motto "Everyone's Watching!" reassures potential customers that this is the place to be.

Finally, it is interesting to consider that while VoyeurDorm is not a home in the traditional sense, but it has recently been declared a home in the legal sense. This designation was hard-won in court, after the city of Tampa attempted to shut down the building that houses Voyeur-Dorm under an ordinance that bans adult businesses from operating in residential areas. Ultimately, VoyeurDorm was allowed to remain, on the grounds that, as a cyber-business, the doings of its residents had no impact whatsoever on the surrounding neighborhood. Though the legal status of VoyeurDorm has been resolved, its social status remains unclear. VoyeurDorm is, I suggest, emblematic of the challenge facing privacy advocates today: to redeem an ideal in a world that can no longer be so easily parsed into tidy domains of public and private.

Beyond Privacy The point of the above is not to argue for abandoning the public/private distinction, nor is it to deny a certain usefulness to invocations of a right to privacy. On a variety of fronts, from the campaign to protect reproductive rights to the effort to halt the expansion of state and private sector surveillance in the post-9/11 era, the notion of privacy has obvious strategic value. Nonetheless, it is important to resist the temptation to overinvest in privacy doctrine as the basis for questioning the legitimacy of encroachments of the state, the market, and society. As I have suggested, judicial recognition of privacy rights for some has come at the cost of the denial of protection for others. Outside of the legal realm, privacy doctrine has too often been appropriated by those who oppose the politicization of power, especially on the domestic front. Finally, there is the risk that in mapping the social world onto the terrain of the public/private divide, we will distort and misapprehend social life, overlooking the complexity and ambivalences that mark the contemporary condition.

Though it is tempting at this juncture in history to seek to revive privacy, to restore respect for clouded boundaries that we imagine were once so clear, I would urge a different course, one that moves beyond the false hopes sustained by the promise of inviolable privacy rights. The appeal of privacy doctrine lies in the comforting notion that there is some principle out there capable of resolving urgent social and political dilemmas of our day: how to balance values like autonomy and security, how to preserve intimacy in the age of publicity. These are questions that need to be faced head-on, not evaded by invocations of a privacy right. In moving beyond the rhetoric of privacy, we have the opportunity to engage in an inquiry about the nature of social life and the possibilities for engagement within it.

Notes

I am especially grateful to Ali Behdad for his incisive and insightful comments on earlier drafts of this essay.

1 The phrase "the unwanted gaze" is taken from Jeffrey Rosen's book of the same name (New York: Vintage Press, 2001). In recent years, a successful publishing niche has been carved out by authors who warn about the faltering state of privacy rights in the United States. Popular titles in this genre include Reg Whittler, *The End of Privacy: How Total Surveillance Is Becoming a Reality* (New York: New Press, 2000); Fred Calls and Michael Armacost, *Privacy in the Information Age* (Washington, DC: Brookings Institution, 1997); and David Brin, *The Transparent Society: Will Technology Force Us to Choose between Privacy and Freedom?* (New York: Perseus, 1999). Other signs of a privacy panic can be found in the recent willingness of legislators, at both the state and the federal level, to consider legislation that would curtail the rights of government and business to control personal information, including the Barr-Nadler bill compelling federal agencies to include a "privacy impact statement" on all proposals, and the recently defeated bill in California aimed at limiting corporate access to personal information.

2 For a more sustained treatment of this topic, see Toby Miller, "The First Penis Impeached," and Catherine Lumby, "The President's Penis: Entertaining Sex and Power," in *Our Monica, Ourselves: The Clinton Affair and the National Interest* (New York: New York University Press, 2001).

3 Jodi Dean, "Introduction: The Interface of Political Theory and Cultural Studies," in *Cultural Studies and Political Theory*, ed. Jodi Dean (New York: Cornell University Press, 2000).

4 See Mary Ann Glendon, *Rights Talk* (New York: Free Press, 1993). S. I. Benn and G. F. Gaus's collection *Public and Private in Social Life* (London: Croom Helm, 1983) provides an excellent survey of the development of the terms public and private. See also Jeff Weintraub and Krishan Kumar, eds., *Public and Private in Thought and Practice* (Chicago: University of Chicago Press, 1997).

5 *Poe v. Ullman*, 367 U.S. 497 (1961).

6 Stephen Holmes, *Passions and Constraint: On the Theory of Liberal Democracy* (Chicago: University of Chicago Press, 1997), 255.

7 Randall Bezanson, "The Right to Privacy Revisited: Privacy, News, and Social Change, 1890–1990," *California Law Review* (1980): 1133.

8 See, for example, Ruth Marcus, "Privacy Takes a Beating as Investigations Progress in Lewinsky, Jones Cases," *Washington Post*, 22 February 1998, final ed., A20; Orlando Patterson, "What Is Freedom without Privacy?" *New York Times*, 12 September 1998, late ed., A27; Ellen Alderman, "The Private Domain," *Newsday*, 28 February 1999, B6; Jeffrey Rosen, "The Eroded Self," *New York Times*, 30 April 2000, final ed., sect. 6, p. 46.

9 "Family of Three Dropping By, Along with Secret Service," *Los Angeles Times*, 18 August 1999.

10 In this regard, it is interesting to consider the significance of the other major privacy case to arise in the 1960s, *Stanley v. Georgia* (1969). This case arose from the prosecution of a man charged with possession of obscene matter. The Court found the Georgia statute prohibiting possession of such matter unconstitutional, thereby extending the right to privacy to cover individuals outside of the context of the marital relationship. Of course, to the extent that one sees the proliferation of pornography as an enabling condition for the perpetuation of the institution of marriage, one that creates a socially sanctioned space of transgression, this decision can be seen as simply an extension of the social logic underlying the *Griswold* decision.

11 *Griswold v. Connecticut*, 381 U.S. 479 (1965).

12 *Bowers v. Hardwick*, 478 U.S. 186 (1986). See also, *Kelly v. Johnson* 425 U.S. 238 (1976) [upholding a regulation regarding the length of policemen's hair]; *Moore v. City of East Cleveland*, 431 U.S. 494 (1977) [overturning a law based on a narrow definition of family]; and *Whalen v.*

Roe, 429 U.S. 589 (1976) [upholding regulations that track purchases of certain highly regulated drugs].

13 Slavoj Žižek, *Welcome to the Desert of the Real* (New York: Verso, 2002).

14 Under the USA/Patriot Act, passed shortly after the 9/11 attacks, Congress radically extended the surveillance power of law enforcement agencies under the guise of protecting national security. In the aftermath, immigrants, particularly those of Middle Eastern background, have been primary targets. In June 2002, the Court held in *Board of Education of Independent School District No. 92 of Pottawatomie County v. Earls* that public schools may subject high school students engaged in extracurricular activities to mandatory, suspicionless drug testing.

15 Peter Beinart, "How the Personal Became Political," *New Republic* (February 1999): 21.

16 John Lloyd, "The Death of Privacy: J'accuse," *New Statesman* 129 (5 March 1999): 12.

17 Jean Bethke Elshtain, "The Displacement of Politics," in Weintraub and Kumar, 172.

18 This literature is often traced back to Carol Gilligan's seminal work, *In a Different Voice: Psychological Theory and Women's Development* (Cambridge, MA: Harvard University Press, 1982). See also Joan Tronto, *Moral Boundaries: A Political Argument for an Ethic of Care* (New York: Routledge, 1993).

19 See Anita L. Allen, "Privacy at Home: The Twofold Problem," in *Revisioning the Political*, ed. Nancy Hirschmann and Christine di Stephano (New York: Westview Press, 1996); Patricia Boling, *Privacy and the Politics of Intimate Life* (Ithaca: Cornell University Press, 1996); and Jean L. Cohen, "Rethinking Privacy: Autonomy, Identity and the Abortion Controversy," in Weintraub and Kumar.

20 Carole Pateman, *The Disorder of Women* (Palo Alto: Stanford University Press, 1989), 131.

21 This is not to deny the obvious sense in which sex scandals like the Clinton-Lewinsky-Starr affair are political, in the sense of politically motivated and promoted to advance certain political interests over others. This is what Benjamin Ginsburg and Martin Shefter mean in calling scandals "politics by other means." See *Politics by Other Means: Politicians, Prosecutors, and the Press from Watergate to Whitewater* (New York: Norton, 1999).

22 For an excellent discussion of these debates, see Krishan Kumar, "Home: The Promise and Predicament of Private Life at the End of the Twentieth Century," in Weintraub and Kumar.

23 http://www.voyeurdorm.com.

The (Too Much) Information Age 231

It Was the Spectacle, Stupid

The Clinton-Lewinsky-Starr Affair and
the Politics of the Gaze

I went to the U.S. Capitol on the day of Clinton's impeachment just to *be there*. To say that the cameras, the costumes, the signs, and the sellers of political kitsch gave the scene a "circus atmosphere" was to miss with an errant cliché the joyless, almost spooky mood. The day was cold and wet. The line for a seat in Congress's citizens' gallery seemed an odd mix of moviegoers queuing up for a hit release and viewers at a wake bracing to see the corpse. On the North Lawn, news teams rooted around to find places to film their live reports without having the background consist simply of other news teams filming live reports. TV reporters, prowling to gauge the feelings of Average Americans, apologized for mistakingly trying to interview other reporters. The scene seemed something out of a science fiction dystopia picturing a society in which actual events and the people capable of making them happen had disappeared, leaving only media to report on each other reporting on each other in an infinite loop.

The public had a modest presence among the thicket of TV people. Moments of true citizen dialogue were rare, drowned out in the semi-articulate rage each side screamed at the other. If I had any civic epiphany, it was a moment of unexpected empathy with what first appeared a garden-variety Clinton basher holding court before a brood of college Republicans. His sense of hurt was genuine; his conviction, almost quaint in an age of boundless cynicism, that the president represented *him* and therefore had a duty to behave with a minimum of honesty, seemed for an instant as valid as my insistence that some sense of proportion must be maintained, reserving impeachment for Nixonesque or even Reaganesque crimes. Our mutual insults gave way to a shared sense of powerlessness over what was happening to our institutions, to America, to *us*. We bonded in the futility of our even having opinions.

Then came the vote, the stream of representatives leaving the Capitol, the hurried conferences of reporters, their impromptu stories in hushed tones, and the incredible silence of the crowd. What to say? Whatever one's side, that day we all lost; those of us there had the good sense to know it, and we mourned in quiet. As the silence lifted, representatives boarded buses for a quick exit. They waved, we cursed or cheered, they left, we murmured, and then we left. Just like that, history was made.

What was it that drew me there that day to play the role of hapless voyeur? What had caused me and nearly everyone else in the United States to follow the Clinton-Lewinsky-Starr affair so intently for all those months? What had so powerfully fixed our gaze, seemingly beyond any force of will or restraint? Was it the story line of the scandal itself, brimming with desire, deception, betrayal, vanity, and other primal drives and weaknesses? Was it the gravity of the "issues" embedded in it, from the fate of privacy in America, to the ways sex and power circulate in the workplace, to the integrity of the rule of law? Was it the drama of the culture war raging in the partisan thrusts and parries?

No, it was something greater than each of these things or the sum of all of them. Something bigger than any person, institution, constituency, or idea. Something utterly seductive and hypnotic, at once cunningly obscure and obscenely obvious. It was the spectacle, stupid.

To reach for the language of the spectacle to describe the inner logic of the Clinton-Lewinsky-Starr affair is to proceed from what may have been its most bizarre and vexing quality: the grinding persistence of the scandal itself and the nation's attention to it, despite the widespread sentiment that it had been blown way out of proportion. Indeed, every major player in the overdetermined drama expressed disgust with, or at least distaste for, the whole thing. Clinton, fearful of political ruin, used repeated denials to try to make it go away. Democrats and others of his reluctant defenders cried foul, warning of egregious harm to the president's agenda and the "spirit of the Constitution" should the inquiry-unto-impeachment go unstopped. Even Clinton's accusers were uncomfortable. They defended their inquisitorial zeal as a regrettable necessity for determining the extent of Clinton's perfidy; it pained them, they explained, to have to initiate something so serious as impeachment proceedings and to discuss such an unseemly thing as sex, even if to restore the rule of law and the nation's moral fiber. The media, conscious of its role in turning a sexual liaison into a national obsession, ritually condemned itself for pandering to prurient curiosities and trivializing politics. Pundits everywhere worried that relentless focus on the affair made the United States look weak and silly before the international community.

Finally, the great majority of the American people felt that far too much was being made of the president's misconduct. The poll numbers are impressive, both for the strong majorities they show and for their consistency, no matter the evidence against Clinton. Right after the release in September 1998 of the Starr report, some 62 percent of the public opposed impeachment, roughly the same percentage as before it had been made public.[1] Following the conclusion in December of the House impeachment hearings, that figure rose to 67 percent.[2] For most of its life, barely a quarter of Americans felt the scandal was of "great importance to the nation."[3] Clinton's approval ratings, widely interpreted as a referendum on whether his wrongdoings warranted such intense scrutiny and, ultimately, impeachment, mirrored these preferences. As the House was set to vote on impeachment, the figure stood at 61 percent; after the vote it rose to 71 percent.[4] For most months of the scandal, the numbers were in the lower 60s, considerably higher than the mid-40s to mid-50s Clinton typically posted in the first six years of his presidency.[5]

When asked point-blank if Congress and the media were paying too much attention to the story, the public was equally adamant. Negative views toward the media set in almost immediately. Ten days into the coverage of the alleged affair, 70 percent of Americans felt that the media was overreporting the story.[6] In December 1998, by which point most allegations had been proven true, the number was only slightly lower (64 percent). By the same margin, the public judged Congress too concerned with the scandal.[7] In fact, poll data show that most of the public disapproved of how *all* of the key actors in the drama—from Clinton to Starr to House Republicans and Democrats to Chairman Hyde—were handling the investigation. In addition, clear majorities felt that the Republicans (70 percent) and the Democrats (61 percent) were motivated by "politics," not principle, as they attacked or defended the president.[8] The overall portrait of the public's response is one of overload, disaffection, and cynicism. Though sensing that there was still more to the story, CNN's Frank Cesno remarked fully six months before its conclusion, "The public probably feels it's time to move on. I'm sure the president . . . would like to move on. I bet a lot of Democrats and probably Republicans would like to move on. . . . Personally, I'm sick of it as well. It's not a fun story; it's not an uplifting story; it's not a good story."[9] By virtual consensus, Americans craved "closure" and the return to discussion of "real issues."

And yet the scandal wouldn't go away, instead building momentum until it could be grasped only in metaphors: the Machine that would go of itself, the Monster that ate U.S. politics, the Energizer Bunny. Despite all the hand wringing, we played our parts. The media reported, investigators investigated, pundits opined, politicians asserted, denied, dissembled, confessed, and spun, and we watched. A journalist described the core irony: the "public was sick and tired of the whole tawdry tale. No one, it seemed, could bear to watch any more. Yet viewing audiences soared—apparently no one could turn away either."[10] This irony is part of the genetic structure of the scandal, whose apprehension calls for scrutiny of the history and characteristics of its overarching form: the spectacle.

In 1967, French philosopher and freelance rebel Guy Debord wrote *Society of the Spectacle* to describe a new logic of commodity production in advanced industrial societies. Though offering a theory of "the whole" in the grand Marxist tradition, Debord's thinking takes the form of fragmentary and frequently cryptic observations that aim to capture in an allusive way the general character of culture and experience in such societies. Thriving on overstatement and meshing poorly with the methods of social science, Debord's theses reward the imagination and the effort to find the place where theoretical insight, experience, and common sense meet.

Debord begins: "Where modern conditions of production prevail, all of life presents itself as an immense accumulation of spectacles. Everything that was directly lived has moved away into a representation."[11] With this statement, Debord speaks most obviously to the dominance of images in the modern era of mass communication, for the spectacle is a fundamentally visual phenomenon that defines subjectivity as a form of viewership. The cover of an English-language edition of the book amplifies his central thesis. It pictures a homogeneous movie audience gazing through 3-D glasses at a screen we do not see. The collective act of gazing constitutive of the spectacle, the photograph suggests, is more important than the viewed images themselves; the medium of the spectacle, which "serves as an instrument of *unification*" by "concentrat[ing] all gazing and all consciousness," indeed is the message (3).

Debord's more challenging point—one that anticipates a key post-modern insight—is that the spectacular realm of representation does not refer to any reality external to itself and to which the subject has access; rather, "the images detached from every aspect of life fuse in a common stream" that constitutes a "pseudo-world *apart*, an object of mere contemplation" in which the "unity of this life cannot be reestablished" (2). Experience, the "directly lived," has somehow passed over into representation. In social and existential terms, we are what we watch.

At its most potent, the spectacle confounds the ontological distinction between reality and representation. Debord insists: "One cannot abstractly contrast the spectacle to actual social activity. . . . The spectacle which inverts the real is in fact produced. Lived reality is materially invaded by contemplation of the spectacle while simultaneously absorbing the spectacular order. . . . Objective reality is present on both sides. Every notion fixed this way has no other basis than its passage into its opposite: reality rises up with the spectacle and the spectacle is real" (8). The binary of reality and representation is not so much dissolved by the spectacle—it remains a condition of possibility for the spectacle's structure and effects—as hopelessly confused or destabilized in a vertigo of reversals.

Debord complements semiotic with social theory with his contention that images, spectacles, are the definitive products of the most modern societies, indeed their dominant commodity form, whose generation constitutes their very raison d'être. Playing on Marx's description of the commodity fetish, he declares the spectacle a "social relation among people mediated by images." If the relations among objects once masked those between people, we have now lost traces of ourselves in the *images* of ourselves. The "deceived gaze," and not the estrangement of labor, constitutes the dominant experience of alienation (3).

The appearance of the spectacle, above all, testifies to the power of the system creating it. Debord elaborates by layering additional definitions: the spectacle is not "an abuse of the world of vision" but a *"Weltanschauung* which has become actual," "both the result and the project of the existing mode of production," "the affirmation of the choice *already made* in production and its corollary consumption," "the total justification of the existing system's conditions and goals." As such, the spectacle has no goal external to itself. Debord explains that "the basically tautological character of the spectacle flows from the simple fact that its means are simultaneously its ends." The spectacle is thus its own telos, demanding "passive acceptance" by virtue of its "monopoly of appearance" (5, 6, 12, 13).

Compelling as a set of descriptions of a new era of mass media, Debord's theses have only grown more relevant, if less shocking, for an age that has become more thoroughly and self-consciously spectacular. Indeed, the nature of gazing has changed with the near compulsory and compulsive use of television and the personal computer, as well as with the sheer multiplication of spectacles, options for viewing, and ways of accessing and manipulating images. Gazing, in short, is less overtly a public, passive, and homogenizing act. (The image of the movie audience, an emblem of democratic conformism within mass society, was already something of an anachronism in Debord's time.) But in becoming more private, atomized, and interactive, gazing has also become more pervasive and alluring. The sociality the spectacle engenders, moreover, is more strictly located in the gaze itself. It matters less that we all watch exactly the same thing in some shared setting than that we are all watching (or pointing and clicking) nearly all the time; the spectacle thus continues to perform its unifying function, even in an age of proliferating media technologies, specialized images, and market fragmentation.

The interpenetration of image and reality, fiction and truth has also grown more conspicuous, evident in the events of our age and in the commonplace language used to describe the qualities of our age. The Persian Gulf conflict of 1991 emerged as the first "TV war" insofar as it seemed to Americans literally to take place on television. Not only did the TV correspondents become national heroes (by virtue of their personalities, not their reportage), but the sanitized images they dutifully broadcast, which made battle appear a bloodless video game, helped ensure its popularity. This support fed, in turn, actual U.S. war strategy. The media, as never before, became players in war itself, while derealizing something as real as death. Opponents of the war, angered by the near total exclusion of their protests from the airwaves, had confirmed the truth of the cynical axiom that unless an event appears on TV, it may as well not have happened.

The O. J. Simpson trial was both the spectacular drama par excellence and a threshold moment in the evolution of the spectacle, perhaps the purest prototype of the Clinton-Lewinsky-Starr affair as a "real-life soap opera" and protracted media event. With its mass and constant viewership, it reunified the country's gaze, bringing us together as an "imagined community" through the shared consumption of images. Its peak moments, the broadcast of the Bronco chase and the verdict, became landmark events in contemporary culture, ones by which we now structure memory (Where were *you*?). The death of Princess Diana had a similar effect, prompting public opinion researchers to remark: "In an era in which virtually *all* Americans share few things, the story . . . captivated the nation."[12] Both dramas, in addition, so thoroughly blurred the line between news and entertainment that they brought into its own a whole media genre: "infotainment." Used just a few years ago to condemn the decline of journalistic standards and the broader erosion of the ability to distinguish the serious from the superfluous, the term is now an essentially neutral description of the form of broadcasting toward which nearly all currents of reportage about the world seem to be converging.

The O. J. trial, proving anew that the truth can be more absorbing than the most fantastic fiction, was a harbinger of more confounding things to come: the reworking of reality itself within the imperatives of the spectacle. In the popular "reality-based" TV programs, the "real world" is intricately contrived for televisual presentation. Deployed this way, reality becomes simply more referential material for the staging of spectacles, whose status is patently neither truth nor fiction. The French theorist Jean Baudrillard, something of an heir to Debord, commented that stucco, first used widely in the Renaissance, was the quintessential substance of the simulacrum insofar as it could be molded into an image of anything.[13] Today, "reality" might be described as the cutting-edge substance of the spectacle, as it is endlessly reshaped within the formal requirements of fiction. MTV's *The Real World*, for example, strives to be a combination of a television situation comedy and drama in which the real-life actors play themselves.

Efforts to reflect critically on this condition point to the confusion over the locus of reality, while ultimately confirming the spectacle's power. In the movie *The Truman Show*, the fabricated environment becomes fully real for Truman, who is not party to the mesmerizing ruse that makes his whole life a hit TV show. The film does not so much warn of a hypothetical, brave new world of inescapable simulation as suggest that the ruse is already upon us—that we are all voyeurs, but also, by some measure, Trumans. Gesturing toward an unseen realm of authenticity, it begs us to leave, like Truman, the order of the simulacrum.[14] For us, however, there is no easy exit, no door from which to escape back to reality. To "Kill Your Television," as a popular bumpersticker implores, may be a theoretical exit route, but it hardly seems a cultural or existential option, should one want to remain tethered to the (pseudo-)world in which reality *appears*.

As a particular spectacle and political drama within a larger "society of the spectacle," the Clinton-Lewinsky-Starr affair was far from unique. Rather, it was a complex organism with multiple origins and genealogical lines, a reorganization of elements that we had quite literally seen before but whose gestalt was without precedent. Those elements, whether narrative tropes or structures of media, were the necessary though not sufficient conditions for its emergence and its identity as the apotheosis of a form. Identifying those histories sets the stage for specifying the spectacular qualities of the Clinton drama and then relating it to a broader analysis of the spectacle.

One hereditary line feeding the Clinton affair was certainly the politics of scandal in the age of mass media, for which Watergate stands as the original type or master code.[15] In Watergate, the country was witness to a televised inquiry, fascinating in its details and profound in its implications, into the misdeeds of a sitting president, the single American, by virtue of the political and symbolic investments in the presidency, whose fate is best able to captivate the nation's attention. The Iran-Contra scandal, with its lengthy hearings about weighty matters, had much the same presentation and gravitas as Watergate, but was already much more a media event. Its central character, Oliver North, used his telegenic personality to turn the hearings from an inquiry into his guilt or innocence into a judgment on the sincerity of his motivations. The Clarence Thomas–Anita Hill hearings complete this troika of precursors, contributing elements directly redeployed in the Clinton-Lewinsky affair. Most obviously, those hearings, like the Clinton scandal, concerned allegations of sexual misconduct by a government official. Equally important, the investigation of Thomas's dealings with Hill went ahead with stunning intensity, despite the absence of any sure sense that his alleged indiscretions were relevant to the question of his qualifications for the Supreme Court. An analogous question hovered over Clinton's deeds. Finally, Thomas's denunciation of the inquiry as a "high-tech lynching" explicitly coded the proceedings as a media-driven spectacle; the medium of television, as never before, was constitutive of the thing itself.

A second stream feeding the turbulent waters of Clinton-Lewinsky was the celebrity trials of the mid-1990s, primarily O. J.'s but also William Kennedy's. Each helped to establish the real-life courtroom drama, covered gavel to gavel and surrounded by ceaseless analysis and scandalmongering, as among the most absorbing television genres, irrespective of its merits as a news item. One could have said about the O. J. trial what two analysts said about the Clinton affair: that "it was a moment of astounding incoherence . . . a historic public event, yet central to it was a debate about whether it was worthy of attention."[16] What this comment fails to broach (and what likely holds for O. J.) is that it was not at all clear that rational judgments about the affair's attention-worthiness had any effect on the amount of attention paid to it. Much more, the O. J. and Clinton sagas posed a conundrum with no answer: Were they so extensively covered because they were so important, or did they appear so important because they were so thoroughly covered?

The Whitewater investigations into the Clintons' real estate dealings in Arkansas may seem to have had little to do with the spectacle. Decidedly uncaptivating, set in the American backwater and far away from the media centers of New York, Los Angeles, and Washington, they failed in their impenetrable detail, sheer drabness, and partisan banality to gain either political traction or much of an audience. Yet Whitewater, in its open-endedness and insoluble drift, established the Clinton presidency and, by extension, U.S. politics, as a never-ending scandal, a condition of permanent investigation and surveillance, poised to convert into the public gaze.[17] Put otherwise, Whitewater was a kind of primordial soup just waiting for the right strike of lightning to come to a life that mattered—one on TV. The catalyst was Monica Lewinsky, a young female intern from Beverly Hills and New York.

The Clinton-Lewinsky-Starr affair was the ubiquitous object of our obsessive gaze. The subject of "nonstop coverage," it was always on. The numbers tell part of the story about the story. In the first ten days after allegations of an illicit affair surfaced, the three major networks devoted 124 segments—fully 67 percent of their news coverage—to the emerging scandal. Princess Diana's death, one of the all-time great "blockbuster stories," generated only 103 reports during a comparable period. In droves, audiences tuned in. In the early days of the scandal CNN posted a 40 percent increase in viewers.[18] Though the numbers fell off some during the many lulls, they remained high. In the three months following the release of the Starr report, the ratings of the all-news cable network MSNBC were up 109 percent from the previous year.[19] The capstone to the saga, Barbara Walter's exclusive, post-impeachment interview with Monica Lewinsky, was watched by 74 million Americans. Only the Superbowl, America's greatest annual spectacle, drew a larger audience.[20]

The qualities of the coverage, fully as much as the quantity, made for the distinct experience of the scandal. Appreciating the synergy of the two demands a focus on the evolving structures and idioms of the great engine of the spectacle: the media. The affair prompted media members and analysts alike to reflect on the compression of the news cycle, driven by newly created means for the instantaneous dissemination of information and the intense competition among ever-proliferating media organizations. (In an era of niche audiences and declining market share, even modest losses or gains in viewers have a big impact on individual networks and programs, further raising the competitive stakes.) One effect of this compression was to speed everything up. As the scandal raged, a professor of communications remarked, "We have accelerated the pace of events in these things to an almost jaw-dropping level. If Watergate was going down in this environment of 24-hour cable channels and Web sites and internet addresses, the entire scandal may have had a life span of 48 hours."[21] Another effect was the quantitative increase of "news." Desperate to be the first with the latest revelation and fearful of falling behind, news organizations elevated each twist or turn in the saga into the next screaming, if fleeting, headline and scrambled to cover stories their competitors broke. In this way, the story gained much of its intensity, intricacy, and sense of being constantly in motion.

Yet the compression of the news cycle became also its elongation, giving the story its contradictory rhythms. Ben Bradlee, the editor of the *Washington Post* during Watergate, observed with respect to the affair: "It used to be that there were maybe two news cycles in a day. . . . But with this constant television coverage we now have, there is an endless cycle. Often it looked like there was a lot of action going on, but in reality, nothing much had happened."[22] Indeed, most days featured news of only very minor developments, followed by exhaustive analysis and then the repeated playback of each. The feeling of speed and absorption was thus balanced by a sense of grueling redundancy, boredom, and numbness, as one followed the slowly moving spirals. As a result, the story often had the qualities of cable television that have been so passionately attacked: always on, never far from us, replete with choices (channels), and oddly mesmerizing, yet offering little or nothing of "true" interest to watch, no matter where one turns. (Bruce Springsteen's cri de coeur was to sing ruefully, "Fifty-seven channels and nothing on.")[23] These observations could well be made about the modern-day spectacle, the broad representational context in which popular images, narratives, and media occur. As if in anticipation of contemporary complaints, Debord wrote, "False choice in spectacular abundance . . . develops into a struggle of vaporous qualities meant to stimulate loyalty to quantitative triviality" (63, 64).

Keith Olberman, the host of MSNBC's daily program *The White House in Crisis*, eventually quit the network in disgust over having covered the Clinton story "28 out of 24 hours." He confessed "to having dry heaves in the bathroom" and "days when my line of work makes me ashamed, makes me depressed, makes me cry."[24] His comments are arresting, both as reflections on the Clinton-Lewinsky affair and as a source of more metaphors for the spectacle. In his phrasing, there was something unnatural about the coverage, as it transgressed the conventional structures of time ("28 out of 24 hours"). He suggests the existence of a new kind of accumulation crisis for a society defined by the generation of spectacles: the overproduction of images. His anguish mirrors the condition of the subject in the thrall of the spectacle, whose "root is within the abundant economy."[25] Overstuffed, he seeks literally to purge himself, as if to simultaneously affirm and expel this excess. But the effort is in vain (dry heaves); he is left paradoxically empty, while not able to rid himself of the images he has both created and consumed.

Demanding that we hurry up and wait, the scandal moved through long valleys of incessant playback and then stunning peaks of the new. To describe this rhythm and topography, Ben Bradlee pointed to the "kerosene effect," whereby, in a journalist's paraphrase, "Every time the long, slow-burning Monica Lewinsky saga showed signs of slowing down, some incendiary event would occur, igniting a sudden burst of journalistic excitement as the story roared to life yet again."[26] This insight reinforces the sense of the scandal as a "real-life soap opera." Far from an idle metaphor, the comparison speaks to essential aspects of the scandal's representation, consumption, and identity as spectacle.

In the Clinton-Lewinsky affair, as in similar spectacles (both prior and since), the country was quickly introduced to the dramatis personae. They became characters in our lives (Bill, Monica, Linda Tripp, Ken Starr, Betty Currie, etc.), to whom we related with striking, almost indecent intimacy, and whose personalities inspired in us often intense attractions, repulsions, and identifications. The characters seemed to personify such distinct human traits as ambition, vanity, temptation, betrayal, and loyalty. Much of the pleasure of following the story lay in watching these surface, recede, and feed on or do battle with one another. The drawn-out drama had, in addition, its plots and subplots, as well as its stock episodes: the denial, the evasion, the interrogation, the disclosure, the confession, and the showdown. The affair thus conformed to the structures of fiction derived less from literature than from daytime television. In a blunt statement of this connection, one columnist described the saga as "Monica's Story," containing a "plot and cast so improbable no soap opera or sitcom writer could have invented it."[27]

The scandal had also its special—and highly titillating—iconography: the cigar, the blue dress, the beret, the embrace, the gifts, the tapes, and, above all, the president's penis. These became a politically and libidinally invested object field within which interest and intrigue circulated. The scandal had, finally, its own vocabulary. This included technical terms turned commonplace (the deponent, subornation of perjury) and vaguely familiar terms now made more precise and urgent (impeachment, high crimes and misdemeanors, the rule of law) and terms that were the utterly unique and highly memorable products of the scandal ("the vast right-wing conspiracy," "I did not have sexual relations with that woman," and, most notoriously, "It depends on what the meaning of the word 'is' is").

Taken together, the characters, icons, and vocabulary made the affair a source of unification, what Debord defines as the chief function of the spectacle. This unity worked in two related domains or registers: that of the story-as-spectacle itself, and that of the consciousness beholding it and being shaped by it. In the first, the scandal appeared a world unto itself, at once familiar and apart, textually self-sufficient. In Debord's language, it had the status of an "autonomous image" composed of internal reference points and self-contained narratives (2). Following the story largely entailed gaining conversancy with its signal personalities, plots, and key words. Once one was fluent, the scandal existed as a parallel, continually accessible cosmos of melodramatic textuality, as the background of life on most days, utterly engaging at moments of high drama. As with a soap opera, one could tune out the saga at will (though never quite escaping it) and then tune back in, picking up the story in medias res and having missed barely a beat.

This pacing was critical to the story's power as a spectacle, given public opinion research showing that surprisingly few Americans were in fact "very interested" in the story. Whatever our recollection of national obsession, in most months of the scandal only between 25 and 33 percent of the public claimed to "follow it very closely." Even during the House impeachment vote, the figure was only 34 percent, making impeachment not even among the "Top Ten Stories of 1998"; just 17 percent watched or listened to the Senate trial each day.[28] These data have been interpreted as a clear expression of the public's disgust with the story and with the volume of coverage; to not follow it closely, or at least to have made this claim, was something of a protest. But it was a largely hollow protest. Given the story's structure, the saturation news, and the endless repetition, one could in fact follow it closely *without consciously following it closely*. Ours was not a fatal attraction to the scandal, in which bursts of uncontrollable passion brought us ruin. Rather, we engaged in an ambivalent, slow-turning romance by grudging peeks and glances.

The reflexivity built into the story enhanced its autonomy. Here the media played a crucial role by making legible the story elements it introduced and covered. The countless expert analysts interpreted the political strategies of the various actors, as is done in any complex political story. But they also performed the indispensable task of deciphering the legal language and structures in which the scandal was embedded. This role signals the judicialization of both U.S. politics and the spectacle more broadly, with profound consequences for political culture.

Describing the Aztec society conquered by the Spanish in the sixteenth century, Tzvetan Todorov observed that a virtual army of functionaries was employed by the Aztec king to interpret the omens, signs, and chronicles that made up the Aztecs' intricate symbol system; their mediation permitted the operation of the Aztecs' entire cultural semiotic.[29] Today, news anchors and analysts with law degrees play a similar role by providing the means for public understanding of the spectacles that so consume and define us. This phenomenon began with Watergate, ripened during O. J. and Clinton-Lewinsky, and has continued to mark subsequent megastories, such as the fate of the Cuban refugee Elian Gonzalez and the 2000 presidential election debacle. All were constituted, mediated, and ambivalently "settled" by the discourse of the law. On the one hand, the pervasiveness of and dependency on the law reinforce a kind of elitism, as knowledge of its technical language confers special authority to represent and speak about matters of public concern. As such, it is a source of division. On the other hand, as the legal language specific to each spectacle was popularized, each developed its own, seamless, cross-referential terminology that became a lingua franca for all who consumed it. To step into the world of a spectacular drama is to pass through its sui generis language and necessary mediations.

In a second expression of unity, the scandal brought the public together by providing a shared story line, language, and tableau of images. It gave us, in colloquial terms, something to talk about "around the water cooler," that idealized space of everyday (white-collar) sociality through which we are constituted as a speaking public. The scene of the water cooler is, however, a far cry from eighteenth-century Europe's coffeehouses; these served, in Jürgen Habermas's influential telling, as the emblematic space for rational deliberation (among the bourgeoisie) and the broader operation of the democratic public sphere. Instead, today's water cooler is a magnet for public gossip and idle opinion about the world, with little regard for any hierarchy of importance. One can talk just as easily about Sunday's football games, a semen stain, the weather, the president's fate, the latest episode of *Survivor*, or the state of the union. Debord's cynicism again rushes to mind: "Under the shimmering diversions of the spectacle, *banalization* dominates modern society" (59).

If the Clinton-Lewinsky affair was always on, it was also everywhere on. In a spontaneous campaign of total mobilization, every conceivable kind of media volunteered in making the affair a megastory. Among these were the daily newspapers, the tabloid press, network television, all-news cable television, countless Web sites, print and TV news magazines, infotainment and celebrity programs, late-night TV, and legal affairs programs. From each, one could get the day-to-day essentials, making it largely irrelevant whether one watched C-SPAN, the *CBS Evening News, Nightline, Hard Copy, The Tonight Show*, or even *Comedy Central*'s "The Daily Show." The scandal, for obvious reasons, even penetrated the world of the pornographic media, which in turn penetrated the scandal. To considerable shock and amusement, *Hustler* magazine publisher Larry Flynt helped bring down the Republican House speaker in waiting and pledged to publicize any other politicians' sexual misconduct his investigations might turn up.

The ubiquity of the story suggests a third form of unity at the level of the medium itself. Combining political, legal, sexual, and pop-cultural elements, the affair had something for everybody; hence, everybody covered it. As a result, it worked against the well-documented fragmentation of both the news media and their audiences. Indeed, in 1998 the Pew Research Center for the People and the Press identified six separate groups of news consumers (e.g., Mainstream News, Basically

Broadcast, Tabloid), each with its distinct preferences and habits.[30] Not only does this fragmentation, according to Pew's analysts, make it hard for any story or news organ to gain a mass audience, but, part and parcel of the diversification of media in general, it has contributed to the "waning [of] interest in all current events."[31] The Clinton-Lewinsky affair seemed to change all that with its ubiquity and high ratings. If the audience remained fragmented in terms of program choices and broader consumption patterns, most everybody was watching a version of the same thing.

The affair is deceptive, however, as the reversal of a trend. Instead, it reflects primarily how the spectacle's means of achieving unity have changed. The fragmentation and diversification of the media exist against the backdrop of the increasing concentration of ownership of all forms of entertainment and broadcasting in the hands of a few corporate media giants. Homogenization exists also in the medium itself. With the interpenetration of styles, contents, and textures, everything increasingly resembles everything else. MTV, for example, transformed the look and pacing of entertainment and news broadcasting alike; the cable sports networks, drawing heavily on MTV's hipspeak in turning the continual playback of the same highlights into absorbing television, has impacted the idioms and rhythms of cable news; cable, in turn, has influenced the composition and style of national network news, which has also incorporated the lifestyle and human interest focus of local news. TV news programs, in addition, increasingly display stock prices, sports scores, weather forecasts, and ticker-tape-style news updates, giving the broadcast the look of an Internet megasite (Yahoo, Excite, etc.). And all media have partly assimilated the orientation to personality and gossip of the celebrity shows, as well as the voyeurism of tabloid TV. (Geraldo Rivera personifies this merging of media genres. Originally a serious investigative journalist with ABC news, he reinvented himself as a daytime talk-and-smut-show host, after which he became the host of a program on CNBC that featured exhaustive coverage of the Clinton scandal.) The effect on the news has been most conspicuous. Though "accuracy and timeliness" remain the qualities valued most by news consumers, "a large segment of the news audience," in the Pew Center's characterization, "wants entertaining and enjoyable news presented by personalities who deliver it in a caring way."[32]

The Clinton-Lewinsky scandal typifies the blurring of genres. Remarkably, a 2001 *New York Times* article casually referred to the whole saga as a "celebrity-sex scandal," not a political scandal, let alone a "constitutional crisis."[33] For some analysts, the melding of news and entertainment lay at the heart of the story. In assessing why the public was generally so forgiving of Clinton, *New Yorker* author Kurt Anderson asserted that "politics in fundamental ways has become entertainment" and dubbed Clinton America's "Entertainer-in-Chief."[34] His core point, in the gloss of editorialist Tom Brazaitis, was that Clinton paid "no more of a price for bad-boy behavior than, say, Hugh Grant or Woody Allen [both the subject of sex scandals]. His personal conduct, like theirs, can be titillating, but has no bearing on our appreciation of his on-screen talents." The implication is that politics has essentially become a media performance, (en)acted, emplotted, and apprehended within a television consciousness. In a near-perfect echo of Debord's description of the confusions wrought by the spectacle, Brazaitis insists, "Make no mistake, the presidency, to the extent that most Americans experience it, happens on television. The motto for TV's premier, all-news channel puts it bluntly: 'Experience Life on CNN.'"[35]

As Anderson and Brazaitis trace the history of the "Hollywoodization of politics," the sense of the merging of public policy and entertainment becomes ever more vivid. Since John Kennedy, presidents and other politicians have actively sought to draw on the glamour and court the influence of the entertainment industry. Not only have they surrounded themselves with all manner of celebrities; for years they have appeared on variety shows, late-night talk shows, and even sitcoms. Clinton, if unintentionally, prepared the way for the intense interest in his private life by presenting himself as the hippest, most approachable president to date. He did this largely through his saxophone-playing appearance on the *Arsenio Hall* show, his masterful Q&A session on MTV, and other moments of televised candor; his ties to Hollywood's powerbrokers are notorious. Media figures have themselves rubbed out some of the lines between the serious and the superfluous. It is now de rigueur that news anchors, competing over celebrity status they and their networks consciously cultivate, perform on the late-night talk show circuit.

The effect of this relentless crossfertilization has been to diminish distinctions within media forms, as well as the significance of choosing among them. The phenomenon of fragmentation thus conceals a broader process of integration. The Clinton scandal, in this light, appears much more the rule than the exception. The fact that it was on virtually every channel and show speaks to our subterranean suspicion, one most likely to surface at moments of overload and numbness, that it is already all one story, all one channel, all one medium, and all one spectacle anyhow.

In addition, the diversity of elements seemingly contained in the story line was in part the product of the limited division of representational labor within the media. It is not just that the story had something for everybody, insofar as it wove together politics, the law, celebrity, pornography, and comedy; all the species of media involved helped to *create* the scandal as this enticing cornucopia. The entertainment and tabloid media invented Monica as the stylish, if overweight, ingenue; *Saturday Night Live* gave us the hilarious portrait of Linda Tripp as the resentful and manipulative glutton; Leno and Letterman cast Clinton as an oversexed, weak-willed, disingenuous, but resilient and oddly charming leader; and a battery of "serious" programs rendered the scandal both a Byzantine drama and a genuine national crisis. Before long, each locus of the media trafficked in all of these characterizations, which combined to form a dominant (though not universal) version of events and personalities.

To focus so intently on the spectacle is to deny the primacy of other analytic vocabularies used to account for how something as seemingly small as a consensual affair could turn into something as big as the impeachment of a president. One important species of explanation highlights Clinton's transgression, presented as far greater than the affair, his perjury, or his breach of the public trust. Toni Morrison provided the most provocative of these theses with her description of Clinton as America's "first black president," insofar as he displayed "almost every trope of blackness: single-parent household, born poor, working-class, saxophone-playing, McDonald's-and-junk-food-loving boy from Arkansas."[36] With the label, Morrison sought mainly to account for Clinton's striking popularity among African Americans. But she also sought, if implicitly, to explain the intense hostility Clinton evoked, evident in the Starr investigation. Her suggestion is that some critical mass of (white) Americans could not ultimately tolerate having a "black" president; the effort to "get" Clinton, therefore, amounted to a figurative lynching. Within this ingenious analysis, Clinton was despised and pursued less for *what he had done* than for *who he was*. The scandal raged under the sign of identity politics.

This view has been recast with other identity categories. Micki McElya asserts that Morrison "woefully misnamed" Clinton as the first black president; he was, instead, the first "white trash" president, insofar as all the attributes of his "blackness" apply also to stereotypical views of poor southern whites and map more precisely onto Clinton. Clinton only *appeared* black by virtue of the common elision of poverty and blackness. To McEyla, Clinton was more disturbing as white trash in that, with his excessive appetites and incorrigible crudeness, he disrupted the expectations that (white) America imposes on its president, while inciting latent white fears of sliding into poverty and its associated stigmas. The tropes of race and class can easily be extended to sexuality, rendering Clinton America's first *queer* president as well. Making just this claim, Tyler Curtain contends that the Clinton-Lewinsky affair provoked chiefly "sex panic." The insinuation is not that Clinton is literally gay but that his transgressive heterosexuality upset the "normatively repressive space of the faith demanding hetero-husband" and was in that sense "queer."[37] Clinton's offense was so great by virtue of the immense symbolic investment made in the president. Because the first family purportedly stands in for the nation as a whole, to disrupt the former is to destabilize the latter. With words that could fit any of these analyses, McElya concludes that Clinton failed to be the "normative, empowered, white male body" he seemed to be and therefore posed a grave "threat to national values."[38]

Fascinating in their own right, these interpretations contest an analysis of the affair centered on the spectacle, while throwing into question the whole critical paradigm of the spectacular society. The first challenge is methodological. Morrison et al. adopt a hermeneutical approach, as they seek the "true" meaning of the scandal beneath the surface meanings offered by standard narratives and interpretations. (A liberal narrative might describe a moralistic minority abusing investigative powers to try to take down a president it could not defeat by legitimate means. A conservative one might portray conscientious politicians trying to make accountable a leader coddled by a permissive culture.) The shared premise is that things were not as they appeared (indeed, Clinton was neither white nor straight!). Getting beyond the realm of appearance entails inventively reading the scandal to discern its symbolic, allegorical, and metaphorical dimensions, where its ultimate significance lies.

Focus on the spectacle, while not denying altogether the importance of the scandal's contents, certainly privileges its form. The ideological element, in this view, lies in the entire apparatus by which appearances and their associated meanings are generated and not in any particular ideological formation or operation. The problem with this emphasis is that it risks looking past how currents of power—indeed, the matrix of race/class/gender/sexuality—operated in and set the stakes of the scandal. More deeply, hermeneutical interpretations contest the autonomy of the scandal-as-spectacle. Far from being a self-contained "pseudo-world," the scandal was implicated in discursive and material contexts that extend beyond it and that constitute the great power play of contemporary politics and society. As the spectacle—merely part of the story—gets mistaken for the whole, the trees vanish in the view of the forest. The danger is not so much of being intellectually lost as of being politically incapable of responding to dimensions of the scandal worthy of response, whether the threat of moralists, the enduring challenges faced by women in the workplace, various breaches of the Constitution, or the repressive norms controlling the symbolism of the presidency.

Above all, efforts to wrest deep, political meanings from the affair suggest a very different attitude toward the spectacle, one in which cynicism and resignation are replaced by renewed enthusiasm for interpretive activism and heightened resolve to do battle on the terrain of representation. Such optimism can be derived from the critique of the spectacle itself. According to Debord, reality and appearance are inextricably interwoven, with "reality" inhering in the image itself. It is a small leap, pace Debord, to conclude that in spectacular societies symbolic struggles are not politics by other, figurative, and lesser means, but politics *as such*.[39]

Accepting this premise, one may recast the spectacle as something other than an intrinsically alienated and alienating medium of distraction and triviality, whose main political effect is to induce public passivity. The O. J. trial, in this revised view, ceases to be at best a highly attenuated and loopy metaphor for race relations and becomes instead the *enactment* of racial conflict. The Clinton-Lewinsky affair converts from a technicolor descent into rank partisanship into a richly political drama through which America staged and partially worked through serious questions concerning sex, power, privacy, the media, and so on. The ultimate lesson is to stop worrying about the loss of "reality" at the hands of the spectacle and learn to love the hyperreal as an arena of contestation and textual play. With this attitude adjustment a measure of agency is restored. Rather than gazing passively at the spectacle, one may read its subterranean currents, renarrativize its elements, and make some public case as to what it means and what should be done in response to it. Spectacular citizenship thus takes on the character of soldiering in Gramscian wars of interpretation, in which critical intelligence is the primary weapon and the antagonists battle for ideological hegemony. The field is by no means a level one, as there exist gross imbalances of discursive power enabling certain institutions and agents, such as the media, the government, corporations, and advertisers, to have their meanings and interests shape public perceptions. Even so, no pure monopoly on meaning exists, making it at all points possible, particularly with the growing use of the Internet and the insurgent "independent media" movement, to articulate some counter-narrative or image.

There are problems, however, with the identity-oriented family of interpretations of the Clinton scandal profiled above, both as explanations of the affair and as bases for reconcieving the spectacle. As explanations, they try in vain to jump over the affair's peculiar shadow by ignoring evidence that most Americans, perhaps even the *great majority* of Americans, were neither so profoundly threatened by Clinton in any of his guises nor all that scandalized by his behavior. Though disapproval of the affair and Clinton's lying may have been universal, true "panic," of whatever origin, appears the reaction only of a vocal minority. If the poll numbers say anything, they seem to say just that.

In addition, focus on transgression relies on a somewhat tired and likely misleading model of old, puritanical America going to absurd lengths to punish sexual and other forms of deviance. Sex, which lies at the root of all of the portraits of Clinton-as-transgressor, remains under the sign of repression, despite Foucault's famous pleadings that we not see sexuality that way. Foucault's attack on the "repressive hypothesis" as a frame for understanding modern sexuality is worth recounting, both for its insights and its evocative, even prescient, phrasing: "Rather than the uniform desire to hide sex, rather than a general prudishness of language, what distinguishes these last three centuries is the variety, the wide dispersion of devices that were invented for speaking about it, for having it be spoken about, for inducing it to speak of itself, for listening, recording, transcribing, and redistributing what is said about it. . . . What is peculiar to modern societies, in fact, is not that they confined sex to a shadow existence, but that they dedicated themselves to speaking of it *ad infinitum*, while exploiting it as *the* secret."⁴⁰ The resonance with the Clinton-Lewinsky scandal is undeniable: the multiple confessions; the tape-recorded phone calls and wiretaps; the titillating euphemisms and bawdy jokes; the suspension, in the name of forensic integrity, of euphemisms and taboos; the affidavits and courtroom testimonies; their mass dissemination; the graphic, if sanctimonious, report; and, as the sum of all this and more, the immense energy expended in discussing, dissecting, and adjudicating something that virtually no one, judging by the common claims, truly wanted to discuss. Foucault's description of sexuality, mapping so well onto the affair, also speaks to the broad dynamics of the spectacle. Like sexuality, the spectacle is fundamentally about revelation and visibility, driven by a dialectic of concealment and exposure.

Finally, hermeneutical approaches may err in tempting us to make peace too easily with the spectacle by downplaying its power and exaggerating our own. There was, for all the sound and fury surrounding the affair, an irreducible kernel of sheer triviality to it, for which the excavation of embedded meanings and paeans to the possibilities of critical reading ultimately offer little consolation. More than anything else, the affair seemed a drawn-out joke on us all that signaled the further degradation of our civic life. We only deepen the joke's cynicism by believing that talking back to our television sets, writing down our thoughts, sharing them with colleagues, students, and the thin ranks of the curious, or even holding a rally or two wins us much power. Debord's own cynicism, though implausibly extreme, is nonetheless instructive in alerting us to the spectacle's one-sidedness and the source of its triumphalism. "The spectacle," he asserts, "is the system's uninterrupted discourse about itself, its laudatory monologue. . . . It is that which escapes . . . reconsideration and correction. . . . It is the opposite of dialogue" (24, 18).

Indeed, the strongest sensation I felt while at the Capitol during the impeachment vote was utter stupefaction that this idiotic pseudo-story had come *to this*. I had been to Washington countless times to demonstrate over issues of war and peace and basic justice. Further, I had always regarded Washington's Mall as near-sacred ground in our democracy, as it provides the most accessible and symbolically important national space for the exercise of civic initiative and democratic vigilance. I had even participated in 1987 in an effort to impeach Ronald Reagan for the covert war in Nicaragua, culminating in our unfurling on the Capitol steps a giant banner with thousands of signatures demanding his removal. Though the gesture was largely theater, it conveyed our honest indignation at what we insisted was the breaking of laws, with the cost measured in death and damaged lives, not damaged reputations.

Yet, on that miserable day in January 1999, we were rendered essentially mute spectators, trapped in the spectacle's maw. Part of my fascination in going was to step inside the image that was on TVs everywhere, to be at ground zero. Without quite anticipating it, I mainly recapitulated the public/private act constitutive of the spectacle, no matter one's location in relation to its apparent "center": gazing, at a remove, at events that seemed simply to happen. In that setting, the events of the day appeared unreal, warped through the funhouse of the spectacle's reality effects. It seemed for an instant that there had been no scandal at all, but only a giant simulation of a scandal as a genre of the spectacle, one whose script we had mastered. All the trappings were there: indictments, subpoenas, interrogations, hearings, polarization, polls, confusion, foreboding, reporters, cameras, and the portentous language of grave crisis. What appeared lacking was either any true crime or any real way to expose the center as hollow, the emperor naked. No matter; if the verisimilitude is sufficiently exact, the illusion becomes real.

The dilemma for democratic citizenship posed by the affair is analogous to the dilemma for subjectivity posed by the spectacle, and vice versa. To fulfill one's civic duty to be an informed, engaged citizen, one had no choice but to follow intently the scandal's twists and turns. But to do so was to grant it a legitimacy it did not deserve and therefore to capitulate to the exaltation of the trivial. Conversely, to ignore the scandal in protest would mean contributing to the willful indifference that renders us a "weak public" in a distressingly weak democracy, given its immense potential. So too with the spectacle. To engage the world necessitates being a regular witness to the great phantasmagoria of images—with all of their commercialism, reductionism, and redundancy—that make up our shared, public life. Tuning out, being offline, means losing an important part of one's social existence. The choice between the two might seem more dispiriting if the spectacle's abundant pleasures and the systematic lowering of expectations were not such effective salves against the gnawing sense that our public life could be, and should be, so much more.

Among the affair's legacies is that we must forever live with the embarrassment of having impeached a president because he had a brief affair and lied to his wife and the world about it. The scandal has already wound its way into U.S. history textbooks. Its inclusion, however jarring, is an appropriate testament to our time, marking less the diversionary or even decadent culture of the "go-go '90s" than the evolution of the spectacular society. In an implied stage theory linking economic and cultural transformations within the broader adventures of the commodity, Debord asserts, "The concentrated spectacle belongs essentially to bureaucratic capitalism" (64; this was likely the spectacle form represented by the film audience). The "diffuse spectacle," which presumably emerges with the fully mature consumer capitalism of the 1960s, "accompanies the abundance of commodities" (53). What might be called the omnipresent, multimedia spectacle so evident in the Clinton-Lewinsky affair accompanies the present form of highly speculative, technology-driven, virtual capitalism, whose paradigmatic environment is the hyperreal.

The part of Debord needing no update is his assertion of the centrality of the spectacle to a culture such as ours. He explains, "The society which rests on modern industry is not accidentally or superficially spectacular, it is fundamentally *spectaclist*" (15). Applied to the present-day United States, this statement suggests that the spectacle is indeed *what we do* as a society: that it is our distinctive national product (as blue jeans, automobiles, and household appliances once were), the means by which we are known to each other and to the world. The spectacular narrative, in addition, has become a national expectation or even addiction, something whose appearance we greedily anticipate and in whose absence we mark time until the next comes along. The Clinton-Lewinsky affair, if this assumption holds, could not possibly be the end of the run of blockbuster stories including O. J., the Jon-Benet Ramsey murder mystery, and the nanny trial (in which a British nanny was accused of shaking to death an American baby). The spectacle did not disappoint. Shortly after the end of the Clinton saga, John F. Kennedy Jr. crashed his plane into the sea, prompting a wave of coverage that revisited the imagery of President Kennedy's "Camelot" and replayed the tropes used for Princess Diana's death. Following that was the months-long obsession with Elian Gonzales, a little boy whose fate, judging from the coverage, seemed to dwarf in importance any aspect of Cuban-U.S. relations over the past three decades. Topping all of these stories was the debacle of the 2000 presidential election, whose ironies in relation to the Clinton scandal are many.

The problem started with the campaign itself. During the Clinton affair, the public's constant plea was to return to consideration of "real issues." We wished for just this; or so we claimed. The two leading candidates went out of their way to downplay any possible differences between them, to limit the debate to arcane disagreements over marginally important policy proposals, and to exclude the third-party challenger. Before long, satirists and pundits alike chastised them for agreeing so loudly and so often. But from this season of relative tranquility emerged one of the biggest stories in U.S. political history: the inability, due to errors in the voting process and vote counting, to declare either candidate the winner. The spectacle was quickly back in the driver's seat, prompting the common sensation of "here we go again." The drama had all of the spectacle's essential elements and then some: a colorful cast of characters; unending and redundant reportage; the language of "constitutional crisis"; the mediation of everything by lawyers; crassly political maneuvering; surreal scenes, such as the live coverage of a U-Haul transporting uncounted ballots (eerily evocative of the televised chase of O. J. in his Bronco); the variously transfixed, perplexed, and stunned public gaze; and the desperate cries for closure.

During the weeks of irresolution, the campaign "issues," already squarely in the back seat, all but vanished. The raging conflict, as in the Clinton affair, appeared vastly more partisan than ideological. The overwhelming concern was with who had won, not what the consequences of having one candidate or the other as president would be. Here again, apparent differences masked structural affinities. As if in anticipation of the resurgent view that our two parties represent only slightly different versions of the same agenda, Debord said with respect to the spectacle: "The struggle of powers constituted for the management of the same socio-economic system is disseminated as the official contradiction but is in fact part of the real unity" (55).

The great power of Debord's theory ultimately lies in its indictment of the spectacular society, not simply its description. For Debord, the spectacle remains a "language of generalized separation" and a "manifestation of alienation" (3). His most immediate complaint is existential, as he insists, "The concrete life of everyone has been degraded into a speculative universe" (19). Several intervening decades of postmodernism, during which the critique of alienation was repeatedly declared an untenable avatar of an essentialism of the self, have not made such laments go away; movies like *The Truman Show* still are made and find some resonance, even if they betray a nostalgia for the real. Debord does not feel, however, that the alienating pseudo-world of images is therefore false. It is, rather, a true expression of a false condition, making the analysis of the spectacle another way of declaring "the whole" false. Debord turns to highly figurative language to express the depth of his disappointment: "The spectacle is the nightmare of imprisoned modern society which ultimately expresses nothing more than its desire to sleep" (21).

That desire may already be partially realized by the spectacle, as it induces a kind of waking sleep. During the Clinton scandal, I have stressed, we purportedly craved focus on the "real issues." The ensuing election raised doubts as to the sincerity of that desire and our ability even to recognize any longer what the real issues are. During our fitful slumber and halfway around the world, an angry, violent, and fanatical subculture was starting to wage a literal war on the United States, insisting that this nation had already begun waging war against it. Among the stated sources of its rage is disgust with the global spread of U.S. culture, in all its decadence, superficiality, and arrogance, conjuring the final of Debord's theses: that the spectacle is "the sun which never sets over the empire of modern passivity, [which] covers the entire surface of the world and bathes in its own glory" (13). This "new war" and the larger conflicts in which it is embedded were among the "real issues" that just recently seemed so elusive. Abuzz with talk of semen stains, cigars, and butterfly ballots, we hardly seemed to notice the storm clouds gathering.

Notes

1 "Pew's Poll Numbers: Clinton Moral Authority Slips," Pew Research Center for the People and the Press, September 1998. All Pew reports available from http://people-press.org/.

2 "Support for Clinton Unchanged by Judiciary Vote," Pew Center, December 1998.

3 "Americans Unmoved by Prospect of Clinton, Lewisnky Testimony," Pew Center, August 1998.

4 "Clinton's Ratings Increase among Republicans and Independents," Pew Center, December 1998.

5 "Popular Policies and Unpopular Press Lifts Clinton Ratings," Pew Center, February 1998; "Support for Clinton Unchanged by Judiciary Vote." The latter report (Pew Center, December 1998) contains month-by-month data on Clinton's approval rating.

6 "Public May Be Saying Enough," *Arizona Republic*, 1 February 1998, A7.

7 "Support for Clinton Unchanged by Judiciary Vote," Pew Center.

8 Ibid.

9 *Jim Lehrer Newshour*, "People and the Press," transcript, 19 August 1998, http://www.pbs.org/newshour/.

10 Deborah McGregor, "Media May Have Fanned the Flames,"*Financial Times*, 12 February 1999, 4.

11 Guy Debord, *Society of the Spectacle* (Detroit: Black and Red, 1983),

section 1. Subsequent section numbers appear in the text in parentheses.

12 "Diana's Death Interested Everyone: A Rare Event," Pew Center, September 1997.

13 Jean Baudrillard, *Simulations*, trans. Paul Foss, Paul Patton, and Philip Beitchman (New York: Semiotexte, 1983), 83–84.

14 The movie *The Matrix* largely replays this scenario while separating the virtual world even further from the human. Generated by a computer after terrestrial existence has been destroyed in an apocalyptic war, even the illusion of reality has been outsourced to a simulation machine.

15 Tellingly, the attachment throughout the English-speaking world of the suffix *-gate* to subsequent controversies marks them as partial replications of the genetic model of Watergate.

16 Lauren Berlant and Lisa Duggan, introduction to *Our Monica, Ourselves: The Clinton Affair and the National Interest* (New York: New York University Press, 2001), 1.

17 The investigation lasted a remarkable six of Clinton's eight years in office.

18 Rankin, *Arizona Republic*, 1 February 1998, A7.

19 McGregor, *Financial Times*, 12 February 1999, 4.

20 Chris Kallenbach, "Smaller Audience Here,"*Baltimore Sun*, 5 March 1999, 1E.

21 Peter Johnson, "A Fast-Frenzy: Now More Than Ever the Chase Is a Race," *USA Today*, 23 January 1998, 1D.

22 McGregor, *Financial Times*, 12 February 1999, 4.

23 Thanks to John McMillian for alerting me to the relevance of this lyric.

24 McGregor, *Financial Times*, 12 February 1999, 4.

25 McGregor, *Financial Times*, 12 February 1999, 58.

26 Johnson, *USA Today*, 23 January 1998, 1D.

27 Tom Brazaitis, "Viewers, er, Voters, Want Their MTV," *Plain Dealer*, 15 February 1998, 3E.

28 "Continued Public Inattention to Trial," Pew Center, January 1999. Captions in the Pew Center report ran "History, but Ho Hum" and "Turned Off Public Tuned Out Impeachment" (December 1998). By Pew's data in 1998, school shootings, military strikes in Iraq and Sudan, and unseasonable weather all ranked above Clinton-Lewinsky in terms of public interest.

29 Tzvetan Todorov, *The Conquest of America*, trans. Richard Howard (New York: Harper Torchbooks, 1984).

30 "Pew Research Center 1998 Poll: News Audiences Fragmented, Online News Use Up Sharply, Local News Interest Strong," Pew Center, May 1998.

31 "Diana's Death Interested Everyone," Pew Center.

32 "Pew Research Center 1998 Poll." The pressure of these audience preferences makes image management a constant challenge for broadcasters. CNN, fearful that viewers increasingly found its *Headline News* program stodgy and dull, recently revamped the show, making an actress from a popular TV drama one of the anchors. An ad for the program pictures a young, uncommonly handsome anchor, with the caption, "New Look. New Headline News. Real News. Real Fast" (seen on Path subway car in New Jersey, October 2001).

33 "The Tabloid Public Is Not the Majority," *New York Times*, 22 July 2001, 4–13.

34 Quoted in Brazaitis, "Viewers, er, Voters."

35 Brazaitis, "Viewers, er, Voters."

36 Quoted in Micki McElya, "Trashing the Presidency: Race, Class, and the Clinton/Lewinsky Affair," in Berlant and Duggan, 156.

37 Dana D. Nelson and Tyler Curtain, "The Symbolics of Presidentialism," in Berlant and Duggan, 41.

38 McElya, "Trashing the Presidency," 157.

39 This phenomenon was brilliantly disclosed in Spike Lee's *Do the Right Thing*. In the movie, a struggle over the racial composition of portraits displayed in a white-owned pizzeria in a black neighborhood erupts into a lethal fistfight and then a riot. The movie is only superficially viewed as a warning that unless some symbolic reconciliation occurs between blacks and whites, "real" violence will surely follow. More astutely, the movie suggests that the passion, the drama, the anger, the injury, and even the violence of racial division are already contained in the symbols *themselves*, whether pictures on a wall, a Jackie Robinson or Larry Bird jersey (worn by black and white characters, respectively), or the juxtaposed portraits of Martin Luther King Jr. and Malcolm X (these are carried by a young, stuttering black man who can articulate his rage and sense of political options only through the semi-inert language of images). The broader point—one missed by critics who complained that the film did not offer flesh-and-blood characters but only MTV-style caricatures—is that in the present-day United States, symbolic conflicts are not merely symptomatic expressions of some deeper experience of division but themselves "real" arenas of struggle. This principle, however counter to conventional materialist wisdom, is ensconced in contemporary hate speech laws that identify the offense in the speech itself, irrespective of its potential to incite hateful action (the old legal standard for the criminalization of language).

40 Michel Foucault, *The History of Sexuality*, vol. 1, trans. Robert Hurley (New York: Random House, 1978), 34–35.

Making (It) Public

> Today occasions for identification
> have to be created—the public sphere has
> to be "made"; it is not there anymore.
> —Jürgen Habermas,
> *The Structural Transformation*
> *of the Public Sphere*

Everyone talked about it for over a year. Whitewater, Flytrap, Zippergate, a Bimbroglio, the Lewinsky affair, the Starr investigation—the events surrounding Bill Clinton's self-destruction were so politically overdetermined that no one name could stick. It isn't even clear precisely what the "it" was that would be named. Were we designating the investigation, the scandal, the impeachment, the response from polls and media? No name was able to contain the seemingly never-ending excesses spiraling out and around the politics of sex, shame, and voyeuristic retribution that preoccupied the United States at century's end.

Much has been said about the Lewinsky affair. Pundits proliferated. Over a holiday meal prior to the House of Representatives' vote to impeach, someone at the table said, "This is an issue anyone can understand. We all have opinions about sex." Monica Lewinsky had turned a boring, complicated set of land and financial deals into a scintillating, easy-to-follow story of intrigue, infatuation, and thong underpants. The Starr report was written for everyone. Like a soap opera or teen diary, it's an inclusive text, just right for democratic consumption. No wonder it was dumped on the Web. Even without graphics and

Java applets, it fits there. And for those unwilling to read hundreds of footnotes, 24/7 news television and talk radio flagged the good ones. With so much said about the Lewinsky affair, theory doesn't seem to be able to add much. Events unfolded rapidly: the House of Representative's decision to impeach, the third act appearance of *Hustler* publisher Larry Flynt, the accusations of "wag-the-dog-ism" flung at Clinton for his bombing of Iraq. In such a cultural context, critique could too easily slide into commentary. Still, an analysis inflected by critical theory and cultural studies might reflect on some of the responses to the events afflicting the Clinton White House. In so doing, it could click on the "pseudo-concrete images" familiar in the mediatized everyday of contemporary entertainment culture, opening a window to the more abstract processes that format our thoughts and experiences and that configure the narratives and representations often presupposed by liberal democrats at the millennium.[1]

What are the ideological processes, the logic and its material underpinnings, presented as the public sphere? How does the Lewinsky affair demonstrate the ideal of publicity?. Do the cameras and cover stories point to the thoroughgoing consumerism of global technoculture in the information age? Or does publicity still have Habermasian connotations of critical investigation and discussion?[2] I argue that the distinction makes no sense. Not only are celebrity and critique linked together in the entertainment-driven politics of late capitalism, but the claim that they can be separated operates ideologically. It secures the normative plea to inclusion masking the secret at the heart of the public that justifies media culture's drive for information. Consumer-oriented publicity, in other words, is inherent in the logic of the public sphere. Thus, the politics of exposure and judgment that brought the Clinton administration crashing toward impeachment is the realization and nightmarish expression of the public sphere. The Lewinsky affair demonstrates why the concept of the public sphere fails to do justice to democratic pluralism in late capitalism's globally networked technoculture.

"I Feel Your Pain" A good portion of the media commentary on the Lewinsky affair was enlightening. The opinions were often well-reasoned and reflective. Those who voiced them had something to say, something well worth one's attention. Reading everything, of course, was out of the question, as was watching all the television coverage or monitoring all the Net chatter. In computer-mediated technoculture, intelligent commentary is widely distributed, "content" available in multiple fora.

"Identity" and "spectacle" are two themes that stood out in the commentary on the Lewinsky affair. Perhaps because of Clinton's empathic presentation of himself, a surprising number of people, of groups, either voiced a sense of identification with him or identified him with disadvantaged populations in the United States. Toni Morrison saw Clinton as "our first black president." "After all," she writes, "Clinton displays almost every trope of blackness: single-parent household, born poor, working-class, saxophone-playing, Mc-Donald's-and-junk-food-loving boy from Arkansas."[3] On December 17, 1998 a prayer vigil on the Capitol steps organized by the Rainbow Coalition brought together unions and women's and African American groups, many expressing the conviction that the "lynching" of the president was an attack on "us." The *Washington Post* highlighted the politics of identification expressed during the vigil, quoting Marino Dona, "a 46-year-old painter from Baltimore": Clinton "represents the working man."[4] Moreover, for the Republican right, as Thomas L. Dumm observes, Clinton symbolically condensed the cultural changes that have impacted the United States since 1968, changes associated with sexuality, abortion, and feminism.[5] These conservatives often identified Clinton with women, in particular women who don't know their place. Fittingly, Betty Friedan was active in the anti-impeachment effort.

The identity politics at work in the Clinton debacle extended to sexual minorities. During the House Judiciary Committee's deliberations over the Starr referral, a commentator on Pacifica Radio compared Clinton to Ellen Morgan, the lesbian played by Ellen DeGeneres whose coming out constituted a primary plot line on the ABC sit-com *Ellen*. Although the comparison lacked substance, it nonetheless indicated why lesbians and gay men might identify strongly with the president: not only was he persecuted for his sexuality, but the sexuality he was persecuted for continues to be illegal in a handful of states. It wasn't "normal," monogamous, sanctified-by-marriage, reproductive intercourse. It violated the terms of orthodox heterosexuality established in the discourse on family values (a discourse that also destroys its fundamentalist authors as it writes itself on their bodies; Robert Livingston's decision not to stand for election to the speakership and to resign his seat in the House because of the revelation of his marital infidelities is but one example). Even Clinton and Lewinsky didn't think their acts "counted" as sexual relations. Oral sex isn't sex; it's just "fooling around."

Although most commentators emphasized the cultural politics that divided around Clinton himself, the politics of identification wasn't confined to the president. The Beltway soap opera was inclusive: there was something for everyone. Folks faithful to straying spouses (and thereby exhibiting the "stand by your man" attitude) could identify with the first lady. That a number of people in fact did identify with Hillary Clinton might explain why her approval ratings rose during the investigation and impeachment. Young women, whether seeking sexual autonomy or victimized by workplace inequities, could identify with Monica Lewinsky, as could anyone who had sought to prolong a relationship with someone no longer interested. Finally, folks outraged by "the death of outrage" could identify with Kenneth Starr and his quest for traditional values.[6] They could perhaps see in him their own struggles for purity and righteousness in a corrupt and unfamiliar culture.

The Lewinsky affair presents as presidential politics an extreme version of identity politics. Anyone and everyone could find themselves in at least one of the central characters in this national psychodrama. All sorts of identities were represented, symbolized, at stake in the attack on the body of the president.[7] The move to impeach Clinton, whether cast as coup or "catching the flag" (the term used by Representative Henry Hyde, chair of the House Judiciary Committee), was the most extreme salvo in the culture war raging through the United States since the 1960s.[8]

With so much—and so many—at stake in the Lewinsky affair, it isn't surprising that a second major theme in the commentary surrounding and producing the event involved its status as spectacle. Circus, scandal, head-on collision, sideshow, carnival, "Super Bowl of gotcha," or "vast right-wing conspiracy," the Starr investigation and congressional debates were characterized as anything but serious, rational discussion of important constitutional questions.[9] The embarrassing, tawdry details of the Starr report stimulated speechifying and condemnation (What would it mean to exchange reasons about Altoids and cigars?). Sex, passion, grandstanding, and calls for retribution and revenge marked most political exchange. Not only did Republican leaders loudly and repetitively call for more and more extensive apologies, admissions, and signs of repentance from the president, but Clinton played along, invoking a narrative of sin, shame, and the hope for redemption that is part of his evangelical southern upbringing and familiar to the nation at least since the tears and confessions of Jimmy Swaggart and Jim and Tammy Faye Bakker during the televangelism scandals of 1987.

That the Lewinsky affair was characterized as spectacle makes sense not only because of the Starr report's soft-porn longings, but also because of the practices of globally networked entertainment culture. With satellite television, twenty-four-hour cable news, and the Internet, not to mention traditional print journalism, it's all news, all the time. We "know" things instantly, before they're reported, when they're only hints, possibilities, suspicions. Media commentators, for example, persistently noted the role of media in the production of the events leading up to the impeachment hearings: *Newsweek*'s and *The Drudge Report*'s exposure of Clinton's involvement with Lewinsky; the leaks from the independent prosecutor's office that kept the issue alive; the television broadcast of Clinton's four-hour videotaped grand jury testimony; the dumping of the Tripp-Lewinsky audiotapes on the Net.[10] At the same time, news analysts criticized themselves for their tabloidization of politics, for appearing as talking heads in countless television interviews, and for their own rabid pursuit of salacious details in the name of the truth. *Time* noted, "Hearings have ceased to be useful. They are now an extension of television."[11] To top it off, although they flagellated themselves for their feeding frenzy while running the excuse that "scandal sells," much print and television media still condemned their audience for consuming, or even caring about, news of presidential sexual liaisons. They lamented the fact that the public wasn't "above it all" even as they produced the public as an audience for a spectacle of sex, judgment, and retribution.

In the contemporary United States, identity and spectacle are linked. Lauren Berlant explains this link in terms of a politics of national sentimentality. "Spectacular forms of identification" such as celebrity, heroism, and scandal overorganize political feelings. Images of sex and narratives of family establish the terms of political debate, the standards of citizens' behavior, and the meaning of the United States as a nation. Berlant's analysis of the images of extremism and hypersexualism that right-wing discourse associates with queers and porn, moreover, applies with particular force to the Lewinsky affair: "Most of the time political discourse about sex in this modality is a way of creating instant panic about the fragility of people's intimate lives; most of the time, extravagant sex is a figure for general social disorder, and not a site for serious thinking and criticism about sexuality, morality, or anything."[12] Identifying with spectacular symbols of sex or decency, people experience their feelings as politics, as action. In the United States at millennium's end, the personal is impeachable.

Exposing the Truth National sentimentality's articulation of identity and spectacle is not the only link structuring the politics of the Lewinsky affair, however. There is another link, located at a deeper level, informing the very logic of the public sphere. That link is the "secret"; what it brings together are the constitutive norms of the public sphere, inclusivity and critical publicity.

The concept of the public requires a contrast with the secret, the private, the hidden, or the unseen. Habermas recognizes this in his classic account of the emergence of the bourgeois public sphere. There he emphasizes the importance of revelation ("Only in light of the public did that which existed become revealed, did everything become visible to all") as well as the public's opposition to secrecy.[13] Claims for the rationality and legality of critical public debate arose to contest—and expose—the secret practices of princely authority.[14] To produce an audience of those who might be counted on as the public, who might be evoked in the justification of a principle or policy, practices of publicity seek to uncover the secret.

That this is the case is clear when we consider statements such as "The public has a right to know." The very notion that public rule depends on access to information, on truth and knowledge, places the secret at the heart of the public. A public of those who know, who need to know, is called into being through the secret's revelation. Revelation gives "us" something to talk about, a way of knowing who and even *that* "we" are. Without a secret to discover, something hidden that can be exposed, there is no public. Today especially, disclosure or, perhaps, exposure seems the very essence of politics. Accepting that there is something left to be discovered, that there is something beyond what we can see before us, somehow seems precisely that act of faith capable of securing "us" as a public.[15]

Although the possibility of a secret seems to generate the public, publicity itself is generative. Publicity produces the secret through its investigations and judgments (What do "we" want to know?). Questions become allegations (Did you have sex with her?). That the primary action of the Lewinsky affair was revealing the secret, uncovering the truth, is thus neither a surprise nor a corruption of the public sphere. It's the embodiment of the very politics demanded, produced by the idea of a public sphere: bringing to light. As William Kristol pronounced in a rage against the president, "He engaged in a shameless and sustained attempt, from January 21 on, to lie to the American people, to conceal, to obstruct all efforts to uncover the truth. These efforts reflect an utter lack of concern for the nation's well-being."[16] Why does Kristol consider Clinton's attempt to conceal his sexual activities an affront on the nation's well-being? Why must "we" know what happened? Because there is no "we" without a secret to call us together. The public is based on knowledge. Its well-being, its very existence, depends on digging out, discovering the hidden.

The processes of discovery, the relentless digging, however, might be thought of as the public's dirty underside, what it needs to suppress, to deny, in order to maintain its aura as a ground for rule rather than simply a form of domination. What makes the Starr investigation, the whole Lewinsky affair, for that matter, disturbing is its all too clear expression of the prurient desire to uncover the secret that motivates the public. We're embarrassed by the too eager search for truth, the excavation of something that can interpellate disparate viewers, readers, hearers, talkers as the public.[17] We don't want to see the process of "making public." Starr is neither an aberration nor a hypocrite; he's the embodiment of the public's need for revelation. He exposes the generation of the public as an audience that cannot be acknowledged if public discourse is to operate effectively as an ideology. The discourse of the public sphere, the claim of critical publicity, is convincing only as long as the process of hunting remains itself hidden or disguised.[18]

Habermasochism   I've argued that the obsessive search for truth marks the Lewinsky affair as the penultimate expression of the logic of the public sphere, again, because of the constitutive place of the secret. The very ideal of the public sphere as the terrain and ground of democracy impels the search for hidden truths and their revelation so as to interpellate the public. One might think, however, that the identity and spectacle around the whole matter in fact prove that Habermas was right. His bleak diagnosis of the decline of the public sphere in the age of mass media seems directly to apply to the emotive, spectacular, and instantaneous processes of information distribution and opinion formation characteristic of late capitalist entertainment culture. The problem is that his description is right, but his diagnosis is wrong. Late capitalist entertainment culture fulfills the logic of the public sphere.

Habermas thinks the bourgeois public sphere came closest to realizing itself in the eighteenth century. By the second half of the twentieth century, he argues, the proliferation of media, advertising, and the business of public relations corrupted the bourgeois public sphere and substituted a "staged or manipulated publicity" for rational critical debate. Increasing the breadth of critical discussion, exposing more people to political issues and including more voices in political discussions, does not, in other words, guarantee the democratization of the public sphere. Habermas reasons that expansions in media, even those giving more people opportunities for cultural production and consumption, may not be accompanied by corresponding increases in the rationality of political discussion. In fact, he argues, the opposite results. Simply put, the public sphere degenerates into a kind of "superslogan" serving the "status quo." Habermas writes: "The public sphere assumes advertising functions. The more it can be deployed as a vehicle for political and economic propaganda, the more it becomes unpolitical as a whole and pseudo-privatized."[19] Habermas thus takes the increase in inclusivity brought about by the expansions in media to mark a decline in rationality, in publicness.

There is a compelling alternative to this story of the fall, however, one that emphasizes the ideological character of the public sphere as an ideal. Slavoj Žižek suggests that "when a certain historical moment is (mis)perceived as the moment of loss of some quality, upon closer inspection it becomes clear that the lost quality emerged only at this very moment of its alleged loss."[20] Habermas claims that the public sphere, a critical discussion potentially including everyone, is lost at precisely that moment when it could actually appear. Not only were there more and more varied media in the twentieth than in the eighteenth century, not only were more people exposed to more media and information more frequently with the rise in literacy and the development of television and radio, but more people had won the right to be heard as race, sex, and property ceased being defensible criteria for political participation. Critical of the sentimentality, commercialism, and consumer orientation of mass media, Habermas not only needlessly totalizes various media as a "mass," but also misses the way they bring political matters to ever larger audiences. The issues, the arguments we engage in collectively and thereby use to constitute ourselves as a "we" might be simple—everyone can talk about sex—but this simplicity increases the number of people who can participate. Simplicity, in other words, fits with inclusivity.

What kind of politics could possibly involve everyone? The ideal of inclusivity that Habermas originally links with secret societies like the

Freemasons and Illuminati (associated in most U.S. political science with conspiracy theory) appears radically political when evoked as a slogan by a small group against a monarch. As a general ideal, however, it is antipolitical. We don't have time to listen to everyone. What would it mean to do so? Much criticism of the Web, for example, is that too many folks are out there talking with not much to say. In the United States, moreover, efforts to attend to "every" voice or position often lead to stereotyping, to presuming that identities and positions are mutually determining. In some circumstances, these efforts toward inclusion become conflated with the public sphere preoccupation with visibility and politics. They end up as the demand that everyone and everything be "made public," a demand that reinforces the media dynamics of transnational consumer entertainment culture.

The public sphere norm of inclusivity leads to the neglect of what happens after folks are included. Focusing on the ideal of "everyone" reasserts an abstract conception of the public sphere as the space of politics. Inclusion, being part of this "everyone," becomes the primary goal of political action. The "where" of politics, the public sphere, displaces attention from more significant "whys" of political inclusion: to engage in conflict over the distribution of rights and responsibilities, for example, or to determine the character of our common engagements.

Of course, Habermas tempers his account of the public sphere's ideal of inclusivity by appealing to rationality. The character of discussion is as important as, or even more important than the number of people participating in it (as in the differences between Rousseau's general will and his will of all). He argues that inclusivity is lost with the rise of mass media because consumerism and corporate capital disrupt rational discussion. Again, this is why more media does not mean more democracy. Still, his appeal to reason could establish unfortunate barriers to democratic discussion, privileging experts and elites, say, or hinting at the necessity of literacy tests. It could suggest that a few could establish for the rest of us what, exactly, will count as reasonable. To avoid this outcome, Habermas turns to his distinction between the critical and the consumer orientations of the public.[21] Critical publicity requires that anything included in public discussion, normative positions or empirical claims, say, must be open to critique. The contents of discussion must withstand critical publicity, the critical gaze and interrogation of the public. Critical publicity thus demands more publicity. The solution to the problem of inclusion is more inclusion.

With regard to media complicity with the Starr investigation, trying to distinguish between consumer-oriented and critical publicity makes no sense. Clearly, media are both at once.[22] Media repeatedly criticize themselves and use this self-criticism to sell copy and generate audience. Reporters interview each other and newspapers report information available on the Net. Talking heads attack the polarizing emotion and spectacle of television shows featuring talking heads. In an eight-hundred-channel satellite TV universe, it's necessary to feed the pundit. Throughout the Lewinsky affair, critical publicity was a norm out of control, a kind of Habermasochism of media self-cannibalization.

Talk, Talk, Talk In contemporary mediatized technoculture, critical reflection is not simply a selling point, not merely a way to generate audience by claiming a rationality and objectivity superior to one's media competitors, but the very hallmark of the ideological component of the public sphere. As Žižek points out, "An ideological identification exerts a hold on us precisely when we maintain an awareness that we are not fully identical to it."[23] Critical commentary on the failures of publicity in the Lewinsky affair reiterates the ideals of the public, holding it out as a possibility. In so doing, however, it feeds the very media machine it criticizes, motivating the talking heads, generating Web copy, feeding the pundits.

The claims to rationality raised in defense of the democracy's basis in the public sphere remain silent with regard to the means of publicity, to the ways in which information is produced and disseminated, the processes through which issues have legs and audiences are interpellated. Media, in particular television, radio, and the Internet, are like pudenda that shame or corrupt real debate with the immediacy of impulse and desire. As they continue to dig for secrets and bring the hidden to light, however, the networked communications of contemporary technoculture follow the operating instructions of the public sphere. Critical publicity, more criticism, more publicity is just a lot of talk. As such, it's an ideology for the information age structuring the political around revelation and conversation. It reduces thinking about action by making visibility, mindshare, celebrity the goals of politics. And this feeds back into late capitalism's media machine. Democracy needs media. Democratic theory, however, can do without the public sphere.[24]

Notes

I'm indebted to Lee Quinby for her comments on an initial draft of this essay and for the conversations that have helped me think through some of these ideas.

1 As Slavoj Žižek writes: "In the good old days of traditional *Ideologie-kritik*, the paradigmatic critical procedure was to regress from 'abstract' (religious, legal . . .) notions to the concrete social reality in which these notions were rooted; today it seems more and more that the critical procedure is forced to follow the opposite path, from pseudo-concrete imagery to abstract (digital, market . . .) processes which effectively structure living experience." *The Plague of Fantasies* (London: Verso, 1997), 1.

2 Jürgen Habermas relies on the distinction between consumer-oriented and critical publicity in *The Structural Transformation of the Public Sphere*, trans. Thomas Burger (Cambridge, MA: MIT Press, 1989). My argument in this essay addresses his arguments in this book. Although Habermas has qualified his position since the original publication of *Strukturwandel*, in particular with regard to his bleak, Adornian characterization of media, he has remained committed to the norms of the public sphere and the general logic of publicity. His critical reflections on the public sphere can be found in Craig Calhoun, ed., *Habermas and the Public Sphere* (Cambridge, MA: MIT Press, 1992).

3 Toni Morrison, "Talk of the Town," *New Yorker* (5 October 1998): 32.

4 David Montgomery and Hamil R. Harris, "For Many, a Political Awakening Rally for Clinton Draws New Voices," *Washington Post*, 18 December 1998, A41.

5 Thomas L. Dumm, "Leaky Sovereignty: Clinton and the Crisis of Infantile Republicanism," *Theory and Event* 2.4, http://muse.jhu.edu/journals/theory_&_event.

6 See William J. Bennett, *Death of Outrage: Bill Clinton and the Assault on American Ideals* (New York: Simon and Schuster, 1998).

7 Michael Rogin draws on Ernst H. Kantorowitz's classic study, *The King's Two Bodies* (Princeton: Princeton University Press, 1957) in his account of presidential self-punishment, "The King's Two Bodies: Lincoln, Wilson, Nixon, and Presidential Self-Sacrifice," in *Ronald Reagan: The Movie* (Berkeley: University of California Press, 1987), 81–114. Rogin notes that the image of the king's two bodies not only separated the person from the office of the king, but aborbed "the realm into the officeholder's personal identity" (82). See also Thomas L. Dumm's discussion of the president's two bodies in *A Politics of the Ordinary* (New York: New York University Press, 1999).

8 An example of media expression of the cultural stakes of the battle around Clinton can be found in Frank Bruni's "A Debate on Something

Bigger Than Words," *New York Times*, 20 December 1998), "The Week in Review" section, p. 6.

9 The phrase "Super Bowl of gotcha" comes from Margaret Carlson, "Our Nattering Nabobs," *Time*, 21 December 1998, 30. For an account of Hillary Clinton's January 1998 remark that her husband's troubles were the product of a conservative conspiracy, see Jodi Dean, "Declarations of Independence," in *Cultural Studies and Political Theory*, ed. Jodi Dean (Ithaca: Cornell University Press, 2000).

10 A detailed account of the early days of the Lewinsky scandal, with particular attention to the ways Linda Tripp nursed the scandal so as to get a book deal from agent Lucianne Goldberg, appears in Steven Brill's "Pressgate," *Brill's Content* (August 1998): 122–37. Brill notes, "A rumor or poorly sourced and unconfirmed leak aired or printed in one national medium ricochets all over until it becomes part of the national consciousness. In short, once it's 'out there,' it's really out there" (136).

11 Carlson, "Our Nattering Nabobs," 30.

12 Lauren Berlant, *The Queen of America Goes to Washington City* (Durham, NC: Duke University Press, 1997), 57.

13 Habermas, *The Structural Transformation*, 4.

14 Ibid., 52–53.

15 I'm indebted to Paul Passavant for this point. See also Dean, "Declarations of Independence."

16 William Kristol, "Impeach and Convict," *Newsweek*, 21 December 1998, 28.

17 Žižek observes, "The excessive opening up (disclosure of a secret, allegiance, obedience . . .) of one person to another easily reverts to an excremental repulsive intrusion. That is the meaning of the famous 'No Trespassing!' sign shown at the beginning and the end of *Citizen Kane*: it is highly hazardous to enter this domain of the utmost intimacy, as one gets more than one asked for—all of a sudden, when it is already too late to withdraw, one finds oneself in a slimy obscene domain" (*The Plague of Fantasies*, 68).

18 My argument here is informed by ibid., 24–25.

19 Habermas, *The Structural Transformation*, 175.

20 Žižek, *The Plague of Fantasies*, 12.

21 Habermas, *The Structural Transformation*, 232.

22 See also Joshua Gamson's nuanced account of sexual minorities on tabloid talk shows *Freaks Talk Back: Tabloid Talk Shows and Sexual Nonconformity* (Chicago: University of Chicago Press, 1998). Gamson points out how outrageous and seemingly exploitative daytime television shows can stretch the field of toleration and provide opportunities for contestation precisely because of their spectacular, inclusive, consumer orientation.

23 Žižek, *The Plague of Fantasies*, 21.
24 For a more detailed account of why the public sphere is inadequate to the complexities of contemporary technoculture, see Jodi Dean, *Aliens in America: Conspiracy Cultures from Outerspace to Cyberspace* (Ithaca: Cornell University Press, 1998) and *Publicity's Secret: How Technoculture Capitalizes on Democracy* (Ithaca: Cornell University Press, 2002).

Notes on Contributors

Paul Apostolidis is an Associate Professor in the Department of Politics at Whitman College, where he teaches political theory, cultural studies, and U.S. politics. He is the author of *Stations of the Cross: Adorno and Christian Right Radio* (Duke University Press, 2000) as well as several articles on critical theory, the Christian right, and U.S. political culture. His current research explores constitutions and contestations of hegemony in the immigration experiences, work lives, and union activism of Latino food-processing workers in the U.S. West.

Jodi Dean teaches political and cultural theory at Hobart and William Smith Colleges, where she is an Associate Professor of Political Science. She edited *Feminism and the New Democracy: Resisting the Political* (Sage, 1997) and *Cultural Studies and Political Theory* (Cornell University Press, 2000). She is the author of *Solidarity of Strangers: Feminism after Identity Politics* (University of California Press, 1996), *Aliens in America: Conspiracy Cultures from Outerspace to Cyberspace* (Cornell University Press, 1998), and *Publicity's Secret: How Technoculture Capitalizes on Democracy* (Cornell University Press, 2002).

Joshua Gamson is an Associate Professor of Sociology at the University of San Francisco. He is a participating author of *Ethnography Unbound* (University of California Press, 1991) and author of *Claims to Fame: Celebrity in Contemporary America* (University of California Press, 1994) and, most recently, of the award-winning *Freaks Talk Back: Tabloid Talk Shows and Sexual Nonconformity* (University of Chicago Press, 1998). He is currently studying the impact of ownership consolidation and concentration in gay and lesbian media and is also writing a cultural history biography of the disco star Sylvester.

Theodore J. Lowi is the John L. Senior Professor of American Institutions in the Department of Government at Cornell University. He has written or edited twelve books, among them *The Pursuit of Justice* (with Robert F. Kennedy, 1964), *The End of Liberalism*, (Norton, 1969, 1979), *The Personal President: Power Invested, Promise Unfulfilled* (Cornell University Press, 1985), and *The End of the Republican Era* (University of Oklahoma Press, 1995). He is coauthor of one of the leading U.S. government texts, *American Government: Freedom and Power* (Norton, 1990, 1996).

Joshua D. Rothman is an Assistant Professor of History at the University of Alabama specializing in the history of the nineteenth-century South. He recently published *Notorious in the Neighborhood: Sex and Families across the Color Line in Virginia 1787–1861* (University of North Carolina Press, 2003). He also has published essays in the *Virginia Magazine of History and Biography* and *Journal of Southern History* and a collection entitled *Sally Hemings and Thomas Jefferson: History, Memory, and Civic Culture* (University Press of Virginia, 1999).

George Shulman is an Associate Professor of Political Theory and American Studies at the Gallatin School of Individualized Study of New York University. He is the author of *Radicalism and Reverence: Gerrard Winstanley and Thomas Hobbes in the English Revolution* (University of California Press, 1989) and *Prophecy and Redemption in American Political Culture* (University of Minnesota Press, 2003). He has also published essays on Toni Morrison, Norman Mailer, James Baldwin, and Richard Rorty.

Anna Marie Smith is an Associate Professor in the Department of Government, Cornell University, where she specializes in contemporary political theory, feminist theory, lesbian, bisexual, and gay studies, theoretical approaches to race and racism, and law and society. She is the author of *New Right Discourse on Race and Sexuality, Britain 1968–1990* (Cambridge University Press, 1994) and *Laclau and Mouffe: The Radical Democratic Imaginary* (Routledge, 1998), as well as numerous scholarly articles. She is currently completing a book entitled *Welfare and Sexual Regulation* (Cambridge University Press, forthcoming 2004), which examines the welfare laws and regulations of all fifty states with a focus on the way such laws regulate the sexual lives of poor single women and promote abstinence education in the schools.

Jeremy Varon is an Assistant Professor of History at Drew University. He is the author of *'Tools of the Revolution': The Weather Underground and the Red Army Faction* (University of California Press, forthcoming 2004). He has also written an essay on revolution in *The New Left Revisited*, ed. John McMillian and Paul Buhle (Temple University Press, 2003). Other works of his, published in "New German Critique," examine the relationship of modernity to mass violence, and issues of violence and representation. He is currently working, with Professor Bella Brodzki, on a study of Holocaust survivors who studied in German universities immediately after World War II.

Juliet A. Williams is an Assistant Professor at the University of California, Santa Barbara, where she holds a joint appointment in the Law and Society Program and the Women's Studies Program. Her research concerns the regulation of sex, gender, and sexuality in U.S. political and popular culture. She is currently working on a project exploring the multiple legal, political, and social meanings of sexual harassment in the United States.

Index

Adorno, Theodor W., 148, 156, 161, 163n20, 165n43
Adultery, 44, 56, 186–87, 191, 203–7
Anti-Communism, 77–78, 90, 141–42, 146
Arato, Andrew, 13
Arbuckle, Fatty, 40
Arendt, Hannah, 174, 178

Bakker, Jim, 44–46, 263
Baudrillard, Jean, 238
Berlant, Lauren, 3, 17–19, 34n16, 162n2, 180, 263
Bowers v. Hardwick, 219
Brown, Divine, 42, 47–48, 55
Bush, George W., 140, 201
Butler, Judith, 24

Callender, James, 27, 102–19
Campaign finance: antidemocratic trends in, 138–39, 150–61; Clinton fundraising scandal and, 6; political action Committees (PACs) and, 91, 150; in presidential campaigns, 202; reform of, 189
Chaplin, Charlie, 40
Chappaquidick scandal, 186
Christian Coalition, 137, 171–72, 190
Christian right: Clinton scandal and, 28–29, 137–40, 168, 181; homosexuality and, 9; Iran-

Contra narrative and, 155–62; privacy rights and, 220; Republican Party and, 137–38, 159; sexual regulation and, 207; Watergate narrative and, 138–47
Citizenship: democratic, 17–25, 34n; in new right discourse, 175; popular culture and, 19; race and, 169; spectacle and, 2, 250–53
Class: class identity and Clinton, 6, 18, 28, 218; class identity and Clinton's partners, 22; Clinton's policies and, 186; democratic accountability and, 148–52, 162; privacy jurisprudence and, 216–17; workers' rights and sexual harassment, 30, 206
Cleveland, Grover, 41
Clinton, Bill: African Americans and, 167–81, 184n13, 248, 261; approval ratings of, 234; bombing of Iraq and, 260; Christian right narrative and, 158–62, 165–66n46; class representations and, 6, 18, 28, 248–49; gender representations and, 18, 28; impeachment of, 12–13, 79–94, 101, 155, 167, 170, 176–82, 186, 190, 232–33, 244, 260; Lewinsky and, 4, 11, 162n2, 191–205, 262; marriage of, 185, 191; media images of, 248; media strategy of, 154–55, 247; Moscow visited by, 137;

Library of Congress Cataloging-in-Publication Data

Public affairs : politics in the age of sex scandals /
edited by Paul Apostolidis and Juliet Williams.
p. cm.
Includes index.
ISBN 0-8223-3276-0 (cloth : alk. paper) —
ISBN 0-8223-3265-5 (pbk. : alk. paper)
1. United States—Politics and government—1945–1989.
2. United States—Politics and government—1989–
3. Scandals—United States—History.   4. Political
corruption—United States—History.   5. Political
culture—United States—History.   6. Political ethics—
United States—History.   7. Politicians—United States—
Sexual behavior—History.   8. Celebrities—United
States—Sexual behavior—History.   9. Sexual ethics—
United States—History.   I. Apostolidis, Paul.
II. Williams, Juliet.
E839.5.P83   2004
973.92—dc22   2003016428